WHAT WOULD THE
FOUNDERS SAY?

ALSO BY LARRY SCHWEIKART

Seven Events That Made America America

48 Liberal Lies About American History

America's Victories

A Patriot's History of the United States
with Michael Allen

WHAT WOULD THE FOUNDERS SAY?

A Patriot's Answers to America's Most Pressing Problems

LARRY SCHWEIKART

Sentinel

SENTINEL
Published by the Penguin Group
Penguin Group (USA) Inc., 375 Hudson Street,
New York, New York 10014, U.S.A.
Penguin Group (Canada), 90 Eglinton Avenue East, Suite 700,
Toronto, Ontario, Canada M4P 2Y3
(a division of Pearson Penguin Canada Inc.)
Penguin Books Ltd, 80 Strand, London WC2R ORL, England
Penguin Ireland, 25 St. Stephen's Green, Dublin 2, Ireland
(a division of Penguin Books Ltd)
Penguin Books Australia Ltd, 250 Camberwell Road, Camberwell,
Victoria 3124, Australia
(a division of Pearson Australia Group Pty Ltd)
Penguin Books India Pvt Ltd, 11 Community Centre, Panchsheel Park,
New Delhi -110 017, India
Penguin Group (NZ), 67 Apollo Drive, Rosedale, North Shore 0632,
New Zealand (a division of Pearson New Zealand Ltd)
Penguin Books (South Africa) (Pty) Ltd, 24 Sturdee Avenue,
Rosebank, Johannesburg 2196, South Africa

Penguin Books Ltd, Registered Offices:
80 Strand, London WC2R ORL, England

First published in 2011 by Sentinel,
a member of Penguin Group (USA) Inc.

1   3   5   7   9   10   8   6   4   2

LIBRARY OF CONGRESS CATALOGING IN PUBLICATION DATA

Schweikart, Larry.
What would the founders say? : a patriot's answers to America's most pressing problems / Larry Schweikart.
p.   cm.
Includes bibliographical references and index.
ISBN 978-1-59523-074-4
1. United States—Politics and government. I. Title.
JK275.S378 2011
320.60973—dc22   2010035006

Printed in the United States of America
Set in Adobe Garamond
Designed by Alissa Amell

To Donald Douglas Dalgleish, mentor and friend

CONTENTS

INTRODUCTION

In February 2009, when the Democrat-dominated U.S. Congress, with the blessing of newly inaugurated President Barack Obama, hurled more than $787 billion at the U.S. recession in an effort to "stimulate" job growth, the results were unexpected, to say the least. Almost immediately—thanks to comments by Rick Santelli of CNBC, who called for a new "tea party" to stop the spending and taxes—spontaneous public gatherings throughout the nation demanded a change of course. "The government is promoting bad behavior," Santelli said. What was needed was a referendum on whether to reward bad behavior: "How many of you want to pay for your neighbor's mortgage, who has an extra bathroom and can't pay their bills?" he asked a group of traders in a speech on the floor of the Chicago Board of Trade. The traders booed. Santelli noted that Cuba used to have mansions and a "relatively decent economy," but they moved from the "individual to the collective. . . . We're thinking of having a tea party in July!"

Santelli's words instantly connected with millions of Americans (certainly by most polls, a majority) who thought that the so-called stimulus bill, often called the porkulus bill for all the pet projects it contained, was not only unnecessary but represented everything that was wrong with American government. This included too much regulation, too much spending, and, above all, too much taxation. The "tea" in *tea party,* in fact, stood for "taxed enough already." Without any significant funding from any established political party or organization, tea parties consisting of Democrats, Republicans, and nonaligned voters organized so rapidly that on April 15—tax day—mass demonstrations took place across the nation with hundreds of thousands turning out. Dayton, Ohio, a city of about 250,000, which had seen several major corporations shut their doors in the previous few years, saw 8,000 gather downtown in Courthouse Square. Other tea parties numbered far more.

While Santelli had provided the energizing phrase that seemed to capture the moment, the grievances of the participants were broad and deep. April 15 tea party speeches repeatedly invoked the Constitution, with orators demanding to know where the authority existed for Obama and Congress to "create" jobs in the first place. Where did the Constitution allow government to advocate one type of activity and investment (e.g., "green jobs") over another? Why did anyone think that government had authority over the environment, much less the global climate? Still other issues lurked beneath the surface of the speeches. If a government had power to seize wealth on such a wide scale, and to distribute it with such blatant partisanship and lack of debate, what other power would it claim? After all, many (if not most) of those voting for the porkulus bill had never *read* it and cheerfully admitted as much. Uncontrolled spending by the Republican Congress prior to 2006 had contributed to growing dissatisfaction with the GOP and permitted a Democratic takeover of the House and Senate that year. Yet instead of controlling expenditures, the Democrats went on a spree that would have made drunken sailors look thrifty.

Before Obama even took office—but with his complete blessing and encouragement—Republican President George W. Bush and the Democratic Congress had staged a massive bailout of the major U.S. investment banks, pouring $700 billion into propping up troubled banks by purchasing mortgage-backed securities through the Troubled Asset Recovery

Program (TARP). Then, when problems spread from banks to the auto industry, Congress (with the blessing of the incoming president) doled out a titanic bailout of General Motors (GM) and Chrysler Corporation in the name of "saving jobs." Few failed to notice the irony that GM's government-approved plan included cutting thirty-one thousand jobs![1] Indeed, the GM bailout largely consisted of bailing out the United Auto Workers and their astronomical pension/retirement/health-care plans, which had been foolishly agreed to by auto executives in the past under threat of strikes. Where in the world did Congress and a president get the power in peacetime to determine which American banks and industries would be saved at taxpayer expense and which (if any) would be allowed to fail? President Bush admitted he had "abandoned free-market principles to save the free-market system,"[2] echoing a sentiment from the Great Depression that somehow by engaging in a light form of fascism, Franklin D. Roosevelt had "saved" capitalism.

But matters were, in reality, far worse. Anyone who had followed Barack Obama's campaign and the actions of the House and Senate since 2006, before they had two-thirds majorities, knew exactly what their agenda was after the 2008 elections. Democratic leaders had promised a national health-care program, "cap and trade" that would supposedly battle "global warming," and "immigration reform" that basically allowed for general amnesty. Then there was the "fairness doctrine," designed to limit opposing voices in radio and on television; "net neutrality," which promised to regulate the Internet so as to prevent, ultimately, individuals from frequenting Web sites that might disagree with an administration; and new "public health" regulations against salt, fat, meat, sugar, and a host of other food items.

During his campaign, Obama had told Joe "the Plumber" Wurzelbacher, an Ohio resident who challenged the candidate's small-business tax policy, that he wanted to "spread the wealth around." Was this within the authority of a president? After taking the oath of office, Obama noted that the United States was "not a Christian nation." Really? Would most Americans have agreed with that sentiment? Obama had moved far from "tolerance" of Islam to embracing it, taking every opportunity to praise the religion, leading many to fear that after prayer had long been banned in schools, favorable references to Christianity would be next. While such concerns were dismissed by the mainstream media as "kooky," they appeared all too plausible given the recent drift in Washington. It seemed that many of the extreme ideas in Washington originated in the public education system, which had taken on a distinct agenda. Schools had become hugely political, with the introduction of classroom materials such as "Heather Has Two Mommies" and curricula sympathetic to homosexual rights groups and hostile to traditional families. Global warming and other unproven environmental doctrines were routinely taught as fact, and young students were urged to "think globally, act locally." Educators and politicians alike consistently undermined American concepts of sovereignty.

Throughout it all, the tea parties objected on the grounds that none of these things were *constitutional*—that the Founders never intended for any of these trends to develop. The tea parties were not the first to spark renewed inquiry into our founding documents and the ideas of the Founders themselves, but they certainly served as a catalyst for the widespread revival of interest in what the Founders thought, dreamed, and would have tolerated. What would George Washington have thought about the government's involvement in the global warming debate? How about Thomas Jefferson? Would he have had a position on the bailout of General Motors? Surely Alexander Hamilton or Benjamin Franklin would have had an opinion on national health care. "What's that?" you say. The Founders never mentioned any of these things? Of course, you would be right for two reasons, the most obvious being that such issues did not exist two centuries ago when the Founders were living. The second reason is that *none* of the Founders would have considered any of these things the business of the federal government. Many wouldn't even have considered them proper subjects for state legislation or regulation.

So does that mean modern American lawmakers and presidents can just run willy-nilly pursuing any agenda that suits their fancy? Absolutely not. While Washington may not have been able to form an opinion on today's school systems, Title IX, or federally funded scholarships, he had quite a lot to say on education, and quite a lot more to say on the role of government in it. When one combines the two, his position on current educational issues becomes fairly clear, and even a little surprising. And while Hamilton may not have advised Tim Geithner or Ben Bernanke on the General Motors and bank bailouts, he certainly voiced his position on whether government involvement in markets, finance, and banks was appropriate, and if so, under what circumstances.

The most difficult part of writing a book that deals with what men of two hundred years ago would have thought about today's issues is that so often the answer is, They wouldn't have thought at all about it. But neither did the Bible give specific instructions on the use of cell phones, automobile safety, or Internet gambling, yet through careful interpretation and analysis, we can glean reasonable conclusions about what the prophets would have said about such things. Just as the Federal Reserve Act made virtually no mention of the gold standard, everyone involved in drafting the bill and in administering the system assumed the existence of gold as a reserve currency. In the film *A Few Good Men,* Tom Cruise as Lieutenant Daniel Kaffee puts Noah Wyle (Corporal Jeffrey Barnes) on the stand and asks him where the mess hall is mentioned in the outline for Marine Corps Recruit Training. The corporal tells him the information is not in the book, to which Kaffee responds, "So how did you know where the mess hall was?" Corporal Barnes replies, "I guess I just followed the crowd at chow time, sir."[3] Like Corporal Barnes, and like the authors of the Federal Reserve Act, the Founders operated on assumptions that were so ingrained, so fundamental, that they didn't feel the need to write down every contingent or conceivable extrapolation of the principles in order to instruct future generations.

Of course, there are those among us who are inclined to a loose interpretation of the Founders' statements. For example, today's social engineers (i.e., those who want to reshape society based on their interpretations of what's in the "best interest" of others) can try to make a case for government intervention in our food choices, particularly if a national health-care system literally makes everyone responsible for the eating habits of everyone else. After all, if your tax dollars are paying for your neighbor's health coverage, you darn sure will make certain he or she isn't wasting your money by sucking down Ho Hos at an unacceptable rate. Bans on cigarette smoking paved the way, allowing people to argue that the personal habits of one affected others. Cigarettes, of course, were only the beginning: a product used by a small fraction of the population, whose health effects on the user were undeniable (but whose health effects on bystanders remained unsubstantiated), tobacco made an easy target.[4] This is, of course, a Saul Alinsky–like strategy, isolating your enemy by cutting out the weakest (in this case, an industry or product) from the herd and forcing a defense of an unpopular or distasteful practice. But those who thought the social progressives, who once sought to ban Coca-Cola and who did temporarily prohibit the sale and distribution of booze, would stop at merely "unpopular" products need to think again. When they come for your Ho Hos, they won't stop until they dictate every morsel that goes into your mouth.

Naturally, such behavior would have horrified the Founders, many of whom smoked, and most of whom drank, sometimes heavily. They would have viewed any attempt by government to regulate their personal habits as not only ill conceived but the essence of tyranny. Can anyone conceive of trying to tell Thomas Jefferson not to consume some of his fine wines, let alone snatching it out of his hands? Would anyone dare to whisk George Washington's mutton and veal off his table?

Determining exactly what the Founders thought is of course difficult. Not all the Founders were consistent in their views throughout their lifetimes. And not all Founders agreed on every issue, with Alexander Hamilton and Thomas Jefferson being the most extreme examples of opposing views. It is worthwhile also to elaborate who the Founders were. While this is not a comprehensive list, and while some spoke more clearly on some issues than others, when I speak collectively of the Founders, I generally mean Washington, Jefferson, John and Sam Adams, Benjamin Franklin, James Madison, James Monroe, and occasionally Patrick Henry, Thomas Paine (though he was a recent immigrant), and George Mason. But certainly where the ideas of John Dickinson or Benjamin Rush were applicable, they too would be welcome in the discussion. The Founders came from two "streams" of liberty, one based on a radical states' rights localized view, and one stemming from the English Whig tradition of a tightly controlled central government dominated by a legislature. Both, however, respected separation of powers, limitations on the ruler(s), and individual rights, so much so that "bills of rights" were considered essential to state (and later, the national) constitutions.

In some cases, the Founders' voices and actions were unmistakable. When it came to private property, all the acts and declarations of the Founders (with the sole exception of Thomas Paine) spoke to its sanctity, and especially to the notion that the government had an obligation to move land that it oversaw into private hands as quickly as possible. (Jefferson went so far as to claim that once in private hands, *no* future generation had a claim on the property or lands of the living.) Here, we have clear and irrefutable evidence of the Founders' intentions, for even before the Constitution took shape, Congress wrote into law the principle of land dispersal in the Articles of Confederation. That Theodore Roosevelt would inaugurate, and subsequent presidents would accelerate, a federal land-grab under the name of "national parks" or "the environment" would have been anathema to the Founders. Despite their ability to look into the future and anticipate the potential for corruption and greed of some in generations yet to come, none of the Founders dreamed that the federal government would, in the name of snail darters and plovers, deny ordinary Americans the ownership and control of land. Fortunately, they spoke with a near-unanimous voice on what should be done with the vast territories owned by the United States of America.

Perhaps most surprising to some will be the Founders' virtually unanimous view of education, which they wanted to extend to as many as possible. Many called for public funding of education—some with fairly radical voices. To the revolutionary vanguard of homeschoolers across this country, it might seem heretical that the Founders wanted kids to attend public, or "government," as Neal Boortz calls them, schools. At the same time, however, the Founders' views as to *what* should be taught were also nearly unanimous, and one cannot separate their support of local public schools from the principles and subjects that they intended those schools to teach.

At times, we do not have to infer much from what the Founders wrote or said. An unmistakable part of their worldview involved individual accountability, including bankruptcy and paying one's debts, government restraint, low taxation, and, above all, a general sense that government should butt out whenever possible. The Founders, to a man, believed in honor, with the dishonor of debt being among the worst sins. When James Madison wrote, "were every one to live within his income or even the savings of the prudent to exceed the devidicts of the extravagant, the balance in the foreign commerce of the nation, could not be against it."[5] To extract individual phrases from the Founders in support of "big government" activity *anywhere* is to wantonly disregard the overall thrust of their intentions and, indeed, their very lives. Government always existed, in their minds, to serve the individual, never the reverse. The term "socialism" had not even been dreamed up by Robert Owen yet (let alone Karl Marx), but the concept of the collective had been abandoned very early in American history when John Smith at Jamestown and the Pilgrims in Massachusetts had each independently rejected the socialist model in favor of, well, "free enterprise." Hence, the issue was so firmly settled that it scarcely required addressing by the Founders.

While the authors of the Declaration and the drafters of the Constitution came from a generation that knew only an economic/political system known as mercantilism, in which individual businesses existed for the advancement of state interests, they had steadily abandoned most mercantilist principles. Virtually none of the Founders believed that wealth consisted only of gold and silver: all of them understood that individual talent and initiative, plus hard work, created goods and services. This is why they put so many protections on private property in the founding documents, including protections of intellectual property. None of them had ever known a system that had anything other than a monarch, yet they rejected that in favor of something entirely new on the earth—a representative democracy that limited the role of government at every level. Thus, while influences of their past cargo can be seen in the tariff or the national bank, so too their awareness of the threats posed by government can be viewed in their treatment of guns, or the militia, or religious freedom. Every step of the way, the Founders intended the system to advance individual liberty, not restrain it, and where government did limit the actions of individuals, it was only to be in clear-cut cases of threats to all.

None of the Founders was heartless, or without compassion. They all believed in charity, and that those who were able should not only work to support their families but also voluntarily help those who could not help themselves. As late as the Civil War, however, few even dreamed that the government at any level—local, state, or federal—"owed" people a job. Not until the late 1800s, when William McKinley ran on the promise of a "full dinner pail," was there a widespread perception that U.S. government policies even could affect labor markets, without yet addressing the issue of whether the government should do so. Rather, most accepted that a well-run government, with low levels of debt and taxes, would promote full employment merely by its fiscal integrity. But in *no case* did any of the founding generation expect that government charity or "make work" was a natural right, nor was it to be used as an economic breakwater to provide "full employment."

It is not possible to examine or attack every goofy and dangerous liberal nostrum circulating today. Most of them are tied in one way or another to the essential questions here. But one has to look only as far as the comment made by the Transportation secretary in the Obama administration in March 2010—"This is the end of favoring motorized transportation at the expense of non-motorized"—to appreciate the pernicious depths to which the Left in the United States has sunk.[6] Or how about the "debate" in Congress as to whether to allow *sex offenders* to receive Viagra? Does anyone who isn't locked in an insane asylum conceivably think that even radical libertarians such as Tom Paine would have entertained this notion for a moment?

What, then, is the solution to our current woes? It helps, when you are lost, to find out where you made the wrong turn. But if you don't know where you started, how can you discover where you went off course? The best way for America to find its way again is to return to the ideas and principles of the Founders. They are far more than "dead white men." They were geniuses because they inherently understood the dangers of big government. Most had experienced it firsthand, and many had paid a high price. Their cautions to modern Americans, whether in their letters or in their legislation, indicate exactly where they would have stood on any issues that did not exist in their own time. We can discover what they would have done (if anything) about global warming based on what they did with property law. We can discern whether they would have allowed prayer in school by finding out when, and where, they prayed. We can understand their philosophy of dealing with unemployment, financial crises, and business failures by observing what they did when faced with those same situations more than two hundred years ago. And we not only can do this, we *must*. The continued existence of the United States as a nation depends on whether we can recapture the spirit of '76 and apply it today, or whether we succumb to modern doctrines that have produced poverty and human misery everywhere they are applied.

The Founders owed it to us to make their positions plain and understandable, and they succeeded. We owe it to them to embrace and apply them.

QUESTION #1

_____

HOW IMPORTANT IS RELIGION, ESPECIALLY CHRISTIANITY, IN MATTERS OF STATE AND GOVERNMENT AND SHOULD THE TWO BE ENTIRELY SEPARATE?

Few subjects have been as contentious in the modern American debate as the role of religion in everyday public life. Almost every American has heard the phrase "separation of church and state," and those who advocate for a completely secular government often pull it out in defense of their beliefs. Quite likely, these people, some of whom may not be able to quote a single phrase or cite a single article from the Constitution, attribute the phrase to that document. Yet it does not appear in the Constitution at all. Nowhere does the Constitution say that there should be a separation of church and state, nor does it say that the federal government cannot use religious symbols, recognize religious holidays, use religious teaching as a basis for law, or prohibit religious teaching or even prayer in state-financed schools or public institutions. And while the First Amendment does provide for freedom to worship any religion, there is little doubt that the Founders all assumed the United States was, and always would be, a Christian nation and that "religious freedom" constituted the freedom to worship any *Christian* faith, not any faith in general.

The context of the Founders' views on religion is crucial, for they emerged from a heritage of religious struggles in England between Catholics and the Protestants eventually known as Anglicans. King Henry VIII's break with the Roman Catholic Church over his desire for a divorce led him to join the broader European Protestant movement, but with a twist because he simply brought the English Catholic structure under the control of his monarchy and placed ecclesiastical authority in England in the archbishop of Canterbury instead of the pope in Rome. When this system soon grew as corrupt as the Catholic Church in Europe, English reformers known as Puritans sought to change it as well. This led to the rise of English Puritanism and to the separatists known as the Pilgrims, who thought England was beyond redemption and eventually settled in the northeastern United States. Knowing this, we see that the Founders came from a tradition of faith as well as suspicion of church authority when associated with government. They believed in the freedom *to* worship, not the freedom *from* worship. Even the less devout of the Founders operated in the context of Christian ideas, principles, and ethical guidelines. For example, the very "rationalist" notion on which science was based came from Christian views that God was knowable by reason as well as by faith, that God established principles that men could ascertain and apprehend, and that He made the world to operate within those principles. Galileo had said as much to Pope Urban VIII in 1623: "Surely, God could have caused birds to fly with their bones made of solid gold, with their veins full of quicksilver, with their flesh heavier than lead, and with their wings exceedingly small."[1] Thus, even those Founders most associated with science worked within a *Christian rational* context.

More than other essays, this one in particular requires a careful review of many primary documents in some detail, and therefore the reader will forgive a few extended quotations. The single mention of "religion" in the Constitution (Article VI) states, "no religious Test shall ever be required as a qualification to any Office or public Trust under the United States." A second reference followed in the First Amendment of the Bill of Rights: "Congress shall make no law respecting an establishment of religion, or prohibiting the free exercise thereof."[2] Although this amendment seems clear beyond misinterpretation that Congress cannot make a law establishing an approved state religion, this principle ran contrary to common practice throughout Europe in 1789, and this single clause has given rise to the commonly held idea that all government in the United States must be strictly secular without any vestiges of any religion present in its laws, forms, or practices. Of course, the same clause makes clear that individual states are *not* prohibited from establishing religions with connections to the state government. Rather, it specifically prohibits the federal government from entrenching a national religion.

As in all of the first twelve articles proposed as amendments to establish a Bill of Rights, the First Amendment had a substantial historical background. In its complete form it says: "Congress shall make no law respecting an establishment of religion, or prohibiting the free exercise thereof; or abridging the freedom of speech, or of the press; or the right of the people peaceably to assemble, and to petition the Government for a redress of grievances." A brief review of the origins and language of this amendment is in order. Although citizen rights originated with German Salic law and were developed over the course of twelve centuries through Old Saxon law to English law in the seventeenth century, the first codified Bill of Rights emerged under King William III and Queen Mary II in a bill entitled "Act Declaring the Rights and Liberties of the Subject, and Settling the Succession of the Crown, December 16, 1689."[3] This act addressed the rights of freedom of speech (in Parliament) and to petition for redress of grievances, but the succession following William and Mary was prohibited to fall to a Papist (Roman Catholic) or a Protestant who married a Papist.[4] This act followed the deposition of James II, a Catholic, in favor of the Protestants William and Mary, and while Anglicanism was not specifically declared the official state religion, that status continued from earlier practices, such as the act by King Charles II that prohibited Papists from sitting in either House of Parliament. England, therefore, had a powerful connection between church, specifically the Anglican Church, and state.

Did the colonists substantially change this system when they arrived in America? Most scholars agree that the world's first written constitution was the "Fundamental Orders," produced by the General Court of Connecticut in 1639. Its originators were Congregationalists who had split off from Massachusetts and settled in the Connecticut River Valley in the Hartford-Windsor area. They made no distinction between church and state because the government and their rights were completely a function of their religious beliefs. (It is worth noting that in the Massachusetts Bay colony, individuals could not participate in government at all unless they belonged to the church.) Any individuals living in Connecticut who professed other than Congregational beliefs, such as the Quakers, were moved out of the colony one way or the other.[5] The Congregational Church remained the official state church until 1818, and all residents were required to attend church services and contribute appropriate financial support. As the colony grew more diverse, other Christian denominations were allowed, but their congregations were required to show evidence of their attendance and support to avoid paying taxes to the Congregational Church.

Connecticut adopted a new constitution in 1818 that disestablished the Congregational Church and allowed for the free exercise of any Christian religion. Article II, Section 4, of the Declaration of Rights states: "No preference shall be given by law to any christian [sic] sect or mode of worship." Article VII states that Christian religions were given the power to tax their members, and, indeed, the article not only infers that any religion other than Christianity would be present in the state, but the wording is oriented solely toward Protestant Christianity.[6] A law allowing Jews to worship freely was passed by the Connecticut state legislature in 1843, and Roman Catholics were allowed freedom of worship in general, although not necessarily by law, from the time of the large Irish Catholic immigration in the 1840s. The reference to Christianity was not deleted until 1965, when the current Connecticut Constitution was adopted and non-Christians were officially granted freedom of worship.[7]

At the time of the writing of the U.S. Constitution, all states but Rhode Island had formal constitutions, but four were particularly influential for the Founders, namely, those of Massachusetts, New York, Pennsylvania, and Virginia. The 1777 constitution of the State of New York, drafted by John Jay, contains several mentions of religion:

• "That all such parts of the said common law, and all such of the said statutes and acts aforesaid, or parts thereof, as may be construed to establish or maintain any particular *denomination of Christians* [emphasis mine] or their ministers, or concern the allegiance heretofore yielded to, and the supremacy, sovereignty, government, or prerogatives claimed or exercised by, the King of Great Britain or his predecessors, over the colony of New York and its inhabitants, or are repugnant to this constitution, be, and they hereby are, abrogated and rejected.

• "Article XXXVIII: And whereas we are required, by the benevolent principles of rational liberty, not only to expel civil tyranny, but also to guard against that spiritual oppression and intolerance wherewith the bigotry and ambition of weak and wicked priests and princes have scourged mankind [a direct reference to Cardinal Mazarin and King Louis XIV of France], this convention doth further, in the name and by the authority of the good people of this State, ordain, determine, and declare, that the free exercise and enjoyment of religious profession and worship, without discrimination or preference, shall forever hereafter be allowed, within the State, to all mankind: Provided that the liberty of conscience, hereby granted, shall not be so construed as to excuse acts of licentiousness, or justify practices inconsistent with the peace of safety of this State.

• "Article XXXIX: And whereas the ministers of the gospel are, by their profession, dedicated to the service of God and the care of souls, and ought not to be diverted from the great duties of their function; therefore, no minister of the gospel, or priest of any denomination whatsoever, shall at any time hereafter, under any presence or description whatever, be eligible to, or capable of holding, any civil or military office or place within this State."[8]

A much opposite thrust was evident in the Constitution of Massachusetts of 1780, drafted by John Adams, who also determined most of its content. The delegates selected John Adams, Samuel Adams, and James Bowdoin to draft the constitution, and Samuel Adams and Bowdoin essentially delegated the actual work to John.[9] The Massachusetts Constitution was riddled with references to religion, as might be expected of the devout Adams and the Puritan/Congregational milieu in which he lived. He wrote in the preamble, "We, therefore, the people of Massachusetts, acknowledging, with grateful hearts, the goodness of the great Legislator of the universe, in affording us, in the course of His providence, an opportunity, deliberately and peaceably . . ." He also stated he was "devoutly imploring His direction."[10] The first articles are almost exclusively devoted to religion and its role in government, education, and the necessity of worship. All denominations of *Christians* are equally under the protection of the law, but no mention is made of non-Christian religions or worship. Like Washington, Adams used terms such as "Supreme Being," "great Creator," and "Preserver of the Universe" in addition to "God." Adams also stated that the "good order and preservation of civil government essentially depend(s) upon piety, religion, and morality . . . by the institution of public worship of God and of the public instructions in piety, religion, and morality . . ." among the people. He gives the people the "right to invest their legislature with power to authorize and require . . . suitable provision . . . for the institution of the public worship of God and for the support and maintenance of public Protestant teachers of piety, religion, and morality."[11] There is no uncertainty about the role of Protestant Christianity and religion here, and Adams would never waver later from this position.

Article II of Pennsylvania's Constitution of 1776, written mostly by Benjamin Franklin, stated:

All men have a natural and unalienable right to worship Almighty God according to the dictates of their own consciences and understanding: And that no man ought or of right can be compelled to attend any religious worship, or erect or support any place of worship, or maintain any ministry, contrary to, or against, his own free will and consent: Nor can any man, who acknowledges the being of God, be justly deprived or abridged of any civil right as a citizen, on account of his religious sentiments or peculiar mode of religious worship: And that no authority can or ought to be vested in, or assumed by any power whatever, that shall in any case interfere with, or in any manner control, the right of conscience in the free exercise of religious worship.[12]

However, each member of the Pennsylvania House of Representatives was required to make and subscribe to the following declaration: "I do believe in one God, the creator and governor of the universe, the rewarder of the good and the punisher of the wicked. And I do acknowledge the Scriptures of the Old and New Testament to be given by Divine inspiration."[13] Clearly this required a legislator to profess the Christian religion, and only in the 1790 rendition of the Pennsylvania Constitution was the wording changed.[14]

Virginia's is the fourth state constitution important for an appreciation of the Founders' views. It was adopted on June 29, 1776, and its writers, George Mason, Thomas Jefferson, and James Madison, constituted Founding Fathers of the highest order. As is commonly noted, Jefferson was a Deist, believing in a God as the creator of the universe, but not one to be revealed in Scripture or to be reached by prayer of supplication. Even so, Christianity makes its appearance in Section 16: "That religion, or the duty which we owe to our Creator, and the manner of discharging it, can be directed only by reason and conviction, not by force or violence; and therefore all men are equally entitled to the free exercise of religion, according to the dictates of conscience; and that it is the mutual duty of all *to practice Christian forbearance* [emphasis mine], love, and charity towards each other."[15] This is a rather un-Jeffersonian writing, explicitly identifying Christianity as the dominant religion about which he wrote.

Other state constitutions—in New Jersey, Delaware, Maryland, North Carolina, and Georgia—also reveal the pervasiveness of Christianity and its influence and position in government. New Hampshire's 1784 constitution contains a Bill of Rights, with Article VI nearly identical to John Adams's Article III in the Massachusetts Constitution, referring to "piety, rightly grounded in evangelical principles," thus clearly stressing Protestant Christianity.[16] New Jersey's Constitution of 1776 stated that only those persons professing a belief in the faith of any Protestant sect could be elected to public office.[17] In addition, no Protestant inhabitant of the colony (State of New Jersey) could be denied the enjoyment of any civil right.

Maryland's Constitution of 1776 features an extremely long article granting freedom of religion, with two additional ones concerning government regulation of gifts and financial transactions concerning religious sects.[18] In all cases the Christian religion is specified as the operational assumption: "all persons, professing the Christian religion, are equally entitled to protection in their religious liberty." In addition, the legislature may "lay a general and equal tax for the support of the Christian religion," and provisions and support of the Church of England (Anglican) were safeguarded. As in other states, admission to any office of trust or profit required a declaration of a belief in the Christian religion.

Although Maryland had originally been designated as a colony to be populated by Roman Catholics, the inability to attract Catholics in sufficient numbers had necessitated the recruitment of Protestants, most particularly the Scotch Irish, and Catholics had rapidly lost their majority in the colony. Adding to the dearth of Catholics was the general acceptance of latitudinarianism as a common policy throughout the state in Catholic parishes as much as in Protestant ones. Catholic laity administered their own parishes through elders, and some even elected their own priests. The Maryland parishes were frequently looked upon with grudging approval by Protestants, and there was little religious animosity in the state. Thus, the Maryland Constitution reflected this harmony with its simple use of the term "Christian religion" to encompass both Protestants and Catholics. An accommodation was even made for Quakers, "Dunkers," and "Menonists," to allow them to make affirmations rather than swearing oaths so that they readily found acceptance and homes in Maryland. There is little evidence that non-Christians were either welcome or unwelcome. The Founders just did not consider their presence to be likely.

North Carolina's Constitution of 1776 says, "No person who shall deny the being of God, or the truth of the Protestant religion, or the divine authority of either the Old or New Testaments, or who shall hold religious principles incompatible with the freedom and safety of the State [e.g., pacifism], shall be capable of holding any office, place of trust or profit, in the civil department, within this State."[19] The constitution of North Carolina was heavily amended in 1835, although the only change in the sections dealing with religion was the substitution of the word *Christian* for *Protestant*. Georgia granted freedom in the exercise of religion in its Constitution of 1777, "provided it be not repugnant to the peace and safety of the State." Like many states, Georgia prohibited clergymen from serving in the legislature, and its oaths all ended with "so help me God."[20] Delaware also specified an oath of office in its Constitution of 1776 with a variation of acknowledging a Christian faith: "[I] do profess faith in God the Father, and in Jesus Christ His only Son, and in the Holy Ghost, one God, blessed for evermore, and I do acknowledge the . . . scriptures of the Old and New Testaments to be given by divine inspiration." Delaware's constitution prohibited the establishment of any one religious sect at the state level, and again prohibited clergy from holding civil office.[21]

A definite pattern can therefore be seen in the twelve state constitutions written by the Founders prior to the U.S. Constitution in 1787:

• Five states granted privileges to specified religions that endured past the adoption of the U.S. Constitution—Massachusetts (Congregationalist until 1833), New Hampshire (Evangelical Christian until 1877), Connecticut (Congregationalist until 1818), Maryland (Christian), and New Jersey (Protestant).

• Seven states expressly guaranteed the freedom to practice one's chosen religion—New York, Pennsylvania, Virginia, Delaware, New Jersey, North Carolina, and Georgia.

• Five states required public office holders to be Christian—Pennsylvania, New Jersey (Protestant), Maryland, Delaware, and North Carolina (Protestant until 1835, Christian until 1876).

• Seven states required public office holders to state that they believed in God—Pennsylvania, Massachusetts, New Hampshire, Connecticut, North Carolina, South Carolina, and Georgia.

• Five states prohibited clergy from holding public office—New York, New Jersey, Delaware, North Carolina, and Georgia.

• No states mentioned any religion other than Christianity or a denomination thereof.

Clearly ten states out of the twelve with constitutions prior to 1787 would fail any modern test concerning "separation of church and state," with only New York and Virginia passing. All ten of these states did what they wished with respect to laws concerning the establishment of state religions, and required oaths of office that would be prohibited for federal offices under Article VI of the Constitution. None of the states that favored certain religions felt the need to amend their constitutions to conform to the U.S. Constitution, and thanks to the Tenth Amendment's protection of state sovereignty and the fact that the Constitution's prohibition of a state religion only applied at the federal level, they were not compelled to do so.

Through these state constitutions, the Founders sent a statement that should have resonated into modern times. While the U.S. Constitution restricted the federal government from certain activities, those same actions were permissible in the individual states. Just as important, and clearly inferred from the Tenth Amendment, communities could take actions or enforce restrictions that neither the federal government nor the states could take or enforce. English common law completely undergirded the states' legal systems, working from a premise that law was passed from God to the people, who then applied the law upward through political structures that became increasingly restricted in their legal power as they became larger. Or, the bigger the level of government, the more Americans put limits on the power of government.

Certainly restrictive laws evolved at the local level: property covenants, zoning restrictions, blue laws, prohibition on the selling of alcohol, education requirements, marriage laws, curfews, and licensing. Religion thus was viewed essentially as a local issue, and certainly did not rise to a national level; hence the prohibition of a national religion.

New York's constitution closely aligned with the U.S. Constitution. In New York, the role of John Jay in the writing of the state constitution is somewhat murky. Jay, a descendant of French Huguenots who were forced to flee from New Rochelle, France, lost all their property after the Edict of Nantes was revoked. Accordingly, an anti-Catholic (and even anti-French) bias pervaded Jay's thought and writing.[22] Joining Jay in writing New York's constitution were Robert Livingston and Gourverneur Morris, plus ten others. Jay introduced many amendments to deny religious toleration to any sects whose doctrines were not considered consistent with state laws. But at the last minute, Jay withdrew that amendment and instead excluded from public life "professors of the religion of the church of Rome" unless they renounced that "dangerous and damnable doctrine."[23] It was defeated, but Jay succeeded in adding an amendment that required Catholics to "take an oath of allegiance to this State, and abjure and renounce all allegiance and subjection to all and every foreign king, prince, potentate, and State in all matters, ecclesiastical as well as civil."[24]

In Massachusetts, John Adams was the guiding light, and multiple times he stated that democracy and a republic could function only in a firm partnership with morality and religion. In 1798, while president, he contended, "Our constitution was made only for a moral and religious people. It is wholly inadequate to the government of any other."[25] He later reiterated the principle that "It is religion and morality alone which can establish the principles upon which freedom and security stand. Religion and virtue are the only foundations . . . of republicanism and all free governments."[26] "One great advantage of the Christian religion is that it brings the great principle of the law of nature and nations—Love your neighbor as yourself, and do to others as you would that others should do to you—to the knowledge, belief, and veneration of the whole people," Adams wrote in 1796.[27] Two years later he insisted, "The safety and prosperity of nations ultimately and essentially depend on the protection and blessing of Almighty God; and the national acknowledgment of this truth is not only an indispensable duty, which the people owe to him, but a duty whose natural influence is favorable to the promotion of that morality and piety, without which social happiness cannot exist, nor the blessings of a free government be enjoyed."[28]

Those sentiments certainly did not mean Adams was "tolerant" in the modern sense. He particularly detested the Catholic Church, writing, "Cabalistic Christianity, which is Catholic Christianity, and which has prevailed for 1,500 years, has received a mortal wound, of which the monster must finally die. Yet so strong is his constitution, that he may endure for centuries before he expires."[29] Adams asked Jefferson if "free government can possibly exist with the Roman Catholic religion."[30]

In Virginia, the primary discussion has always focused on George Washington, Thomas Jefferson, and James Madison (usually to the exclusion of the staunch Christian Patrick Henry). Washington and Jefferson were both low-church Anglicans (under vestry control), while Madison was less than forthright about his religious background. Consequently, it is useful to look at these three men.

George Washington did not attend church services regularly, although he was a vestryman in his parish. As many historians have pointed out, he rarely mentioned the name of Jesus Christ, and most, if not all, leftist historians have concluded that he was a Deist. They generally take a modern-day bias into their studies, using modern secularism to interpret what Washington meant. Such writers usually overlook Washington's many names by which he referred to God—by one count at least 104 different terms, not all of which can be applied by any stretch of the imagination to a Deist concept of an impersonal force of nature represented as God.[31] In an exhaustive study, Michael and Jana Novak concluded that the preponderance of evidence indicates that Washington was indeed a Christian, professing to be an Anglican, and certainly acting at all times according to Christian principles.[32] Washington attended many churches, spreading his faith around, as it were, in part because it was good politics. But that did not diminish his own personal religious views.

Perhaps the most stunning evidence of Washington's Christianity is found in an authentic handwritten manuscript book dated April 21–23, 1752, in which he wrote a prayer: "O Most Glorious God, in Jesus Christ, my merciful and loving Father, I acknowledge and confess my guilt in the weak and imperfect performance of the duties of this day." He concluded his prayer with, "I humbly beseech Thee to be merciful to me in the free pardon of my sins for the sake of thy dear Son and only Savior Jesus Christ who came to call not the righteous, but sinners to repentance. Thou gavest Thy Son to die for me."[33] Billy Graham would have been pleased with such a confession of faith at any of his crusades!

So how would Washington view modern secular progressives who insist on wiping out any vestiges of Christianity in American government? The answer is perhaps formulated best by examining Washington's Farewell Address. He stated, "Where is the security . . . if the sense of religious obligation desert the oaths. . . . And let us with caution indulge the supposition, that morality can be maintained without religion . . . reason and experience both forbid us to expect, that national morality can prevail in exclusion of religious principle."[34] When taken in concert with John Adams's opinions on the necessity of religion, a concrete principle emerges: that there can be no democracy without a majority of citizens being virtuous; that virtue requires morality; and morality requires religion and belief in a higher power than oneself.[35] Without religion—and some have even argued that such religion must be Christianity, while others go even further to argue that it must be Protestantism featuring latitudinarianism—there can be no effective representative democracy, and no United States. It is perhaps not a stretch to think Washington would agree.

So would Washington have supported the Supreme Court decision in *Everson v. Board of Education* in 1947? This was a groundbreaking case where the Supreme Court held that the "establishment clause" in the First Amendment ("Congress shall make no law respecting an establishment of religion") applied equally to states by virtue of the Fourteenth Amendment's due process clause ("No State shall make or enforce any law which shall abridge the privileges or immunities of citizens of the United States; nor shall any State deprive any person of life, liberty, or property, without due process of law"). The plaintiff, Arch Everson, a New Jersey tax-payer, contended that his school district used taxpayer funds to reimburse students attending private religious schools instead of public schools and that this constituted support for a religion in violation of the due pro-cess clause. The Court (with Justice Hugo Black authoring the language) agreed that the Constitution "was intended to erect a wall of separation between Church and State," effectively overthrowing 160 years of consti-tutional law.[36]

The phrase "wall of separation" was originally Jefferson's, written in a single private letter to a committee of the Danbury Baptist Association in Connecticut, where the State still supported Congregationalism as the state religion. In it, he wrote, "Believing with you that religion is a matter which lies solely between Man & his God, that he owes account to none other for his faith or worship, that the legitimate powers of government reach actions only, & not opinions, I contemplate with sovereign reverence that act of the whole American people which declared that their legislature should 'make no law respecting an establishment of religion, or prohibit-ing free exercise thereof,' *thus building a wall of separation between Church & State* [emphasis mine]."[37] Most astounding, Jefferson then concluded by asking for their "kind prayers for the protection & blessing of the common father and creator of man." Jefferson's personal view was that this was what was intended by the "establishment" clause, but in fact Jefferson was not at the Constitutional Convention, nor did he cite any of those who drafted the clause as to their intentions. Nor did he participate in drafting the Bill of Rights. Jefferson did not presume to impose the federal will as expressed in the Constitution on the State of Connecticut (obviously recognizing the illegality of doing so), but rather indicated his support of the Baptists' position in high-sounding phrases. On such flimsy evidence as this from a single individual, the Supreme Court, by a vote of five to four, overturned 160 years of precedence.

Jefferson certainly was a complex character, professing the Anglican faith, regularly attending church services, but alternatively castigating Christianity as harshly as the most devoted Deist. But the question is, what role did he expect Christianity to play in the United States, and what would be the interplay between the federal government and religious denominations? Jefferson issued a thanksgiving and prayer proclamation as governor of Virginia, and attended church services regularly in the House of Representatives chambers in the Capitol while president. It seemed he had no objections to services on government property as long as they were voluntary. He encouraged religious services at the University of Virginia: "we suggest the expediency of encouraging the different religious sects, to establish, each for himself, a professorship of their own tenets on the confines of the university, so near as that their students may attend the lectures there and have the free use of our library and every other accommodation we can give them," and even supported religious worship each morning by students.[38] Thus Jefferson looked remarkably conventional in his practices of religious observance.

As his main antiestablished religion activity was geared toward representing Baptist and Presbyterian dissenters against the official Anglican state church before it was disestablished, one is tempted to conclude that Jefferson played at being the religious doubter while keeping church and state intertwined on a voluntary basis, except when any sort of money or funding was involved. Like Washington and Adams, he no doubt would have been aghast at the unintended consequences realized by the increasingly hostile interpretations toward religion issued by the judiciary through the First and Fourteenth amendments. Given that he was absolutely a "minimum government" advocate who steadfastly believed in state sovereignty, every new federal initiative taking power from the states and increasing the federal bureaucracy would have alarmed him.

However, Madison did spend a great deal of time with Presbyterian Scotch-Irish ministers and laity, attended college at Princeton University, a Presbyterian school, and fell under the spell of "New Light" Presbyterianism under his tutor, Rev. Thomas Martin, and at Princeton.[39] He defended Presbyterians and Baptists strenuously against laws supporting Anglicanism as Virginia's state religion before it was disestablished, and warned against the "evil" of the "indefinite accumulation of property" by "ecclesiastical corporations," which "never fails to be a source of abuses."[40] "I have," he said in 1818, "ever regarded the freedom of religious opinion and worship as equally belonging to every sect."[41] In an interesting letter to Mordecai Nash that year, regarding the "Consecration of the Jewish Synagogue," he praised the "spirit in which your Sect [i.e., Jews] partake of the common blessings afforded by our Government and Laws."[42] Citing the preceding century, he noted that in fact civil government could exist "without the prop" of a religious establishment, and, conversely, that "the Christian religion itself . . . would perish if not supported by a legal provision for its Clergy." Virginia, he noted, was a perfect example of this principle.[43] Madison thought that when government and religion united, it produced corruption for both.

Madison was similar to Jefferson, and used the phrase "separation of church and state," or some variation thereof, a number of times after leaving the presidency. Perhaps the most famous is from his letter to Robert Walsh in 1819, saying, "the devotion of the people have been manifestly increased by the total separation of the Church from the State."[44] Other examples include his letters to Rev. Jasper Adams in 1832 and to Edward Livingston in 1822.[45] In all of these letters Madison claims that religion will function and prosper better without financial backing and involvement from the state, much like modern libertarians believe the economy will always function and grow better without interference from the federal government. Madison's concern about the financial connections between church and state led him to share Jefferson's views in that area.

Madison had earlier faced a political battle with George Mason and Patrick Henry over religion in the Virginia Constitution. The prime mover behind the Virginia Bill of Rights was Mason, but Madison objected to his wording on the religious freedom clause. The two were able to agree on the final wording, and then Madison tackled Jefferson's draft of a Statute for Religious Freedom. Patrick Henry emerged as his main antagonist, and Jefferson even wrote Madison from France, "What we have to do I think is devoutly pray for his [Henry's] death."[46] As matters turned out, Madison was able to neutralize Henry through political maneuvering. Interestingly, the entire debate between Madison and Henry centered around what type of Christianity the state should support.

Madison also reveals other feelings and opinions in a group of writings called "Detached Memoranda" from the period between 1817 and 1832.[47] In these writings, normally shunned by secular theorists, Madison is concerned with the growth of wealth in churches through government ties at the expense of the citizenry and to their detriment. He mentions that in some European countries the church has amassed perhaps half the property of the nation. However, he has no objection for religion to be present within government and in public places as long as it is voluntary and done at nongovernmental cost. "If Religion consist[s] in voluntary acts of individuals, singly, or voluntarily associated," he wrote, "and it be proper that public functionaries, as well as their Constituents shd [sic] discharge their religious duties, let them like their Constituents, do so at their own expense." This writing opens up a whole new side to Madison, and explains why he could freely attend religious services in the House of Representatives, as did Jefferson despite his wariness of state or national religions.[48]

Jefferson's and Madison's writing and behavior indicate that both would look favorably on religious symbols, monuments, writing, chaplain services, praying, and other religious functions, activities, and features in government as long as they were voluntary and did not cost the government money. Certainly both men would have been unwilling to have any government pay for religious accommodations such as washing feet in public places.

Of Thomas Paine's suspicion of organized religion there is little doubt. He dismissed Christ's divinity, sought to debunk the Bible, and otherwise made enemies out of almost all his former supporters. He was a very recent English transplant, to be certain, yet even Paine said, "Spiritual freedom is the root of all political liberty. . . . As the union between spiritual freedom and political liberty seems nearly inseparable, it is our duty to defend both."[49] In 1776 he wrote, "It is the will of the Almighty, that there should be a diversity of religious opinions among us," which constituted strange words to put in God's mouth, given that certainly the Judeo-Christian God utterly rejected such equality of faiths. Yet again, even Paine seemed to operate from the "Judeo-Christian umbrella," for he concluded by saying, "I look on the various *denominations* among us, to be like children of the same family."[50] He noted in *Common Sense,* "As to religion, I hold it to be the indispensable duty of *all government,* to protect all conscientious professors thereof, and I know of no other business which government hath to do therewith."[51]

Last, there is Benjamin Franklin, who is constantly depicted as a Deist, and even proclaimed himself as such in his *Autobiography.*[52] Yet for a "Deist," he acted like an unabashed advocate for Christianity, going so far as to say, "History will also afford frequent opportunities of showing . . . the excellency of the Christian religion above all others, ancient or modern."[53] He also echoed Adams and Washington in the need for virtue in the population for a republic: "Only a virtuous people are capable of freedom. As nations become corrupt and vicious, they have more need of masters."[54] Keeping in mind that a Deist believed prayer to be ineffectual, Franklin recommended that the Constitutional Convention open its daily sessions with a prayer, and at a key moment when the proceedings threatened to break down, he asked the delegates to pause and pray. Franklin seemed as far from a Deist as one could get.[55]

But despite all the evidence indicating the Founders advocated religion, especially Christianity, as the foundation for good government, politicians and courts have been quick to say otherwise. The ruling by the Supreme Court in 1962 in *Engel v. Vitale* (370 U.S. 421) carried the separation of church and state to the extreme, striking down prayer in public schools, finding that prayer is a religious activity and, as such, constitutionally impermissible.[56] For the Founders—who, as we will see later in my discussion of education, universally thought that schools should teach religion (i.e., Christianity) as one of many courses—such a ruling would have been a travesty. Benjamin Rush said, "Without religion, I believe that learning does real mischief to the morals and principles of mankind," and added in 1806, "The only foundation for a useful education in a republic is to be laid in religion. Without this there can be no virtue."[57] The current "wall of separation between church and state" would not be recognizable to the Founding Fathers, and they would seriously question what insanity had erected it. Certainly, it would have been none of their doing.

They would remind us that their references to the evils of priests corrupting government were targeted at the Roman Catholic Church, not Christianity in general, and that it is civil law that is corruptible by priests as the law descends downward. Law going up from the people cannot be corrupted in the same way. Europe is still following the old corruptible ways today with state religions and priestly intervention in government, and a new threat is emerging from theocratic Islamic states. Indeed, studies by Rodney Stark and his colleagues have shown that the more competition that exists in religious views, the more vibrant and deeply held those views are, and the more often Christianity thrives and grows. Nevertheless, in Europe, secular progressives are attempting to counter those threats by marginalizing American Christianity and accommodating Islam—a strategy akin to organized suicide.

The Founders are often misquoted and taken out of context on the notion of church and state. Often some wording in the Treaty of Tripoli—"The Government of the United States is not, in any sense, founded on the Christian religion"—is falsely attributed to a nonexistent letter by George Washington. No such letter has ever been found, and there is no documentary evidence that Washington was ever aware of the treaty language. Nonetheless, more than fifty Web sites perpetuate this falsehood. Another bogus quotation involves a letter Jefferson wrote to a group of Baptists in Virginia in 1808. Supposedly this letter is another reference to the "wall of separation" that Jefferson mentioned in his letter to the Danbury Baptists in 1802. However, the entire paragraph featuring this wording was not part of Jefferson's original letter—it was inserted before the letter by an editor, Eyler Robert Coates, as a commentary. Originally posted on the University of Virginia's Web site, it has since spread to hundreds of sites.[58]

The key to understanding the Founding Fathers' attitudes toward Christianity and its role or lack thereof with the federal government lies in looking at the actions of the Founders, not just their documents. For example, Jefferson represented dissenting groups, particularly Baptists and Presbyterians, before the Anglican Church was disestablished in Virginia. What he wrote to the Danbury group was, therefore, encouragement to a sect he had represented in the past. One should consider modern lawyers and their communications to their clients or supporters—do they always reflect their true inner feelings? Jefferson's actions, like Franklin's and Madison's, reveal a Christian soul acting with Christian behavior.

All the Founders, like all people at all times, went through transitions in their views at different times in their lives. Hamilton, who began his life fairly devout, drifted in his thirties, only to return to affirmations of the divinity of Jesus Christ before his death. Paine's hostility to religion grew over time. Washington remained fairly consistently faithful throughout his life. And Franklin? It often depended on what day one caught him. But what could not be questioned was that *all* accepted the existence of God (and almost all within the context of a Judeo-Christian God). They *all* saw a close connection between the practice of religion, the presence of virtue, and good government. They *all* thought God and liberty were inseparable—even Jefferson in his *Summary View of the Rights of British America* insisted that "the God who gave us life, gave us liberty at the same time."[59] John Witherspoon noted that Jefferson was "the best friend to American liberty, who is most sincere and active in promoting true and undefiled religion," and Adams wrote to Jefferson in 1815, "the question before the human race is, whether the God of nature shall govern the world by his own laws, or whether priests and kings shall rule it by ficticious miracles."[60] Today, with "ficticious miracles" such as universal health care and multicultural one-world-ism abounding, Adams's question looms more immediate than ever.

QUESTION #2

WHAT IS THE FUNCTION OF EDUCATION
AND HOW MUCH CONTROL SHOULD THE
FEDERAL GOVERNMENT HAVE OVER IT?

O f all the issues on which the Founders agreed, education stood out as the most prominent. Virtually every one of the Founders agreed that some form of public education was necessary in order for a true democracy to function. John Adams wrote in his *Dissertation on the Canon and Feudal Law* (1765), "The preservation of the means of knowledge among the lowest ranks is of more importance to the public than all the property of all the rich men in the country."[1] What was the nature of that "knowledge"? How was education to be provided, and who was to provide it? Should religion play a role in public education? And, above all, what was the role of the federal government (if any) in overseeing the education system?

When talk show host Neal Boortz refers to "government schools" and the "propagandizing" of American children, and when up to 2.1 million (K–12) American children are homeschooled because of concerns about what is being taught in public schools, then the debate over whether the federal government is overinvolved in public education is more than hot rhetoric. Part of the concern involves religion—the subject we just addressed—and the systematic exclusion of Christianity from education over the past century. But there are secular homeschoolers as well, and many of them are concerned more about the declining quality of a system that seems to appeal to the lowest common denominator. A majority of Americans tell pollsters that they think schools nationally are poor, but that their own educational institutions are better.[2] However, other polls show that almost half of the respondents think schools are "dabbling in topics in the classroom in which they have no business," and American students continued to fall well behind the performance of students in other countries.[3] Particularly in math and science, American students fall below the average of other developed nations. This, of course, was the reason behind the Bush administration's "No Child Left Behind" program of mandatory testing, which is now reviled by many of the same people who complained about student performance. Yet increasingly, stories emerge about schools teaching gay and lesbian studies, environmentalism, global warming, and a host of what might be called nonacademic subjects (most of them highly politicized), while genuine critical skills of "readin', writin', and 'rithmetic" seem to decline or evaporate altogether. How would the Founders have reacted to modern educational trends?

The best way to determine what the Founders would say about such issues today is to examine what they said in their own lifetimes about education. George Washington's views on education were often expressed in his letters to relatives. Writing just a year before his death to his nephew William Augustine Washington, the former president commented on the 1700s version of homeschooling, in which a tutor was hired, and explained, "the reason which you assign for giving the rudiments of education to your sons at home is a weighty and conclusive one; but much will depend upon qualifications, and fitness of the Preceptor you employ, to render it more or less beneficial."[4] He went on to add, "To a certain point, tuition under the eye of parents or guardians of youth is much to be preferred; because the presumption is, that the propensities and passions, will be watched with more solicitude and attention by them, than by their tutors: but when the direction of these are unfolded, and can be counteracted by the discipline of public schools, and the precepts of the professors. Especially too, when the judgment is beginning to form; when pride becomes a stimulus; and the knowledge of men, as well as of books are to be learnt; I should give the preference to a public seminary."[5] Some of this had to do with the fact that, as today, in the 1700s both parents worked—but the wife's work "inside the home" was all-consuming and full-time, often with older children helping out raising the younger ones. On another occasion, Washington wrote to George Chapman, "the best means of forming a manly, virtuous and happy people, will be found in the right education of youth. Without *this* foundation, every other means, in my opinion, must fail; and it gives me pleasure to find that gentlemen of your abilities are devoting their time and attention in pointing out the way."[6]

What, however, should be taught? None of the Founders thought that good citizens could survive without strong moral codes. As Washington put it to his nephew Steptoe Washington in 1790, "a good moral character is the first essential in a man, and that the habits contracted at your age are generally indelible, and your conduct here may stamp your character through life. It is therefore highly important that you should endeavor not only to be learned but virtuous."[7]

Washington's comments revealed several basic elements of the Founders' view of education. First, they all revered books. "With us," Madison wrote of Americans, "there are more readers than buyers of Books. In England there are more buyers than readers of Books."[8] Jefferson insisted, "Read good books because they will encourage as well as direct your feelings," and Washington said, "a knowledge of books is the basis upon which other knowledge is to be built."[9] Books, Jefferson said, "constitute capital. A library book lasts as long as a house, for hundreds of years. It is not, then, an article of mere consumption but fairly of capital, and often in the case of professional men, setting out in life, their only capital."[10] (Certainly that was true of Abraham Lincoln.) Americans' appreciation of books—stemming from the founding generation—lasted until the 1830s when Martin Van Buren created the Democratic Party and pushed through government subsidies for partisan "newspapers" that were little more than propaganda organs. Then, and only then, did Americans' reading habits shift from books to the ubiquitous newspapers.

A second element easily discernible in the Founders' view of education entailed their approach to learning in the context of faith in God, and far more explicitly than many anti-Christian scholars insist. Washington, for example, in 1783 lectured the "Learned Professions of Philadelphia," saying, "For the re-establishment of our once violated rights; for the confirmation of our independence; for the protection of virtue, philosophy, literature: for the present flourishing state of the sciences, and for the enlarged prospect of human happiness, it is our common duty to pay the tribute of gratitude to the greatest and best of Beings."[11] Benjamin Rush, for example, insisted, "the blessings of knowledge can be extended to the poor and laboring part of the community only by the means of FREE SCHOOLS [emphasis in original]. . . . To a people enlightened in the principles of liberty and Christianity, arguments, it is hoped, will be unnecessary to persuade them to adopt these necessary and useful institutions."[12] Rush went on to write to John Armstrong, "without religion, I believe that learning does real mischief to the morals and principles of mankind."[13]

The connection between Christianity and education was obvious to almost all of the Founders, and they did not see a contradiction between the "free schools" that Benjamin Rush described and Christian education. For many, it was a tradition dating as far back as the early colonies. The first schools in Massachusetts taught students to read with the *New-England Primer,* which taught the alphabet using phrases such as "In Adam's Fall, We sinned all" to "Zacheus he did climb the Tree, Our Lord to see." Massachusetts passed a law in 1647 that required a school in every town, "it being one chief project of that old deluder, Satan, to keep men from the knowledge of the Scriptures," and therefore every town of more than fifty people was required to "forthwith appoint one within their town to teach all such children as shall resort to him to write and read."[14] These views did not fade out as the nineteenth century unfolded. As James Monroe said, "An institution which endeavors to rear American youth in pure love of truth and duty, and while it enlightens their minds by ingenious and liberal studies, endeavors to awaken a love of country; to soften local prejudices, and *to inoculate Christian faith* and chastity, cannot but acquire . . . the confidence of the wise and good [emphasis in original]."[15] As I showed in the last chapter, Benjamin Franklin proposed that the teaching of history in schools would help demonstrate the importance of religion and the superiority of Christianity.[16] Both Fisher Ames and Benjamin Rush (often called "the father of public schools in America") wanted the Bible to be the primary textbook in all schools, and even Jefferson, as president, made the Bible a primary text for Washington, D.C., schools.[17]

Just as the connection between God and knowledge stood obvious to all, so too was the connection between an educated people and a free people. "Children," John Adams said, "should be educated and instructed in the principles of freedom."[18] "Liberty cannot be preserved without general knowledge among the people," he wrote. "The preservation of the means of knowledge among the lowest ranks is of more importance to the public than all the property of all the rich men in the country."[19] James Madison flatly stated, "It is universally admitted that a well-instructed people alone can be permanently a free people."[20] His Virginia colleague, James Monroe, agreed: "In a government founded on the sovereignty of the people," he told the Virginia General Assembly in 1801, "the education of youth is an object of the first importance. In such a government knowledge should be diffused throughout the whole society, and for that purpose the means of acquiring it made not only practicable but easy to every citizen."[21] Thomas Jefferson explained the only "safe depository" of public powers was the people themselves, and "if we think them not enlightened enough to exercise their control with a wholesome discretion, the remedy is not to take it from them, but to inform their discretion by education." That, he concluded, "is the true corrective of abuses of constitutional power."[22] James Madison similarly insisted that "a diffusion of knowledge is the only guardian of true liberty."[23] "Here then lies the foundation of civil liberty," wrote Nathaniel Greene in 1771, "in forming the habits of the youthful mind, in forwarding every passion that may tend to the promotion of the happiness of the community, in fixing in ourselves right ideas of benevolence, humanity, integrity, and truth."[24]

The Founders also noted the value of understanding and remembering the American Revolution. James Madison wrote in 1819, "The origin and outset of the American Revolution contain lessons of which posterity ought not to be deprived," and two years later he stated, "No studies seem so well calculated to give a proper expansion to the mind as Geography and History."[25] Jefferson once quipped, "History, in general, only informs us what bad government is."[26] Thomas Paine, in *The Crisis,* reasoned, "A too great inattention to past occurrences retards and bewilders our judgement in every thing."[27] And while the tendency to color the truth through the passions or prejudices of the writer posed a problem, the solution, Jefferson thought, lay in time: "history may distort truth," he noted, and "the opening scenes of our present government [will not] be seen in their true aspect until the letters of the day, now held in private hands, shall be . . . laid open to public view."[28] While many Founders worried that, as Adams said, "nothing but misrepresentations, or partial accounts" of the Revolution would survive, his own son, John Quincy Adams, insisted, "the interior working of the machinery must be found."[29] Appreciating and treasuring one's own history did not mean despising that of others. Benjamin Rush insisted that students "must be taught how to love [their] fellow creatures in every part of the world, but he must cherish with a more intense and peculiar affection, the citizens of Pennsylvania and of the United States of America."[30] In a statement that could be taken as a direct broadside against multiculturalism, Rush explained, "I do not wish to see our youth educated with a single prejudice against any nation or country; but we impose a task upon human nature, repugnant alike to reason, revelation, and the ordinary dimensions of the human heart, when we require him to embrace with equal affection the whole family of mankind."[31] Patriotism demanded that a young man be taught that "this life 'is not his own'" when the safety of his country requires it."[32] For a man who served in the Revolutionary army as General Washington's chief physician, Rush knew the sacrifices for which he called.

Benjamin Franklin, who insisted that a good education was necessary, embraced Dr. Turnbull's *Observations on Liberal Education* as his own: "Whatever else one may have learned, if he comes into the World from his Schooling and Masters, quite unacquainted with the Nature, Rank and Condition, of Mankind, and the *Duties of human Life* . . . he hath lost his Time; *he is not educated;* he is not prepared for the World; he is not qualified for Society; he is not fitted for discharging the *proper Business of Man.*" Turnbull continued, "The Way therefore to judge whether Education be on a right Footing or not, is to compare it with the END; or to consider what it does in order to accomplish Youth for choosing and *behaving well* in various Conditions, *Relations* and Incidents of Life. If Education be calculated and adapted to furnish young Minds betimes with proper Knowledge for their Guidance and Direction in the chief Affairs of the world, and in the principal Vicissitudes to which human Concerns are subject, then it is indeed *proper or right Education.*"[33] Writing to Samuel Johnson in 1750, Franklin insisted, "nothing is of more importance for the public weal, than to form and train up youth in wisdom and virtue. Wise and good men are . . . the *strength* of a state: much more so than riches or arms, which, under the management of Ignorance and Wickedness, often draw on destruction, instead of providing for the safety of a people."[34]

What Franklin called "general virtue" was more likely obtained from the "*education* of youth, than from the *exhortation* of adult persons," and he praised "the talents for the education of youth" as "the gift of God; and that he on whom they are bestowed, whenever a way is opened for the use of them, is as strongly *called* as if he heard a voice from heaven."[35] John Adams told Jefferson that education was a "subject so vast, and the systems of writers are so various and so contradictory . . . that human life is too short to examine it; and a man must die before he can learn to bring up his children. The phylosophers, divines, politicians and paedagogues . . . who have published their theories and practices in this department are without number."[36] Minister Samuel Phillips Payson observed, "the slavery of a people is generally founded in ignorance of some kind or another. . . . Hence knowledge and learning may well be considered as most essentially requisite to a free, righteous government."[37]

According to the Founders, the primary purpose of education was to teach young people how to be good citizens and instill within them civic virtue and a sense of moral responsibility so they could lead their communities later on. It must be noted that the Founders' ideal system for doing this consisted of a network of taxpayer-supported, locally driven primary education in public schools, religious schools, or even the equivalent then of homeschooling. Each citizen would receive a few years of schooling under this system, and at some point qualified and talented students would advance to a middle school or a high school, but this was based solely on performance and scholastic merit, not on a general "right." It would, necessarily, involve a smaller number of students. Primary school, therefore, was to focus on reading, writing, government/civics, mathematics, history, geography, and the priority of religion—all considered necessary by the Founders for the preparation of a good citizen. High schools would allow for those pursuing specialized studies, while colleges were intended for the study of law, science, religion, and languages.

This system was advocated by Thomas Jefferson, who, in keeping with his Rousseauian roots, wrote an essay in 1779 called "A Bill for the More General Diffusion of Knowledge." In it, he called for a plan in which every local district would create three-year schools for children between seven and ten years of age and a set of county schools for the top students, capped by a state college for the best of those students.[38] As Jefferson outlined it, there would be a "free school for reading, writing and common arithmetic; to provide for the annual selection of these best subjects from these schools who might receive at the public expence [sic] a higher degree of education at a district school; and from these district schools to select a certain number of the most promising subjects to be completed at an University [sic], where all the useful sciences should be taught. Worth and genius would thus have been sought out from every condition of life, and completely prepared by education for defeating the competition of wealth and birth for public trusts."[39] He intended a meritocratic system—an "aristocracy of talent"—that would be distinctly secular, focused on "training citizens, rather than Christians."[40] Writing to George Wyeth, Jefferson implored, "Preach, my dear Sir, a crusade against ignorance; establish and improve the law for education [of] the common people. Let our countrymen know that the people alone can protect us against these evils, and that the tax which will be paid for this purpose is not more than the thousandth part of what will be paid to kings, priests, and nobles who will rise up among us if we leave the people in ignorance. . . . [American] learned men are too few in number, and are less learned and infinitely less emancipated from prejudice than those of this country [i.e., England]."[41] Education, in Jefferson's view, provided a safeguard against the aristocratic class system that had arisen elsewhere, and reinforced his view that there was no inherent inequality in birthright.

Such a position was supported by Robert Coram, who wrote to Washington in 1791 with "Political Inquiries, to which is added a plan for the establishment of schools throughout the United States." Coram argued, "Let public schools then be established in every county of the United States, at least as many as necessary for the present population; and let those schools be supported by a general tax."[42] Rush did not disagree: "Let our common people be compelled . . . to give their children (what is commonly called) a good English education. Let schoolmasters of every description be supported in part by the public."[43] In 1797, the American Philosophical Society sponsored an essay contest on the topic of the creation of public education for the sake of a democratic government, with most of the submissions outlining state-funded systems that would produce literate and knowledgeable citizens.[44] Jefferson party journalist Samuel Harrison Smith, who shared the prize with Samuel Knox, was the youngest of the essayists. While men had "engraven upon his heart certain great principles of duty . . . it remains uncontested that these principles are few and undefined and that they do not comprehend half the relations which men stand towards each other."[45] The "diffusion of knowledge," he insisted, "actually produces some virtues, and without it would have no existence, and that it strengthens and extends all such virtues as are generally deemed to [exist] independent of uncommon attainments."[46] Once again, like others of the age, he noted that "human happiness depends upon the possession of virtue and wisdom . . . [and] that knowledge itself cannot possibly be too extensively diffused."[47] It bears repeating that the Founders thought a democracy required the majority of citizens to be virtuous; and that virtue required morality; and that morality demanded religion, with its belief in a power higher than oneself.

Smith continued to note that the "elements of education," citing reading and writing, were "so obviously necessary" that it wasn't worth the time to write a defense of them, while mathematics was "of nearly equal importance," but so too was geography, as "it becomes the duty of the citizen to have just ideas of the position, size, and strength of nations."[48] Everyone would benefit, including, he maintained, the farmer and the mechanic. He concluded by arguing "this, then, appears to be the era, if ever, of public education."[49] Smith advocated a combination public/private elementary and high-school system, with a publicly funded national university. Such a system, he predicted, would result in "many of the most enlightened of our citizens [traversing] the globe with the spirit of philosophical research."[50]

Samuel Knox similarly championed a publicly funded system and wrote that to establish the best education system, "it is necessary that the community be so convinced of its importance as to cheerfully furnish every accommodation."[51] Deeply concerned about violations of religious freedoms in public schools, Knox nevertheless acknowledged "the direction and all-powerful protection of that BEING who is the ineffable source of all knowledge, excellence, and happiness attainable by man."[52] But even Knox noted there would "appear to be no infringement of this liberty in its widest extent for the public teacher to begin and end the business of the day with a short and suitable prayer and address to the great source of all knowledge and instruction."[53]

Jefferson, of course, remained cautious even about *state* funding of education, and would have recoiled at the prospect of any federal intervention. Instead, he proposed a "radical bottom-up approach, in which smaller communities formed the basis for most education, with progressively smaller elites emerging at each point."[54] Noah Webster agreed: "In our American republics, where government is in the hands of the people, knowledge should be universally diffused by means of public schools."[55] Moreover, to Webster, having a domestic education was a prerequisite to patriotism. "It is therefore of infinite importance that those who direct the councils of a nation should be educated in that nation . . . their first ideas, attachments, and habits should be acquired in the country which they are to govern and defend."[56]

One proposal about which many of the Founders agreed was a national university. Thomas Pinckney's draft of the U.S. Constitution included a clause to "establish and provide for a national University at the Seat of Government in the United States."[57] Mulling over what might be taught, Adams wrote to Jefferson, "When you asked my opinion of a university it would have been easy to advise mathematiks, experimental phylosophy, natural history, chemistry, and astronomy, geography, and the fine arts, to the exclusion of ontology, metaphysicks, and theology. But knowing the eager impatience of the human mind to search into eternity and infirmity, the first cause and last end of all things I thought best to leave it, its liberty to inquire till it is convinced as I have been these 50 years that there is but one being in the universe who comprehends it; and our last resource is resignation."[58] In his first annual address to Congress, Washington sought funding for "the promotion of Science and Literature" and urged Congress to debate "whether this desirable object will be best promoted by affording aids to seminaries of learning already established, by the institution of a national University, or by any other expedients."[59] In November 1794 Washington said that "a National University in this country is a thing to be desired, has always been my decided opinion; and the appropriation of ground and funds for it in the Federal City, have long been contemplated and talked of," but admitted that the plan still lacked details.[60]

But Washington returned to the issue of a national university in his final address to Congress in 1796, again urging Congress to establish both such an institution and a military academy. He argued that the seminaries of higher learning were "highly respectable and useful," but "the funds upon which they rest . . . are too narrow . . . to command the ablest Professors." He reasoned:

The more homogeneous our Citizens can be made in these particulars, the greater will be our prospect of permanent Union;
and a primary object of such a National Institution should be,
the education of our Youth in the science of Government. In a
Republic, what species of knowledge can be equally important?
and what duty, more pressing on its Legislature, than to patron-
ize a plan for communicating it to those, who are to be the
future guardians of the liberties of the Country?[61]

When Washington left office, he told St. George Tucker that while
his desire for a national university had not receded, "the Sentiments of the
Legislature have not been in unison therewith," and he postponed further
consideration of the project to see if he could devise a different plan to create such an institution.[62]

With the exception of a national university, it is important to real-
ize that at *no time* did the Founders advocate *national* or *federal* public
schools. Rather, the Land Ordinance of 1785 was meant to give the states
land on which to found their own schools. John Adams set the pattern
during the American Revolution when he wrote the Massachusetts state
constitution and included a passage to require cities and towns to provide
for "the public worship of God and the support and maintenance of public
Protestant teachers of piety, religion, and morality" in the schools.[63] He
insisted that schools should inculcate all citizens in "Public and private
charity," "industry and frugality," and "honesty and punctuality."[64] In the
Northwest Ordinance, a similar sentiment was expressed: "religion, morality, and knowledge being necessary to good government and the happiness
of mankind, schools and the means of education shall forever be encouraged."[65] Thus, three principles in early constitutions and legislation were
established about education: (1) that it was a necessity for a free people; (2)
that it consisted of a certain measure of Christian, religious teaching; and
(3) that it would be funded at the local level with state encouragement.

These institutions of higher learning supposedly remained under
state control, and even in the general education wave of the 1830s and
1840s, when public schools were established by the hundreds, those doing

so continued to believe that the "Schools and churches were allies in the quest to create the Kingdom of God in America," and thus the evangelicals moved into school founding with verve.[66] Horace Mann, one of the leading proponents of a public school system, insisted, "The Bible, the whole Bible, and nothing but the Bible, without note or comment, must be taken as the text-book of religious instruction" within the schools.[67] Another leading common school proponent, Samuel Lewis, was a Methodist minister who pressed for the creation in Ohio of a superintendent of Common Schools in 1837. Lewis, like Mann, argued, "It can not be too deeply impressed on all minds, that we are a Christian, as well as a Republican people; and the utmost care should be taken to inculcate sound principles of Christian morality."[68] While both Mann and Lewis sought to avoid "sect" or "catechism" or "creed," they focused on obtaining "broad common ground" where "all Christians and lovers of virtue meet."[69]

Later, the pattern of nearly universal education, strongly controlled at the local or state level, repeated itself in the Morrill Act (also called the Land Grant College Act). Morrill provided federal land to states for the purpose of establishing technical, agricultural, or industrial schools, as well as teachers' schools. The act sought, "without excluding other scientific and classical studies and including military tactic, to teach such branches of learning as are related to agriculture and the mechanic arts, in such manner as the legislatures of the States may respectively prescribe, in order to promote the liberal and practical education of the industrial classes in the several pursuits and professions in life." Two private universities, Cornell and the Massachusetts Institute of Technology, were funded by land scrip that authorized a state to acquire federal land in other states to fund institutions within a state's own borders. But most schools were public institutions, such as Alabama A&M, the University of Arizona, Colorado State, the University of Delaware, the University of Florida, Florida A&M, Purdue, Kansas State, Iowa State, Louisiana State, the University of Maryland, and many more.

Meanwhile, tensions arose between the goal of having an educated electorate (enforced by mandatory school attendance) and a free society, where people should be free to opt out of state education. This was especially true when it involved state authority to coerce taxes from citizens for public schools. In 1922, a group of Oregon churches initiated a referendum that would require all children between eight and sixteen to attend public school. The state's Catholic parochial schools challenged the law, and the resulting case, *Pierce v. Society of Sisters* (1925), ruled that it was a violation of property rights to deprive Catholics of their school organizations. Compulsory education did not mean compulsory *public* education. A subsequent host of cases involving Jehovah's Witnesses engaging in the "Pledge of Allegiance" ultimately led Justice Robert Jackson to conclude, "Free public education, if faithful to the ideal of *secular instruction and political neutrality* [emphasis mine], will not be partisan or enemy of any class, creed, party, or faction."[70] But of course, as we have seen, the Founders were neither "secular" in their intent for education nor "politically neutral," for their entire premise in supporting public education was to perpetuate and energize a free republican form of government, not despotism, monarchies, or cults of any shape or size.

At that point, political correctness and multiculturalism entered public schools. Some interpreted Jackson's reasoning to mean that "a democratic system must embrace all citizens, with their wide range of opinions and creeds, and *make all welcome and learn from them* [emphasis mine]."[71] This led to a liberalization of education (an early form of political correctness) wherein creationism could not be taught and Islam could be referred to only as a "religion of peace." In the world where all religions have something to teach us, animism, which holds that all objects, including plants and animals, have a soul, was on deck by the early twentieth century as a genuine "alternative" faith.

The implications of these principles took on federal proportions in 1946 when Harry S Truman, in his State of the Union message, proposed federal aid to "assist the States in assuring more nearly equal opportunities for a good education." Thus, the federal camel's nose entered the tent. He inadvertently suggested that people were entitled, through education, to a certain opportunity of outcome. Moreover, critics pointed out that federal money meant federal control—always under the auspices of "watching the taxpayer's dollar"—and that federal control in one aspect of education would soon spread, like a virus, to all others. This, again, was something the Founders absolutely would have abhorred. Federal involvement cut both ways, however, and when local schools provided busing to and from schools, parochial schools proverbially jumped on board arguing spending discrimination against religious schools.

With the Elementary and Secondary Education Act in 1965, Lyndon Johnson pushed more than the camel's nose inside the tent. The act included funding for the preschool Head Start program, plus other support for low-income families. It also established book budgets for school libraries to kids in both public and private elementary and secondary schools, after-hours programs, and curriculum materials. Most of these funds came through Title I, and while they were to be, at first, administered through the states and localities, and were to be available to parochial schools as well, the act opened the door still wider to federal control of elementary education. In essence, the Elementary and Secondary Education Act "bought off" Catholic opposition by including the parochial schools.

After World War II, a pair of trends contributed to further federal involvement in public schools. The first involved a combination of national defense concerns and economic benefits because the cold war dictated that we should have a scientifically literate and educated workforce, and the federal government began seeking ways to fund lower-level science and mathematics. The second involved a steadily growing emphasis on the increased earnings capacity that education brought. By the 1960s, it was a commonly held opinion that everyone "needed" a high school diploma to succeed and that college degrees were becoming a necessity as well. Studies showed the higher wages and salaries of college graduates compared with high school graduates, while at the same time underscoring the economic benefits to the nation as a whole of having a more educated populace.

A third trend more specifically affected elementary and high schools, however, and played a key role in insinuating the federal government even further into the public school systems—racial discrimination and *Brown v. Board of Education*. Challenging the 1896 *Plessey v. Ferguson* principle of "separate but equal," *Brown* immediately plunged education into a struggle between states and the federal government, as President Dwight Eisenhower sent in the 101st Airborne to protect black students after Governor Orval Faubus had called out the Arkansas National Guard to protect the segregationists during the integration of Little Rock public schools. Underlying these struggles was the assumption that equal resources would produce rough equality of outcomes, educationally, economically, and even socially. But now the assumptions changed: only the federal government could assure the equality of opportunity, giving it still more license to become involved in public education.

At the same time, schools themselves shifted their emphasis from the talented students who performed well to the disadvantaged, and tried to figure out why they weren't performing as well.[72] In part, this came back to the notion that through education, individuals could be more productive and not be a "drain" on society. Yet with minimal government intrusion, incomes had steadily grown more equal prior to the Great Society: by 1962, income disparities dropped dramatically. This was before the impact of *Brown v. Board of Education* could even be felt, let alone measured.[73] Put another way, the presumption that *Brown,* by offering wider educational opportunities, also sparked economic equality was simply mistaken, and, in fact, quite the opposite occurred as suddenly (thanks in large part to the Great Society programs themselves) inequality increased as the number of female-headed households increased.[74]

Even then, government asked the wrong question. It was irrelevant if schools made the population more or less equal. The Founders would have said, "Did it leave them more or less *educated*?" By "educated," the Founders meant patriotic, informed of science and the humanities, and aware of God and the Christian faith. But with the creation of the Department of Education in 1979, a federal department explicitly charged with overseeing education below the college and university level was directed to create programs to generate funds for education and to enforce civil rights laws. Now the federal government had made itself a permanent, necessary presence in the local classroom with the acceptance of *any* federal funds. Colleges and universities quickly discovered this when they accepted students with federal scholarships and grants, and only a handful of universities and colleges—most notably Hillsdale College and Grove City College—

have refused to accept students who entered on federal money, instead providing them with private scholarships to offset the financial loss. Equality had displaced good citizenship and learning as the primary focus of the educational system in the eyes of the government.

Once again, it was an ironic turn that "higher education" had been transformed from an almost entirely religious institution to a nearly completely secular and antireligious one. At one time, for example, "such a large percentage of [Harvard's] graduates entered the ministry that many referred to the college as the 'school of prophets.'"[75] Indeed, it would not be a stretch to say that the national university many of the Founders envisioned was viewed as necessary only because they expected the system of higher education would remain overwhelmingly religious. As one student of the university system noted, a rash of new colleges appeared in the middle of the 1700s, a development explained by the Great Awakening.[76] Eight of the nine Colonial colleges had a religious affiliation: Harvard (Puritan), William & Mary (Anglican), Yale (Congregational), Princeton (New Light Presbyterian), Columbia (Anglican), Brown (Baptist), Rutgers (Dutch Reformed), and Dartmouth (New Light Congregational). (Only the University of Pennsylvania, founded by Benjamin Franklin, was essentially secular.) Three of these—Brown, Rutgers, and Dartmouth—stemmed directly from the revivalistic fervor sweeping North America, and while most of these institutions were private, Harvard, William & Mary, and Yale were all chartered by the established church in the colony and as such had a relationship to the state, receiving substantial financial aid from the Colonial governments. A similar religious character could be observed in the typical curriculum in such colleges, which contained heavy doses of logic, Greek, Hebrew, rhetoric, and divinity—between two and four times the amount of hours dedicated to math or physics.[77]

Much has been made of Thomas Jefferson's letter to the Danbury Baptists, discussed at some length in the previous chapter, which contained no public authority or legal bearing whatsoever. Why so many have latched onto his "separation of church and state" sentiment as indicative of the will and wishes of the entire Revolutionary generation—over, say, those of Franklin, Washington, Adams, or others—is obvious: only Jefferson uttered an opinion that stood apart.[78] Virtually everyone else, including early justices of the U.S. Supreme Court, acknowledged only that "*Congress* shall make no law" abridging the freedom of religion, but that the states were perfectly within their rights to support—or not support—whatever religion they chose. In 1833, U.S. Supreme Court Justice Joseph Story (1811–1845) wrote, "The whole power over the subject of religion is left exclusively to the State governments, to be acted upon according to their own sense of justice and State constitutions."[79]

Any understanding of "public" education in the early republic, then, must begin with the premise that virtually all of the Founders expected that schools could be either private—and, as such, tied to a particular religious denomination—or public. Regardless, the schools would instruct students in becoming good citizens (by which they meant possessing an understanding of history, politics, logic, and, above all, Christianity), and public monies used to fund public schools would be controlled at the local level, even if the funds came from the state. Never was the federal government to be involved in elementary school education, and only in the case of a national university would the federal government have any role in the governance of any institution. Moreover, at every level, in every school of every type, the fundamental assumptions were that the purpose of the schools was to educate an electorate not only in basic knowledge of literature, mathematics, geography, history, and politics, but also in the moral elements of wisdom, virtue, and religious faith.

To have drifted so far away from these principles so that multiculturalism, political correctness, and tolerance have become the standards for many public schools would have shocked and outraged the Founders, most likely enough that they would have added provisions into the Bill of Rights erecting a "wall of separation" between the federal government and education. Indeed, it would not have been a surprise—if the Founders could have seen how the educational system and the university networks have evolved—to have recanted on their favorable comments about a national university as well. For a generation of men who mentioned "God," "The Divine," "Providence," and "Jesus Christ" at almost every conceivable *public* event to see that virtually all mention of such terms had been driven from schools, it's entirely likely that they would have contemplated another revolution.

A final, related point to education involves the federal government and the arts. The Founders were no sticks-in-the-mud: Jefferson was a multitalented musician, architect, and writer; Washington—while musically inept himself—loved both "classical" tunes and the Irish and Scottish folk songs of the day; and Patrick Henry frequented the home of Colonel Nathaniel West, whose parties included "games aplenty in every room, and minuets, reels, jigs, and marches performed in the ballroom to the accompaniment of violins and horns."[80] Washington said, "The arts and sciences essential to the prosperity of the state and to the ornament and happiness of human life have a primary claim to the encouragement of every lover of his country and mankind."[81] "To promote literature in this rising empire," Washington observed, "and to encourage the arts, have ever been amongst the warmest wishes of my heart."[82]

Jefferson would not have disagreed: "I am an enthusiast on the subject of the arts," he gushed. "But it is an enthusiasm of which I am not ashamed, as its object is to improve the taste of my countrymen, to increase their reputation, to reconcile to the respect of the world & procure them its praise."[83] Some of Jefferson's love of the "arts" really constituted a pragmatic interest in architecture, noting that "as we double our numbers every 20 years we must double our houses."[84]

James Monroe wrote to his daughter, Eliza, in 1805 not to forget that "among all of y[ou]r useful acquirements, the comparatively trivial one of playing & singing several airs upon the harp. . . . That is an accomplishment that will be really useful to you."[85] His fellow Virginian James Madison encouraged private arts and sciences, noting that "some of the most important discoveries [in both fields] come forward under very unpromising and suspicious appearances."[86] Thomas Paine, likewise, saw the connection, saying "every principal art has some science for a parent."[87]

John Adams, of course, had outlined a pecking order of education:

The Science of Government it is my Duty to study, more than
all other Sciences; the Art of Legislation and Administration

and Negotiation, ought to take Place, indeed to exclude in a manner all other Arts. I must study Politicks [sic] and War that my sons may have liberty to study Mathematicks [sic] and Philosophy. My sons ought to study Mathematics and Philosophy, Geography, natural History, Naval Architecture, navigation, Commerce and Agriculture, in order to give their Children a right to study Painting, Poetry, Musick [sic], Architecture, Statuary, Tapestry and Porcelaine [sic].[88]

Thus, government was foundational—until the principles of government were understood, there could be no education in mathematics, history, or the arts. As government was presumed to rest on public virtue and religion, one could say that to the Founders, education in religion and morals ensured good government, and good government permitted the pursuit of the arts. However, just as the federal government was to stay out of state and local education, so too the Founders expected that the arts would remain outside the purview of government. The ultimate conflation of malpractice, they would have agreed, would have been federal support for arts education!

In sum, the Founders emphasized education and did everything they could to ensure that states and territories had what they needed to establish their own schools. At the university level, many Founders favored a single, national secular university that would stand beside the half dozen major religious-oriented universities. They never would have entertained a federal presence in local education to the point that it could dictate curriculum, admission, or sports policies. In short, they never would have envisioned, or tolerated, what we have today. Nor would they look favorably on multiculturalism, or the elimination of American exceptionalism, for they all believed in it. American history was the story of a nation blessed by God, with a particular system of government that surpassed all others, but the Founders well knew that the system was potentially so fragile that it depended on public virtue to function, and that education remained foremost in shaping that virtue.

QUESTION #3

IS THE GOVERNMENT RESPONSIBLE
FOR PROTECTING THE LAND
AND THE ENVIRONMENT?

Land was something many of the Founders felt a deep connection to, something that constituted more than a livelihood, and the embodiment of their entire concept of liberty. When Thomas Jefferson wrote, "the true foundation of republican government is the equal right of every citizen in his person and property *and in their management* [emphasis mine]," he was addressing the fundamental principle accepted by most of the Founders that individuals were responsible for the land.[1] He went on to write, "A right to property is founded in our natural wants, in the means with which we are endowed to satisfy these wants, and the right to what we acquire by those means without violating the similar rights of other sensible beings."[2] Jefferson believed that every citizen was entitled to his own property through his own efforts, and that government provided the structure for the individual to acquire property, but not the entitlement.

The Founders' concern with property rights, often portrayed by the Left as an obsession with wealth, in fact displayed a deep understanding of the stewardship of the earth. This was seen in the extensive attention they paid to inheritance laws. After all, if one uses up or destroys his property, what is left for his children to inherit? At the same time, however, assumptions about what "improved" property were nearly universal: land was to be cleared (of trees, rocks, and any other obstacles to farming), game was to be hunted for food and pleasure, and the water supply was to be protected at all costs. But notions of clearing land for farming were not unique to European settlers, as some agricultural tribes of Indians had been clearing land for years. What was different about the English who arrived in America was that they brought with them the concept of individual land ownership, and that meant individual land development and protection. It is common today to see a forest as something to be preserved, but that is an entirely ahistorical reaction. To the settlers in the New World, forests represented both a nearly endless supply of fuel and an impediment to greater productivity and wealth through agriculture, which, of course, meant feeding more people.

George Washington, John Adams, Thomas Jefferson, and many other Founders who either worked their land themselves or oversaw slave labor forces understood the relentless mathematics of agricultural productivity. Simply put, one's land had to produce more than the workforce consumed; and to survive from year to year, it had to produce enough of an excess to make a profit. Gilder's Law (a concept introduced by economic theorist George Gilder, which holds that a society will consume cheap resources to preserve dear resources) was in effect: Americans consumed cheap resources (wood, land, game) to preserve precious resources (human life). Europeans, as a rule, did not share many of the Indians' view of the "sacred" nature of land. Although later, philosophers such as Ralph

Waldo Emerson and Henry David Thoreau would wax romantic about being connected to the earth, Revolutionary-era Americans had a thoroughly utilitarian view of land: it existed to produce. This, of course, had its roots in biblical teaching, wherein Jesus, in Matthew 7:19, admonished the disciples that "Every tree that does not bear good fruit is cut down and thrown into the fire," and in Mark 11:12–14, "He cursed the fig tree that had not borne fruit." Land was to yield its crop—of course it could do so only if well tended and cared for—and unproductive land was worse than useless: it was consuming resources (space, water) without giving back to society. And while most of the Founders had not yet immersed themselves in the capitalist doctrines of Adam Smith, he said the same thing, namely, that the individual would seek to sell his own labor dearly and purchase the fruits of others cheaply. The primary imperative of capitalist activity was that one had to serve his fellow man before reaping a reward.

From the outset, property in America was understood by all to be an *individual*, not a collective, right. Individual property rights ensured both a measure of equality and liberty. It was a by-product of these that, in general, land, water, and other resources were protected by the self-interest of individuals, not government. These property rights existed long before they were permanently fixed in the Constitution. Both the Plymouth Company and the Massachusetts Bay Company tied voting rights in the infant colonies with ownership rights in the companies, and early on, both Jamestown and Plymouth quickly abandoned communal property rights for individual property rights when they began to starve.

Certainly by the 1700s, the concept of private property, protected by the state, was nearly universal in the colonies. The Reverend Elisha Williams had said in his tract *A Seasonable Plea* (1744) that "Reason tells us, all are born thus *naturally equal*, i.e., with an *equal Right* to their *Persons*; so also with an equal Right to their *Preservation*; and therefore to *such Things* as Nature affords for their *Subsistence*. . . . Thus *every Man* having a *natural Right* to . . . his own *Actions* and *Labour* and to what he can honestly acquire by his *Labour*, which we call *Property*; it certainly follows that no Man can have a Right to the *Person* or *Property* of *another* [emphasis in original]."[3] That same year, John Dickinson noticed the logical connection between having control of physical property and having control of one's self: "Great Britain claims a right to take away nine-tenths of our estates—-have we a right to the remaining tenth? No—To say we have, is a 'traiterous position' [sic] denying her supreme legislature. So far from *having* property, according to these late found novels, *we are ourselves a property*."[4]

The Articles of Confederation had many faults, including an ineffective system of government revenue raising and the absence of a central treaty-making process. But under the articles, the infant government of the United States passed two monumental land bills that, perhaps more than any other subsequent legislation or rulings by the U.S. Supreme Court, have shaped the American attitudes toward land and citizenship. With settlers already moving out into the "West" (then defined as Kentucky, Ohio, and western Carolina), Congress had to make several decisions about the relationship of the government and land, and the nature of private property rights and citizenship rights. For example, past societies such as Rome had jealously guarded their citizenship privileges, granting them to only a few of their conquered peoples; and they deliberately sought to make citizens property owners to prevent non–property owners from using public resources for corrupt activities. Other western states, while grudgingly admitting that people were subjects (and, occasionally, citizens), differentiated rights and privileges based on the amount of land one owned.

Not in America. Already land had played a critical role in shaping the future economic growth of the United States, and put the nation on a path toward relentless innovation and invention. As the settlers arrived, the abundance of land profoundly influenced labor prices: virtually anyone at any time could sing the old Johnny Paycheck song "Take This Job and Shove It," then head for open land to become a farmer. While certainly not all farmers were successful, all who wanted to could *try*, and for immigrants coming from societies where land that could be owned and developed was nonexistent or phenomenally expensive, that meant that the pull of available land acted as a constant prod to productivity in all businesses. Firms—even early, small ones—found themselves substituting machinery for labor. Almost every scheme and trick to encourage new laborers to come to the English colonies failed. Headright, the process by which Englishmen who emigrated to British America could receive up to 250 acres for themselves and their families, merely created hundreds of new independent farmers, not a new labor pool. Indentured servitude proved impossible to enforce. The final alternative, slavery, was cheaper than free labor, but only when it was subsidized, supported, and protected by the machinery of government, and half the nation soon refused to provide that support on ethical grounds. So even as the Confederation Congress passed two momentous land acts, the die was cast for a system that constantly drove the wages of free employees up, and forced businesses to relentlessly replace laborers with slaves or cheaper technology—a pattern that continues to this day.

What the Founders did under the Articles was confront this westward expansion on two levels, one related to property rights and development, the other related to political rights and citizenship. As early as 1776, Jefferson proposed a grant of fifty acres to any Virginian who did not own that amount of land, and nearly a decade later, he met a pauper woman in France whose destitute condition he attributed to the absence of land ownership in France. He had already concluded that land was an essential ingredient in human happiness:

> The earth is given as a common stock for man to labour and live on. . . . It is too soon yet in our country to say that every man who cannot find employment but who can find uncultivated land, shall be at liberty to cultivate it, paying a moderate rent. But it is not too soon to provide by every possible means that as few as possible shall be without a little portion of land.[5]

This was a suggestion that struck at the very essence of English aristocracy and its inherited lands.

Moreover, in 1778, he actively suggested a means to provide each with that "little portion of land" through a return to the headright system "for the Encouragement of Foreigners," but also extending to native Virginians a birthright of seventy-five acres.[6] Virginia's legislature did not embrace Jefferson's plan, but he advanced the concept to the Articles of Confederation Congress. Jefferson wrote the Virginia deed that generously conveyed that state's backlands to the United States, in which it was required that the region be formed into states having "the same rights of Sovereignty, Freedom, and Independence" as the original thirteen states. Whether his language specifically shaped the subsequent Land Ordinance of 1785 remains a matter of historical debate.[7] Nor was his motive entirely honorable. In a letter to Madison in February 1784, he urged, "For God's sake put this at the next session of assembly [as it] is for the interest of Virginia to cede so far immediately; because the people beyond that will separate themselves, because they will be joined by all our settlements beyond the Alleghaney if they are the first movers."[8] Similarly, he told George Washington that Virginia had to cede immediately or risk losing control altogether.[9] But what is not at issue is that Congress established a survey system that would lay out new areas (such as Ohio, where the survey was to start) in a grid, a large box called a "township," consisting of thirty-six one-mile squares called "sections." After the survey, the townships would be opened up for sale to the public, usually at remarkably low prices. Anyone could purchase as much as he wanted, but the government attempted to ensure that all purchases occurred in a systematic and orderly manner to provide for a "critical mass" of settlers who could defend themselves against Indian attacks. In other words, the government wanted to sell section one, then two, and so on, rather than jumping from section one to section twenty. In the Land Ordinance of 1785, the government not only provided for the survey of sections and townships but held back five sections out of every township for itself, four to be sold off in case of future revenue needs, or to build an armory, and one given to the people for the purposes of constructing a public school. (With reference to the entry on education, it should be noted that the public school clause did not reserve power to the federal government, but instead devolved power again to the state and local governments after providing the land.)

It is somewhat ironic, therefore, that the "small government/states' rights" Jefferson favored government activism when it came to distributing land. Instead of fighting to have Virginia retain its land rights, or even to redistribute western lands among the states (certain to cause objections among the "landless" seaboard states), Jefferson called for "cultivat[ing] the idea of our being one nation, and to multiply the instances in which the people shall look up to Congress as their head."[10] In October 1778, the Continental Congress, urged by the Virginia delegates, resolved that all ceded lands "shall be disposed of for the common benefit of the United States, and be settled and formed into distinct republican states, which shall become members of the federal union, and have the same rights of sovereignty, freedom and independence, as the other states."[11] Moreover, the legislation stipulated that every state "so formed" would have a minimum and "suitable extent of territory," namely, at least one hundred acres square. But other conditions the Virginia delegation put on the cession, including restraints on speculators, kept the proposal tied up for three years, and another proposal to carve out a specific state for former officers also occupied Congress.

Immediately reality intervened to alter the plans of those who drafted the Land Ordinance. Settlers moved into the "Northwest territory" so fast that they outpaced the survey teams in short order. Instead of clean and orderly sections shaped like a box—necessary for defense against Indians—settlers staked out lands based on geographic markers, such as a tree, a river, a large rock. Worse (from a "planner's" point of view), they spread inland, settling far from the first survey points and often on land reserved by treaty to the various Indian tribes as illegal squatters. This produced a critical challenge for the young nation: rein in the settlements and force them to conform to "planned growth," or trust the people, allowing a system of informal law to evolve and then later conform the legal codes to reality. They chose the latter. Operating under the concept of "preemption," or "squatter's rights," a practice that became codified in the law wherein if people settled and maintained land for seven years without being evicted, and showed some proof of having developed the land (a farm, a house), they acquired ownership of that land. As Hernando de Soto noted in his book *The Mystery of Capital*, this process quickly separated the United States from many other parts of the world by providing a rapid system of title deed acquisition.[12] De Soto found that rapid, and sometimes almost immediate, access to the process of acquiring legal title to land in America produced a stunning certainty of ownership. Thus, entrepreneurs (who frequently had to borrow on a home or other existing property to build a new business) could leverage their wealth, whereas in Egypt or Peru, de Soto found, it could take as long as a decade and up to 150 separate steps to acquire title deed to wealth one already possessed.

When it came to land in the hands of the citizens, the small-government-minded Thomas Jefferson did not hesitate to acquire Louisiana in 1803, with the intention of disbursing it among the nation's population. Completely unauthorized within the strict construction of the Constitution, Jefferson justified the purchase by asking, "is it not better that the opposite bank of the Mississippi should be settled by our own brethren and children, than by strangers of another family? With which shall we be most likely to live in harmony and friendly intercourse?"[13] Dealing with the procedural objections, Jefferson issued an amendment that prevented settlement of Louisiana north of the thirty-third parallel until Congress produced enabling procedures. And even at that, Jefferson admitted that the general government had no "power of holding foreign territory, & still less of incorporating it into the Union," yet he did so anyway.[14] Congress obediently rushed through such legislation, but it would not be the last time such elasticity would be needed when it came to land. In the case of Spanish Florida, which was not contained in Napoleon Bonaparte's transfer of Louisiana, Jefferson began efforts to effect Florida's "natural" incorporation into the United States. He expanded funding of commerce with the Indians, particularly those who had "superfluous lands" and were willing to part with them, hoping they would "find it in their interest, from time to time, to dispose of parts of their surplus and waste lands for the means of improving those they occupy."[15] The final outcome, in his mind, was a natural progress of assimilating Indians into American life, and with them, their lands.[16]

Among the reasons the Founders permitted squatter's rights to be given such legal authority was their desire to avoid the creation of large European-style landed estates in which property remained in the hands of a few. If someone did not police his boundaries often enough to find a squatter, the Founders reasoned, he had too much land to develop anyway and was hoarding it, not using it. Squatter's rights also dovetailed with a more unpleasant tradition, that of paying property taxes, which shared the same philosophical objectives: land should not lie dormant and must be productive. Thus, property taxes ensured that people did not "sit" on vacant land and merely keep it out of circulation. In 1785, Jefferson again tied the concept of property ownership to natural rights: "Whenever there is, in any country, uncultivated land and unemployed poor, it is clear that the laws of property have been so far expended as to violate natural right."[17] Every inclination of the Founders was to encourage development of the land over its mere acquisition.

Along with the Land Ordinance, the Articles of Confederation Congress addressed the issue of citizenship. What happens when settlers arrive in, say, Ohio? This was not one of the original thirteen colonies; how should they be treated? The Founders still felt the sting of their colonial status under the British, and resolved never to repeat that mistake. With the Northwest Ordinance of 1787, they created a process that allowed newly settled areas to become, first, territories, then states on an equal footing with the original thirteen. Once a territory had five thousand residents, it could seek territorial status with Congress, which would appoint a territorial governor to work with the territorial legislature elected by the people. U.S. marshals and federal judges would also "ride the circuit" to ensure law enforcement and adjudication of disputes. When the population rose to sixty thousand, the territory could submit a constitution to Congress and, if approved, be granted statehood status with all rights and obligations contained therewith. Above all, it meant that the "colonies" had a pathway to equality with the existing states, and that no one would remain in a colonial status, but that all would have the opportunity for full citizenship within the United States. This was something truly new under the sun. *No* republic or empire in history had ever routinely granted full citizenship to all newly acquired areas. Even today, the United States is one of only five countries in the world that awards citizenship on the legal principle of jus soli (place of birth) as opposed to jus sanguinis, (parents' place of birth). Yet the Americans did it with little debate, and almost overnight.[18]

Many of these ideas derived from the influence of Thomas Jefferson, whose view of "pursuit of happiness," contrary to popular misunderstanding, was not self-sufficient agrarianism, but rather a nation of prosperous planters who could farm in the morning and play music or design buildings at night. For Jefferson, everything depended on getting land out of the hands of government and into the hands of the people. Economic historians Jonathan Hughes and Louis Cain noted that Jefferson "feared the potential abuse of power by the national government and wanted the land, whenever possible, removed from its grasp."[19]

Moreover, Jefferson viewed the land as an element of generational sovereignty. In a letter to James Madison, Jefferson used the same "self-evident" phrase to address the question of whether "one generation of men has a right to bind another. . . . I set out on this ground 'that the earth belongs in usufruct to the living.'"[20] He went on to add,

> If the society has formed no rules for the appropriation of its lands in severality, it will be taken by the first occupants. These will generally be the wife and children of the decedent. If they have formed rules of appropriation, those rules may give it to the wife and children, or to some one of them, or to the legatee of the deceased. So they may give it to his creditor.[21]

Jefferson and other Founders considered property rights "an unquestioned assumption."[22] James Madison, writing in 1786 to James Monroe, noted, "Government is instituted to protect property of every sort; as well [as] that which lies in the various rights of individuals, *as that which the term particularly expresses* [emphasis mine]."[23] The phrase "which the term particularly expresses" might have referred to "various rights," except that Madison went on to say that a government "which [even] indirectly violates [individuals'] property in their actual possessions is not a pattern for the United States."[24] Without doubt, then, the "various rights of individuals" is "particularly express[ed]" in the term "property of every sort." Or, put another way, individual rights *begin* with property. Indeed, one authority on property rights insisted that for Madison, the acquisition of property "was a necessary by-product of the freedom of action he deemed an essential part of liberty."[25] Madison even introduced an amendment to the first Congress declaring that "government is instituted and ought to be exercised for the benefit of the people: which consists [among other things of] the right of acquiring and using property."[26]

John Adams in 1776 insisted, "Each individual of the society has a right to be protected by it in the enjoyment of his life, liberty, and property, according to the standing laws . . . no part of the property of any individual can, with justice, be taken from him, or applied to public uses, without his own consent, or that of the representative body of the people."[27] A year later, he warned that the "moment the idea is admitted into society that property is not as sacred as the laws of God, and that there is not a force of law and public justice to protect it, anarchy and tyranny commence."[28] Noah Webster placed private property rights *above* those of free speech, which was ironic given Webster's claim to fame, writing in 1787, "The liberty of the press, trial by jury, the Habeas Corpus write, even Magna Carta itself, although justly deemed the palladia of freedom, are all inferior considerations, when compared with a general distribution of property among every class of people. The power of entailing estates is more dangerous to liberty and republican government, than all the constitutions that can be written on paper, or even than a standing army."[29]

Madison argued that violations of private property and oppression were inextricably tied together. In October 1788 he noted, "If *all* power be suffered to slide into hands not interested in the rights of property which must be the case whenever a majority fall under that description, one of two things cannot fail to happen; either they will unite against the other description and become the dupes and instruments of ambition, or their poverty and independence will render them the mercenary instruments of wealth. In either case, liberty will be subverted; in the first by a despotism growing out of anarchy, in the second, by an oligarchy founded on corruption."[30]

At the heart of the Founders' positions lay the assumption that private property ownership was natural and the right of every man, but also that private property itself provided yet another brake on government power, and the less land the government controlled, the less mischief it could make. Further, as Hamilton would later argue in the assumption and funding debates, it lay in the interests of the nation to ally those of property with the government, rather than seeking—as it appears so many politicians do today—to ally the government with the property-less. Only those who had a stake in the "system," they claimed, could possibly make sound judgments about the future of the nation.

Virtually all the Founders' legal views on individual property owner-ship had a long tradition in English law. The Founders looked to the En-glish legal giants William Blackstone and Edward Coke for their property law philosophy, but of course took their broader views from John Locke, who wrote, "The great and *chief end* [emphasis in original], therefore, of Mens uniting into Commonwealths, and putting themselves under Gov-ernment, *is the Preservation of their Property*"[31] [emphasis in original]. Locke argued whenever the legislators endeavor to take away *"and destroy the Property of the people* . . . [emphasis in original] they put themselves into a state of War with the people. . . ."[32] Blackstone interpreted Locke as saying that property was an inherent right of "every Englishman," and that the right consisted of "free use, enjoyment, and disposal of all his acquisi-tions, without any control of diminution, save only the laws of the land."[33] But even those laws enacted by Parliament had to be restrained, he noted: "So great moreover is the regard of the law for private property, that it will not authorize the least violation of it; no, not even *for the general good of the whole community*"[34] [emphasis in original]. Blackstone said a property owner could forfeit his lands only "by doing wrong."

These, and other property rights concepts, weighed heavily on the minds of the delegates to the Constitutional Convention and during the ratification process. The Declaration of Rights proposed by Virginia greatly influenced the amendments that James Madison submitted to the House. Two of the provisions were:

> First, that there are certain natural rights which men, when they form a social compact cannot deprive or divest their posterity, among which are the enjoyment of life and liberty, with *the*

means of acquiring, possessing and protecting property . . . [emphasis in original] [and also] that no freedom ought to be taken, imprisoned, or disseised of his freehold, liberties . . . or deprived of his life, liberty or property but by the law of the land.[35]

Subsequent language in other states' ratification recommendations was similar.

An exception had to be made for "public use," which appeared in the Fifth Amendment: "No person shall . . . be deprived of life, liberty, or property without due process of law; nor shall private property be taken for public use, without just compensation." During the Revolution, George Washington commandeered animals, food, and even boats to cross the Delaware, rendering the owners IOUs to be paid after the war, and the Constitution recognized that there could be certain national needs that might exceed those of the individual when it came to property. This principle became known as eminent domain, loosely referred to as "takings." Takings never applied to those engaged in illegal activities and were generally applied to acquiring land for a clear public purpose, such as an armory or, later, highways. In normal circumstances, however, the key phrases in the Constitution were "public use" (i.e., something benefiting the entire public) and "just compensation." Few owners who had their land seized by the government ever thought they received just compensation, but the alternative was to allow individuals along, say, the path of a needed road to hold out for vastly inflated prices well outside the boundaries of "just" compensation and bordering on extortion.

Moreover, the "takings" clause involved a substantial amount of ambiguity. Chief Justice Lemuel Shaw, in 1839, wrote that it was "difficult, perhaps impossible, to lay down any general rule, that would precisely define the power of the government, in the acknowledged right of eminent domain."[36] As Richard Epstein pointed out in his classic study, *Takings* (1985), "public use" implies an openness to all who meet minimum requirements of fitness (i.e., the use of public highways) as opposed to preferences for a small group of individuals who may or may not eventually benefit the general public.[37] Systems of land recordation, for example, "alter the priority of title and thus take the property of those who fail to register," but the registration process is open to all.[38] But Epstein did point out that the Mill Acts (a series of state-level decisions in the early 1800s in which courts ruled that individuals who dammed up rivers to build flour mills provided a public good and, therefore, the damages claimed by those up- and downriver were denied) constituted a problematic and vexing issue for the law. Even after the U.S. Supreme Court attempted to sidestep the issue by claiming the acts were merely "regulatory" and did not involve fundamental "takings" issues, the question of when one person's alteration of property in the public interest affected the value of others' property still remained.

Other aspects of property rights emerged in the early republic, including whether sale of property, even under suspicious circumstances, constituted a contract. Chief Justice John Marshall, writing in the *Fletcher v. Peck* case (1810), overruled a Georgia law that repealed the sale of lands—even though the original law enabling the sale was the result of bribery of state legislators—on the grounds that the sale was a binding contract. It established early in the nation's history property rights and the sanctity of contracts. A second case in 1815, *Terrett v. Taylor,* struck down a Virginia law that would have deprived the Episcopal Church of its property; and yet again, in 1829 (*Wilkinson v. Leland*), the Court affirmed that legislatures were limited in their rights to restrict ownership rights, with Justice Joseph Story insisting, "government can scarcely be deemed free, where the rights of property are left solely dependent upon the will of the legislative body."[39]

In short, English law, American state constitutions, and the U.S. federal Constitution with the Bill of Rights all reiterated the critical nature of property as a "natural right." Because property was a natural right born of the individual's necessity to improve his own lot in life, the Founders thought that the individual would best protect the land against the incursions of others. This included forms of pollution or human-induced destruction. But after the grazing laws were introduced in the West, the concept was subtly applied to forests in the 1890s, wherein these principles were changed from an individual right to a collective right. These forest acts allowed the president to place national forests in areas called "reserves" (i.e., reserved *from* private acquisition and *for* the government). By 1905, the term "public domain" meant all lands other than these reserves—land that still lay open for settlement.

As cattlemen (and sheepmen, later) combined into large state livestock associations, they began individually to fence off boundaries of ranges, which they policed individually and collectively against newcomers. The Wyoming Stock Growers Association, for example, established in 1879, divided the range into roundup districts, named foremen to head up each roundup, and set the dates of the roundups, and their zeal for catching "rustlers" led in part to the Johnson County War of 1892. For the most part, the government acquiesced in this administrative structure—the ranchers handled most of the property upkeep themselves, and some states even allowed them to engage in land-use regulation. What was important, however, was that in most cases the ranchers *did not own the lands* but simply allowed their herds to occupy open land. Naturally, however, a conflict ensued when any new homesteader decided to fence off some of this land. Instead of "reserving" the land for settlement (i.e., for the people) or offering it for sale to the ranchers, however, the government tore down the (often illegal) fences put up by the ranchers and then sealed off *all* the land as national forests.[40] Thus the debate that emerged posited a false set of choices between open grazing lands controlled (but often not owned) by livestock associations and national forests owned and controlled by the federal government. Lost in the mix was the average homesteader's right to acquire the land.

Another challenge to traditional homesteading came in the nature of the remaining land, which often was arid and impossible to cultivate without irrigation. Thus lobbying efforts by farmers often turned to the federal government in an attempt to secure water rights, particularly in the long and intense struggle between California and Arizona over the Colorado River. Again, just as the federal government had shied away from demanding that ranchers pay their own way, federal money helped build massive water projects that, in turn, allowed bureaucrats to delve into how much acreage was needed to support a family and to regulate land use by virtue of the fact that Uncle Sam provided the water. Instead of opening up the West and allowing individuals to determine how best to use the land, the government involved itself in regulation and "planning" to shape the American frontier. And with each new regulation came more government authority over the land.[41]

The Taylor Grazing Act of 1934 essentially cemented the view that "public lands" would be put under the control of the federal government instead of sold. All federal lands not already awarded to homesteaders or reserved for federal conservation were removed into grazing districts and soon put in the charge of the Bureau of Land Management, a subdivision of the Interior Department. Admitting ranchers into the forest lands to graze now put them at the mercy of the *Use Book,* a guidebook establishing classes for grazers. Gifford Pinchot, the former chief of the forestry division of the Agriculture Department, who had been at the center of a nasty controversy with President William Howard Taft and Interior Secretary Richard Ballinger over the proper use of public lands, gushed that after transfer of the forests to the Agriculture Department, "we could say, and we did say, 'Do this,' and 'Don't do that.'" Aided by *Light v. United States* (1911), a cattle trespass case, the government gained final authority over rules and regulations of the national forests.

By 1995, the United States held 660 million acres of land—nearly 29 percent of total surface area of the country! Of the roughly 260 million acres of public land in the contiguous western states, the BLM supervised nearly 170 million acres. For all intents and purposes, federal land ceased to be available to Americans.[42] The Wilderness Act of 1964 set aside 9.1 million acres in Arizona, California, Colorado, and other western states; then in 1968, Congress set aside yet another 800,000 acres of western land, followed by another 161,000 acres a year later, and yet another 200,000 acres the year after that. Each year saw more land taken out of the hands of people and put under the control of government, both state and national: 1 million acres in 1972, 547,000 in 1974, 1.7 million in 1976, 5.5 million in 1978, 520,000 in 1982 and 1983, 8.6 million in 1984, another 250,000 from 1985 to 1987, and so on.

Once the land was in the hands of governments—both federal and state—it became possible for the environmental movement to hijack the very concept of "public land" with a much different agenda. Teddy Roosevelt's view of conservation, in which *some* land was set aside for use by *all,* and access by *all,* to enjoy a natural, pristine experience, by the mid-twentieth century had taken on a more ominous and threatening character. "Public lands" became the excuse by which the environmental movement sought to take control away from individuals and the free market: it was so much easier than battling through those nasty courts, which would still occasionally find in favor of private interests. Thus the Sierra Club, Wildlife Federation, Greenpeace, National Resources Defense Council, and Friends of the Earth all actively joined the effort to remove more and more private lands from development through government acquisition. (Keep in mind that acquisition did *not usually mean "purchasing from the owners,"* but rather, by fiat and executive order, involved taking land off the sales market.)

The results have been truly horrific. Michigan's Department of Environmental Quality had the power to impose $25,000 *per day* fines under its "wetlands law," and prosecuted one contractor who created an award-winning ecosystem that supported 150 bird and mammal species and created a habitat for another 120.[43] He was convicted for not having proper permits and had to flee the state. Among other federal laws protecting the environment or endangered species, "annoying" a kangaroo rat could result in a fine of $100,000 and a year in jail, and merely shining a flashlight on such an animal could be considered annoying.[44] The environmental and wildlife rules had grown so absurd and bizarre, not to mention numerous (adding two hundred pages of new rulings and regulations *per day* to the Federal Register by 1995), that federal mandates alone related to the environment cost each American household more than $6,000 per year.[45]

Environmentalists have used arguments such as "aesthetics" to defend stealing the property of others; or cited "unknown effects," under which absolutely *no development at all* could occur because no one can ever know the ultimate effects of anything (including government action).[46] And while he was somewhat out of step with most of the Founders on this, Jefferson explicitly argued in his "usufruct" comments that in fact *no* future generation has claims on the living—that they exist and prosper only on the goodwill of those alive, and that the first concern must always be in seeing that those alive at present prosper enough to ensure a future generation at all. While none of the Founders, as best can be determined, were wanton with their lands, virtually all cleared their properties, burned brushes and some forest, and uprooted any trees that prevented them from cultivating the land. Almost all hunted and fished, and all knew that you left land to be fallow for a time. Anyone trained in Scripture knew Ecclesiastes, that there was a "time for every season," and that included letting land recover.

But the notion that governments would dictate one's land use—barring clear and present threats to neighbors (brewing a toxic liquid whose gas would kill the neighbor's farm animals)—was anathema. Certainly they understood that no one had the right to poison others, either by tainting the water or by so obviously fouling the air that someone literally could not breathe. It is doubtful, however, they would have agreed to ban DDT on such flimsy evidence as was introduced in the 1960s that it could affect human life, particularly when equally strong evidence was introduced showing that humans would suffer the most from the famines that would ensue without DDT.[47] In short, the straw man argument that conservatives who followed the thinking of the Founders "couldn't anticipate" threats we now face, and want to "foul the air and poison the skies and streams," is exactly that, a straw man.

What the Founders saw as the major threat was not man's destruction of the environment, for both other men and the market would right that in time, but a runaway government obsessed with its own godlike powers intruding into everyday activities. Certainly the Environmental Protection Agency crossed that line long ago. More ominous now, though, is the *international* threat introduced in the United Nations' "Agenda 21," which promotes "sustainable development." This is a code phrase for a lifestyle that would put the world back into pre-Egyptian levels of civilization. Under the rubric of Agenda 21, the secretary general of the UN's Rio Earth Summit stated that American middle-class lifestyles were "unsustainable," as were high meat intake, plowing of soil, single family homes—virtually anything associated with private property.[48] "Optimistic scenarios," stated the *Global Biodiversity Assessment*, "envision several possible mechanisms for averting global crisis including . . . sacrifice of future growth in consumption on the part of wealthy nations in order to allow future growth in the developing world and direct transfer of resources and technology to developing countries."[49] This constituted nothing except a blatant confiscation of individuals' property.

Not only has the Founders' principle that the land should be managed only by the government until it can be transferred to individuals been trampled flatter than Wyoming grass, but the government is rapidly allowing international bodies to determine American property rights by referencing the United Nations' Agenda 21, which calls on participating countries to engage in "sustainable development" in an effort to protect the environment. ("Sustainable," of course, is a bureaucrat's definition of what the earth should provide.) For example, in 2009, Senator Chris Dodd (before he retired as a result of a scandal) introduced the "Livable Communities Act," which created in the office of Housing and Urban Development the Office of Sustainable Housing and Communities.

Were the Founders to magically reappear at this time and observe the pernicious intrusion of the United Nations into property rights, they would close down that monstrosity, evict all the freeloading diplomats, and issue a new Declaration of Independence from meddling do-gooder globalist busybodies. As for the land-baron status of the federal government, the Founders likely, to a man, would insist that the BLM be burned down, and that the lands be unloaded as quickly as possible. And given his skills as a surveyor, George Washington probably would volunteer to survey the first section for sale back to individual Americans.

QUESTION #4

IS THE HEALTH OF THE PEOPLE CONSIDERED PART OF THE "GENERAL WELFARE"?

At President Barack Obama's health care summit in February 2010, Speaker of the House Nancy Pelosi declared that all Americans were entitled to quality health care, and that the bill before Congress was not just about "health care for America; it's about a healthier America."[1] Good health care, she said, required "accessibility" and "affordability" to health care services, and it was necessary to "expand access to quality health care for all Americans." Perhaps most astoundingly, she admitted, "health care reform is *entitlement reform* [emphasis mine]."[2] She was largely echoing what Ted Kennedy had said as early as 1978 that health care was "a matter of right and not of privilege."[3]

What would the Founders have said to such a proposition? How would they have reacted to the massive government program directed at ensuring that all Americans have access to health care that subsequently passed (though barely)? Would they have objected? Would they have rebelled again? In that comment, Pelosi revealed the ultimate objective of the government's program, which was to control the dietary, exercise, and very living habits of Americans.

What would Thomas Jefferson have said if you told him that in an effort to create a "healthier America" he couldn't drink his wine or toast his country? How do you think John Adams would have reacted if the government had taken his tobacco away? Would George Washington have allowed *any* public authority to tell him he could not eat meat? Of course, the answers are obvious. No Colonial American would ever have submitted to government restrictions on something as private as diet and drink. Perhaps a parish minister could have some sway when it came to drinking habits—but the government? Never.

As the monster health care bill—that most legislators had not read—inexorably became law, more and more red flags surfaced suggesting it would be detrimental to most Americans' health. In polls, doctors in droves announced they would leave the profession if the bill became a reality, and already under the weight of new government burdens, American companies began raising prices for their goods, thus lowering sales and ensuring layoffs that would cause *fewer* people to have health care. Some simply skipped the middle step and laid off employees in anticipation of new burdens. Government requirements under the bill that individuals purchase health insurance or pay a fine (or even go to jail), while repugnant in themselves, really only constituted the first step in true health care reform, because to control prices, it will eventually be necessary to control behaviors that the government deems unhealthy. Already this approach has been taken nationwide by virtually banning smoking in public places. In some places, such as New York City, local governments have gone even further by banning trans fats and other supposedly unhealthy food components.

To truly understand the effects of health care "reform," one need look no further than Massachusetts, which passed a prototype version of the national bill in 2006. The results were obvious: costs to individuals went up.[4] But in fact the bill was the result of *decades* of agitation, work, and indoctrination in which the United States has steadily been aping Canada and Britain, both of which have publicly funded health care. In 1975, the Canadian government published a report called "A New Perspective on the Health of Canadians," in which Marc Lalonde, the Minister of National Health and Welfare, bluntly stated that "Self-imposed risks and the environment are the principal or important underlying factors in each of the five major causes of death between ages one and seventy, and one can only conclude that unless the environment is changed and the self-imposed risks are reduced, the death rates will not be significantly reduced."[5] A few years later, a prominent speaker at a health forum in America, John Knowles, insisted that "the costs of individual irresponsibility in health have now become prohibitive. The choice is individual responsibility or social failure. Responsibility and duty must gain some degree of parity with right and freedom."[6] Jimmy Carter's Health and Human Services secretary, Joseph Califano, in his introduction to the surgeon general's report in 1979 wrote, "Indulgence in private excess has results that are far from private. Public expenditures for health care are only one of the results."[7]

That this language leads to government control of individuals' bodies on the most fundamental level—eating, drinking, and exercise, not to mention risky but (so far) legal activities—should be abundantly obvious. In the late 1800s, courts began to attempt to limit alcohol consumption on the grounds that the public morals and the public safety may be endangered by the "general use of intoxicating drinks."[8] Later, Prohibition would seek to implement such ideas with what are now considered universally disastrous results.[9] Ironically, it was the automobile, and auto accidents, that most significantly reopened the door to the notion that there were "public costs" to individual health choices. Much of the debate about seat belts involved "externalities" that were born by others when someone lacking a safety belt died in a car crash. (A typical comment comes from an "ambulance chaser" legal Web site: "The cost of unbuckled drivers and passengers goes beyond those killed and the loss to their families. We all pay for those who don't buckle up in higher taxes, higher health care and higher insurance costs.")[10]

The current health care bill is too fresh to discuss in terms of its final results. Certainly, Sarah Palin's concerns that there would be "death panels" seem to be confirmed both in existing British and Canadian programs and even in Medicare treatments.[11] Commonsense economics suggests that a scarce good (e.g., medical treatment), when confronted by unlimited wants and demands (i.e., made free to all citizens), must be rationed either by the market or by the government.

Such notions were so far outside the realm of the Founders' experiences that few had any comments that even remotely addressed whether government should involve itself in everyday people's decisions about medicine, diet, or lifestyle. Of course, they did have a lot to say about the dangers of an overly expansive government. Thomas Paine, for example, warned that "Society in every state is a blessing, but government, even in its best state, is but a necessary evil; in its worst state, an intolerable one."[12] Richard Henry Lee cautioned that chains were chains, even if made of gold; and Madison stated that "No axiom is more clearly established in law, or in reason, than that wherever the end is required, the means are authorised."[13] What is different today from the intrusions on freedom more than two hundred years ago is that today's tyrants always insist they are "protecting" people from themselves, and that they have only the best of intentions when they restrict people's choices.

We do have, however, a clear record of what the Founders thought when it came to restricting or controlling their food and drink, and perhaps this area best illuminates for us what they would have said about the current health care debate. While the American Revolution began, in its most fundamental way, over taxes, the issue behind the taxes was control of a key food item in the colonists' diet—tea. But the infamous Tea Act was hardly the first time the British had singled out a food product for special regulation and taxation. In 1733, Parliament passed the Molasses Act, which proved a failure and was universally avoided. The motivations behind the Molasses Act were financial and regulatory: Britain needed new revenues, while West Indian plantation owners wanted to limit trade from Colonial competitors. Instead of prohibiting non–West Indian molasses outright, Parliament used a common back-door method of eliminating competition, namely, a tax that made non–West Indian molasses so expensive that New England in particular quit buying it. When the act was about to expire in 1763, the British government needed new revenue. Hence, Parliament passed the Sugar Act of 1764, halving the previous tax on molasses but—setting a foolish precedent that would haunt the government in the 1773 Tea Act—ramping up enforcement and increased duties on sugar and wine. Parliament's intention was to "force the colonists to shift to port, supplied via England, at a duty of ten shillings per double hogshead as compared with the new impost on Madeira of an impossible seven pounds, fourteen times as much."[14] Colonists reacted by imposing a boycott on "Punch and Madeira," and shifted to New England rum, cider, and beer.

Perhaps in more prosperous times, the colonists wouldn't have resisted the Sugar Act so much, but coming as it did during a depression, the act sparked major protests. Historian John Miller, in his history of the American Revolution, stated that the act caused greater alarm in New England than did offensives by the French and Indians in the Seven Years' War.[15] American colonists, led by Samuel Adams and James Otis of Massachusetts, saw the resistance gained in organization and strength, with fifty Boston merchants refusing to procure British luxury goods. Before the colonists could become too incensed about the Sugar Act, Parliament passed the infamous Stamp Act and hell truly broke loose. The Stamp Act carried a surcharge on liquor licenses on top of local licenses already being paid. Popular outrage exceeded that directed at the Sugar Act, and in 1766 Parliament was forced to repeal the Stamp Act, while the Sugar Act was quietly also rescinded and replaced with a generic Revenue Act that reduced the tax on all molasses imports. The message here was clear, namely, that early on Americans saw a distinct connection between the taxing powers of the government and its ability to regulate all kinds of personal behavior and infringe on personal liberty.

But the British had certainly not learned their lesson. With the Tea Act of 1773—another attempt by government to assist a private company by giving it monopoly control—Parliament again attempted to impose a tax on the American colonists, who commonly smuggled tea into America at a ratio of almost two to one over the amount the East Indian Tea Company imported. There were at least three components to Colonial concerns over the Tea Act: (1) it constituted a revalidation of the Townshend Acts of 1767, which, while an "indirect tax," included new duties on lead, paint, paper, glass, and tea imported into the colonies; (2) it seemed to reaffirm the legality of writs of assistance (search warrants); and (3) if enforced, it constituted a general price hike in the cost of most tea.[16] More to the point, though, the colonists clearly discerned a connection between the government's use of *taxation* as a means of social control and as a means of revenue raising, for if Parliament could decide what tea colonists could drink, could it not decide *if they could drink tea at all*? Responses included forcing the return of some British East Indian tea to England, or, in Charleston, to leave it on the docks to rot. Of course, the most famous reply came with the Boston Tea Party, during which colonists dumped casks of tea into the Boston Harbor. In the end, the Tea Party was less about tea than it was about the regulations over it, just as the outrage over the Stamp Act was more about the way it was imposed and less about what it actually taxed.

Buried in these protests, however, was a deep understanding by the Founders of the power of government—that when it was empowered (by taxes or any other device) to intrude on *anything*, the door was open for it to intrude on *everything*. It was ironic that one of the first areas in which this was appreciated involved slavery: George Mason noted that while "There is no clause in this Constitution to secure [slavery]; for they may lay such a tax as will amount to manumission."[17] Sam Adams also perceived the slippery slope of using taxation to intrude on all aspects of people's lives. Writing in 1764, Adams asked, "For if our Trade may be taxed, why not our Lands? Why not the Produce of our Lands & everything we possess or make use of?"[18] Of course, modern American governments—local, state, and national—have often simply skipped straight to banning products in the name of public health rather than going through the interim step of taxing them out of existence.

To know how the Founders would have reacted to modern government restrictions on "trans fats," or the implementation of the "food pyramid," or the imposition of "dietary guidelines," one should start by looking at how the Founders themselves ate and drank. How did they see food? What were their concerns about food? Certainly during the American Revolution, George Washington had a great deal to say about provisions and the need to keep armies fed. But many of the Founders, including John Adams and Thomas Jefferson, were farmers at one time or another, and understood the nature of planting and raising crops, and the delights of dining.

Thomas Jefferson, a man of the land, commented more than many of the other Founders on the physical pleasures of food and drink. He once called coffee the "Favorite drink of the civilised world," and listed in those things he deemed a "necessary of life" salad oil, salt, and wine. He purchased wines (Montepulciano, "in black bottles, well corked & cemented, and in strong boxes") from Thomas Appleton, from whom he requested "annually . . . about the same amount, this being a very favorite wine, and habit having rendered the light and high flavored wines a necessary of life with me."[19] He noted, "I double . . . [Dr. Benjamin Rush's] glass and a half of wine, and even treble it with a friend; but halve its effects by drinking the weak wines only. The ardent wines I cannot drink, nor do I use ardent spirits in any form. Malt liquors and cider are my table drinks, and my breakfast, like that also of my friend, is of tea and coffee."[20]

Unlike George Washington, Benjamin Franklin, or John Adams, Jefferson, while no vegetarian, ate little meat—or so he said. His granddaughter also once described him as living "principally on vegetables. . . . The little meat he took seemed mostly as a seasoning for his vegetables."[21] He particularly liked peas and cucumbers. But the account books of Monticello suggest no shortage of protein. During a single month in 1772, for example, Martha Jefferson recorded opening a barrel of flour; two loaves of sugar; having seven ducks, one lamb, and one pig killed; buying six pounds of coffee and eleven pounds of butter; and supervising the brewing of one cask (fifteen gallons) of beer.[22] Moreover, one of his granddaughters wrote that to "think of anything but beef and pudding" while in the kitchen was "out of the question."[23] Two historians of eating in America note that Jefferson "assured himself a rich and varied food supply at Monticello by keeping his woods stocked with game (deer, hare, rabbit, turkey 'and every other wild animal' except of course predators); his ponds and streams with fish; his fields with cattle, sheep, goats and swine; [and] his poultry runs with chickens, pigeons, guinea fowl and peacocks."[24] In 1819, he wrote to Doctor Vine Utley, "I have lived temperately, eating little animal food, and that not as an ailment, so much as a condiment for the vegetables, which constitute my principal diet."[25] But Captain Edmund Bacon insisted that especially as a younger man, Jefferson "was especially found [*sic*] of Guinea fowls; and for meat, he preferred good beef, mutton, and lambs. . . . [His] broad-tailed sheep . . . made the finest mutton I ever saw."[26]

Jefferson drafted a daily menu for the University of Virginia. Breakfast consisted of wheat, corn bread with butter, and coffee or milk; lunch, of a small portion of meat; and dinner, soup, salt meat, fresh meat, a variety of vegetables, and corn or wheat bread. Recipes from Monticello that survive included a flair for continental cuisine, such as blancmange (almond cream) and *nouilly à maccaroni* (a pasta dough), and he enjoyed Italian olive oil and French mustard. (Daniel Webster once characterized Monticello dinners as "half Virginian, half French.") Indeed, while minister to France in 1784, Jefferson acquired a spaghetti-making machine from Italy, which he brought back to the United States, along with a waffle iron from Holland.

> As president, Jefferson hosted a dinner described by a guest as follows: "Dinner not as elegant as when we dined before. Rice soup, round of beef, turkey, mutton, ham, loin of veal, cutlets of mutton or veal, fried eggs, fried beef, a pie called macaroni. . . . Ice cream very good . . . a dish somewhat like pudding . . . covered with cream sauce—very fine. Many other jimcracks [nuts, sweetmeats, and fruit], a great variety of fruit, plenty of wines."[27] This was similar to a dinner Washington gave in New York in 1789, described by a guest as follows: First was the soup; fish roasted and boiled; meats, gammon, fowls, etc. This was the dinner. The middle of the table was garnished in the usual tasty way, with small images, flowers (artificial), etc.; then iced creams, jellies, etc.; then water-melons, musk-melons, apples, peaches, nuts.[28]

Washington seldom dined alone, and he and Martha often entertained twenty dinner guests or more. Based on records from Mount Vernon, he started every day with cornmeal hoe cakes drenched in butter and honey, and drank three cups of tea; he had two iceboxes to keep ice cream on hand. Fish was a staple of Washington's diet, and he included at least one fish meal a day. At lunch and dinner, he had wine, particularly Madeira, as well as beer, and ate garden-grown vegetables that included cabbage, lettuce, squash, carrots, and herbs—often having them preserved or pickled. Cooks at Mount Vernon made a type of ketchup from walnuts and mushrooms. Ice cream, also, was a staple at Mount Vernon. His household possessed two pewter ice cream pots, and during a single summer, he spent two hundred dollars on ice cream—a fortune in the 1700s. He served ice cream at every formal dinner and in 1784 bought a "Cream machine for making ice" in Philadelphia. (Jefferson too had an ice cream machine that he acquired in France in 1789, with a recipe for the dish so elaborate that it required eighteen separate operations. Unlike Washington, Jefferson preferred his ice cream wrapped in a crust of warm pastry, an early version of baked Alaska.)[29]

Above all, Washington was a meat eater, consuming pork, mutton, goose, duck, turkey, roast beef, ham, bacon, and other smoked meats doused in onions. He also favored a cream of peanut soup, mashed sweet potatoes with coconut, and for dessert, mince pies, fruits, nuts, and cheeses. Even Washington's slaves ate a great deal of meat, and over time, meat constituted up to half of the food consumed by slaves at Mount Vernon.[30] Washington supervised much of the fishing, and "chose to do the bulk of his fishing during April and May at several spots along the Potomac when the herring and shad spawn. The catch brought in by the huge nets was salted to preserve as provisions for slaves as well as to sell if there was a surplus. According to documents, twenty salted herring were given to each slave every month."[31] After abandoning tobacco farming in 1765, Washington shifted Mount Vernon to wheat, but experimented with sixty field crops and fished extensively with nets. Washington's estate inventory reveals an extensive library of volumes dedicated to botany, husbandry and gardening, anatomy, physical health, diseases, medicine, and diet.[32]

Although he never commented on the government's appropriate involvement in regulating the diets of citizens, Washington was acutely sensitive to the need for regular food as a part of compensation packages, whether to soldiers or civilians. When it came to provisioning troops, as early as 1756, Washington conducted a tour of frontier garrisons and towns, observing that pay for soldiers often was insufficient to cover the food allowances of the troops, and he wrote to Robert Dinwiddie a year later of the need to meet the dietary needs for soldiers marching through the countryside.[33] His correspondence with Edmond Atkin about ten Indian prisoners noted that sickness among the natives was likely the result of an unfamiliar diet.[34] Sensitive to the cost of food, he asked Robert Dinwiddie to intervene with the British to ensure that Colonial commanders "be treated as gentlemen and officers, and not have annexed to the most trifling pay, that ever was given to English officers, the glorious allowance of a soldier's diet,—a pound of pork, with bread in proportion, per day."[35]

Preparing for war in 1775, he attempted to ensure good relations between quartermasters and local farmers: "Complaints have been made that some of the Soldiers ill treat the Country People, who come to Market; The General most positively forbids such behavior."[36] Good policy, as well as the health of the troops, "depends upon supplies of Vegetables," and "if we drive off the Country people and break up the Market—The healthy will soon be sick, and the sick must perish for want of Necessaries."[37] Washington, it seems, understood not only health and diet but the free market as well.

"It is expected that the Colonels will frequently visit their Mens Barracks, and see that they are kept clean and decent; their Victuals properly cook'd &c.—nothing contributes more to the health of the troops or can add more to the reputation of the Officers than Men to be seen healthy, clean, and well dressed."[38] He wrote to General Horatio Gates, "It is to be regretted that our Supplies of so Esential [sic] an Article, are extremely scanty, and by no means equal to the necessary demands. I should be happy, if they were larger, as a more frequent use of Salt food, I am well convinced, would contribute greatly to the Health of our people."[39]

When the Revolution started, Washington kept close watch on the diet provided the sick by the surgeons and the general hospital, and he wrote Brigadier General Alexander McDougall from Morristown in 1777 that the health of the army "cannot be preserved without a due portion of vegetable diet."[40] He wrote the Continental Congress with blistering criticisms about its ability to feed the army:

> With respect to Food, considering we are in such an extensive and abundant Country, no Army was ever worse supplied than ours with many essential articles of it—our Soldiers, the greatest part of last Campaign, and the whole of this, have scarcely tasted any kind of Vegetables—had but little Salt and Vinegar, which would have been a tolerable substitute for Vegetables, have been in a great measure strangers to—neither have they been provided with proper drink—Beer or Cyder seldom comes within the verge of the Camp, and Rum in much too small quantities. Thus, to devouring large quantities of animal-food, untemper'd by vegetables, or vinegar, or by any kind of Drink but water, and eating indifferent Bread (but for this last a remedy is providing).[41]

In 1780, Washington wrote to the president of the Continental Congress, Joseph Reed, "much will depend on the State of Pennsylvania. She has it in her power to contribute without comparison more to our success than any other state; in the two essential articles of flour and transportation."[42] In August of that year, Washington sent a circular to the states reporting that "the Army is again reduced to an extremity of distress for want of provision. The greater part of it has been without Meat from the 21st." He expected only 120 head cattle from Pennsylvania to be delivered and 150 from Massachusetts, but had no idea when those would arrive, and found coercion to be an ineffective means of supplying the army. Hence, he sent "small parties to procure provision for themselves."[43] "We have not yet been absolutely without Flour, but we have *this* day but *one* days [sic] supply in Camp, and I am not certain that there is a single Barrel between this place and Trenton."[44] And Washington loved his salt: "I shall be happy, if they were larger, as a more frequent use of Salt food, I am well convinced, would contribute greatly to the health of our People."[45] Later, in 1782, he warned against the "vile practice of swallowing the whole ration of liquor at a single draught," ordering sergeants to ration it and mix the liquor with water, whereupon the drink "instead of being pernicious . . . will become very refreshing and salutary."[46]

Washington's compatriot, and future vice president, John Adams, "throve well on turtle, jellies, varied sweetmeats, whipped syllabubs, floating islands, fruits, raisins, almonds, peaches, wines, especially Madeira" while he was in Philadelphia. Unlike Washington, however, Adams suffered from chronic heartburn. His physician, Dr. Nahum Willard, prescribed a milk diet, urging Adams to avoid meats, spices, and wine in favor of bread, milk, and vegetables, but the heartburn persisted, which Dr. Willard treated with tea.[47] He also smoked well into his seventies, and chewed tobacco. And like both Washington and Jefferson, Adams loved his drink. In May 1777, the British interrupted trade and the importation of his (and Jefferson's) favorite Madeira wine. Adams wrote to Abigail in Massachusetts, "I would give three guineas for a barrel of your cyder. Not one drop of it to be had here for gold, and wine is not to be had under sixty-eight dollars per gallon, and that very bad. I would give a guinea for a barrel of your beer. A small beer here is wretchedly bad. In short, I am getting nothing that I can drink, and I believe I shall be sick from this cause alone. Rum is forty shillings a gallon, and bad water will never do in this hot climate in summer where acid liquors are necessary against infection."[48] Adams was not above the occasional purge—he once wrote it "worked seven times and wrecked me"—but as he lived to be ninety years old, there is little to suggest that anything in Adams's diet harmed him.

Patrick Henry, another farmer, early in life worked as a bartender but eventually drank little at all, and, according to one relative, worked diligently to end what he viewed as a drunkenness epidemic after the Revolution. He sought to make a beverage that contained less alcohol, experimenting with grains to develop a new beer. Late in life, he could not stand the smell of tobacco, and house servants had to hide their pipes from him.[49]

Few had as many opinions—most of them good—as Benjamin

Franklin. Of course, Franklin had a great deal to say when it came to food and diet. In *Poor Richard's Almanac,* he laid out "Rules of Meat and Drink," in far too great a number and detail to be completely recounted here. But among them were the following:

- "If thou art dull and heavy after Meat, it's a sign thou hast exceeded the due Measure; for Meat and Drink ought to refresh the Body, and make it cheerful, and not to dull and oppress it. If a Man casually exceeds, let him fast the next Meal.

- "If a Man casually exceeds, let him fast the next Meal and all may be well again, provided it be not too often done; as if he exceed at Dinner, let him refrain a Supper, &c.

- "A sober Diet makes a Man die without Pain; it maintains the Senses in Vigour; it mitigates the Violence of Passions and Affections. It preserves the Memory, it helps the Understanding, it allays the Heat of Lust; it brings a Man to a Consideration of his latter End; it makes the Body a fit Tabernacle for the Lord to dwell in; which makes us happy in this World, and eternally happy in the World to come, through Jesus Christ our Lord and Saviour."[50]

Franklin clung to the notion that a fever was to be fought with more food and drink, for fevers "are Diseases that are not caused by Repletion, and seldom attack Full-feeders."[51] To Deborah Franklin, in 1772, who suffered from pains in her head and side, Benjamin Franklin advised, "Eat light Foods, such as Fowls, Mutton, &c. and but little Beef or Bacon, avoid strong tea, and use what Exercise you can; by these Means, you will preserve your Health better, and be less Subject to Lowness of Spirits."[52] Whether they consumed a great deal of meat, as did Washington, or little, as in Jefferson's case; whether they purged or gorged; whether they drank wine, ale, or tea (or, in Adams's case, milk), these were all decisions left to the individual with no role for government. It is important to note that while much is made about *federal* government power in the twenty-first century, it would have been abhorrent to these Founders that *any* government—federal, state, or local—attempt to butt into what were private choices. Even the most innocent connections could have social consequences. For example, Virginia permitted its citizens to pay taxes in tobacco notes, which de facto placed a government price on what the value of tobacco was. Explicit in such entanglements was a link between what people produced and what they consumed.

When Jefferson wrote, "The care of human life and happiness, and not their destruction, is the first and only legitimate object of good government," he certainly meant it in the narrowest of definitions. Government was only legitimate when directly protecting life and liberty, not infringing upon it in any way. It is not our duty, John Dickinson wrote, "to leave wealth to our children; but it is our duty to leave liberty to them."[53]

Perhaps the greatest connections in the early republic between government power, particularly federal government authority, and consumption of food products involved alcohol, which was already regulated in its distribution to Indians and slaves. Although there is some evidence that early Native Americans fermented grapes and had forms of wine, by the 1760s drinking among Indians was viewed as a problem on both sides of the color line. As Ottawa leader Pontiac said, "Our people love liquor and if we dwelt near your old village of Detroit, our warriors would always be drunk."[54] Georgia's trustees attempted to ban alcohol entirely in the 1730s, declaring that "no Rum, Brandies, Spirits or Strong Water" be allowed into the colony.[55] Otherwise, virtually everyone drank ale, beer, some wine, or even hard spirits from time to time: John Adams pounded down a pitcher of hard cider with every breakfast. Jefferson prided himself on his wine cellar, which the British took great pleasure in destroying when they sacked his home. Although he drank no hard spirits, he kept plenty around for guests.

Above all, the omnipresent drink everywhere in early America, rum, constituted an important part of the economy, and as two historians of food note, "if the Revolution had not been sparked by tea, it might have been by rum."[56] Rum found itself in an unintended holy alliance with slavery, as slaves and rum were often imported together, and slaves were routinely traded in the West Indies for rum and sugar. But where rum was commonplace, Madeira became a symbol of defiance against British rule (particularly after the tax of 1764), and the tax and subsequent boycott probably helped shift American drinking patterns a bit. George Washington, no stranger to ale, used alcohol for more pragmatic purposes, elections. When he ran for the Colonial legislature in 1758, his agent poured out more than three gallons of beer, wine, rum, or cider for every voter![57] Bribing the electorate, it seems, predated ACORN, although Washington paid for these goodies himself. By the time Jefferson became president, however, he complained that "the habit of using ardent spirits by men in public office . . . has often produced more injury to the public service, and more trouble to me, than any other circumstance that has occurred in the internal concerns of the country during my administration."[58]

After Franklin wooed the widow of the philosopher Helvetius and was spurned while on a trip to Paris, he returned to his table, stocked with red Bordeaux and white, including some very old vintages, champagne and "*white mousseux,*" red Burgundy, and sherry to wash down the two principal dishes of meat and poultry (or game), followed by "two kinds of *entremets,* two dishes of vegetables and a platter of pastry, with hors d'oeuvre of butter, pickles, radishes, etc. Two bowls of fruit in winter (flour in summer), two sorts of stewed fruit, a platter of cheese, one of cookies, one of candies."[59]

If Franklin sought to drown his sorrows, he certainly had the right equipment. In drink, however, Franklin, Washington, and Jefferson resembled most Americans of the day, in that laborers often received part of their wages in rum or whiskey, while the elite drank hard liquor routinely. Thus, as two historians of food and drink in America noted, Europeans visiting the United States were "astonished at two things—the American consumption of meat and the American consumption of strong drink," particularly at the habit of Americans to imbibe hard liquor at breakfast. Young or old, male or female, most Americans began their day with "a tumbler full of rum or whiskey taken upon arising as an 'eye-opener.'"[60]

Not surprisingly, it was alcohol—and its dangers to the family and society—that evoked the first campaign against any food product in the United States, and equally unsurprisingly, the temperance movement needed a villain. In this case, it was the beer barons, but later, as Upton

Sinclair's attack on the meat industry unfolded, it was the "beef trust." Americans typically are leery of imposing regulations on themselves or others, unless the argument can be framed in the context of an oppressive force ("big tobacco" or the "sugar trust") whose power can be portrayed as having disproportionately shaped or controlled consumer demand.

Sinclair's war on meat initiated the first full-fledged government offensive against a food group, but Sinclair never bothered to go to a Chicago packing-house to see conditions for himself, choosing instead to rely on the assertions of others. After Sinclair's scare-mongering book appeared, the Department of Agriculture's Bureau of Animal Husbandry issued a report providing a detailed refutation of his most outrageous accusations, some of which the investigators called "willful and deliberate misrepresentations of fact," "atrocious exaggeration," and "not at all characteristic."[61] Even Teddy Roosevelt, a die-hard Progressive, said, "I have utter contempt [for Sinclair]. He is hysterical, unbalanced, and untruthful. Three-fourths of the things he said were absolute falsehoods. For some of the remainder there was only a basis of truth."[62]

Perhaps even more surprising, hundreds of state and even federal inspectors were checking meat and other products before the 1906 Meat Inspection Act, and not one ever "registered any complaint or [gave] any public information with respect to the [adulteration] of meat or food products."[63] Meat, however, was only one product that felt the investigative power of the federal government, which for several years had engaged in low-level sniping against drugs, particularly the opium trade. It was the concern about the presence of cocaine in Coca-Cola that led to an assault on that soft drink by Dr. John Harvey Wiley shortly after the Food and Drug Administration (FDA) was created.

There was some tradition in English culture of the government inspecting and protecting the food supply: in 1202, King John issued the Assize of Bread, which prohibited the adulteration of bread with ground peas, beans, or fillers. The U.S. Constitution granted Congress the authority to set weights and measures, and one could argue that an implied authority against adulteration of food existed. Certainly some of the states thought so, setting standards and permitting inspection of certain foods.[64] During the Mexican War, some suppliers provided impure or diluted foods to the troops, contributing to the exceptionally high rates of cholera, yellow fever, dysentery, and other diseases, and resulted in passage of the Drug Importation Act of 1848. England had passed a general food purity law in 1860, banning poisonous chemicals in food products.

As with most reforms, food "reform" came with the best of intentions. During the Civil War, the Department of Agriculture (USDA) was created, ostensibly to increase yields for the army, but quickly one of the first administrators, a chemist named Charles Wetherill, detoured into trying to determine if by adding sugar to grape juice during winemaking, the grower adulterated the product. This later grew into an entire department within the department, the Department of Chemistry, headed by none other than the infamous Dr. Harvey W. Wiley, who would lead the offensive against Coca-Cola.[65]

Wiley became obsessed with the patent medicines and cure-alls that circulated around the country—products such as Lydia Pinckham's Vegetable Compound and Kickapoo Indian Sagwa. Such suspicious elixirs had to be tested for poison, he insisted, setting up a "poison squad" of otherwise healthy young men to become human guinea pigs. The men were monitored as they ingested food laced with ever-increasing doses of additives, which, of course, produced side effects. In what would typify government's haste to "fix something" before completely contemplating all ramifications, Harvey sent the volunteers off to their meals with no consent forms, no animal studies, no lab tests, and no institutional medical oversight.[66] They ate large doses of borax, salicylic acid, formaldehyde, sodium benzoate, and copper salts, swallowed in gelatin capsules halfway through their meals, making "several men so sick they couldn't function." Remarkably, at the end of the five-year testing period, the average subject was observably healthier than at the beginning, most likely because he had received (otherwise) nutritious meals for a long period of time and none drank anything except water.[67] Wiley thought that the few who had experienced severe adverse effects, however, probably offered a good warning sign, and he ceased the tests, recommending that all chemicals used in the study be banned, though only formaldehyde was. Given that the study wasn't conducted under scientifically controlled standards, industry officials had reason to be concerned. As some of the findings leaked out, in 1906 the House Committee on Interstate and Foreign Commerce held hearings on benzoic acid (aka borax), which was one of the primary means used to cure and preserve meat to determine if it posed a health risk. As the hearings unfolded, however, much of the committee's attention was focused on the ethics of Wiley's use of human subjects in uncontrolled tests.[68]

Naturally, the big overhauls of food regulation came during the terms of the so-called Progressive presidents, Woodrow Wilson and Franklin Roosevelt. They started with Prohibition, then followed up by enacting the Food, Drug, and Cosmetic Act of 1938, which essentially fleshed out the modern FDA's policing powers. Prohibition *did* partially succeed in improving public health by getting family men out of corner saloons. Norman Clark and others have shown that alcohol-related diseases were cut by half or more as a result of Prohibition, and the traditional males-only corner bar was replaced by the elite "speakeasy," which catered to men and women. Thus, in some sense, Prohibition universalized the behavior it sought to end but made it more respectable.[69] Yet in the end, the intrusions on personal choice and the other undesirable effects of Prohibition convinced most people that in the arena of alcohol, the government's reach should be limited. Ironically, by doing so, it became almost immune from subsequent "do-gooder" health crusades, and the 2010 health care legislation scarcely mentions alcohol as a threat to public health.

Whether the Constitution mandates that the government is responsible for protecting the public from "unhealthy" products is highly debatable. The medieval rule of caveat emptor—originally a consumer-empowering tradition because it allowed consumers to physically inspect materials, foods, and products—remained in force as a positive principle in the free market system in that people could buy, or not buy, whatever they chose. Only recently has it become viewed as a negative concept. But even if one can find a constitutional argument under the "general welfare" clause that empowers the federal government to protect the public from harmful products, poisons, and drugs, the thin line between regulation for public safety and control of public health for political reasons has certainly been crossed in the last fifty years. It's one thing for the federal government to prohibit elixirs that contain poisons, but it's quite another to ban products from the market because they do not do what they promise. Carter's Little Liver Pills were not harmful, but the Federal Trade Commission ruled in 1951 that the word *liver* had to be dropped because the pills didn't ostensibly affect the liver. Of course, the medical community has now confirmed that so much of physical health is psychological and mental. Knowing this, at what point does a person's *belief* that a product is beneficial actually start to produce physical results? Since that question is unanswerable, the Founders almost unanimously would have argued that government should stay out of individual choices as much as possible.

By the 1950s, however, the FDA and public health officials had stretched their authority to a new level, moving from careful monitoring of poisons in the American food and drink supply to recommending to the public what foods to eat and what drinks to consume. As I showed in *Seven Events That Made America America*, this trend accelerated with Dwight Eisenhower's heart attack and opened the door for the fusion of medicine, science, politics, and public health.[70] Rashly determining that Ike's heart attack had been caused by cholesterol, and that his diet was to blame, the medical/government axis rushed to dictate to all Americans how to restructure their eating habits, minimizing meat and fats and maximizing carbohydrates. Beginning with incomplete and unconfirmed studies by a single researcher, Ancel Keys, a group of activist researchers pushed for a reduction in the fat/meat intake of Americans. (Government had already started to "educate" people about their diets with the famous food pyramid of the 1980s.) In 1977, the McGovern Committee's "Dietary Goals for the United States" inserted the federal government as an active player in the diets of average Americans. Unfortunately, the assumptions of all these groups were based on contested, flawed, inadequate, or simply erroneous evidence. As a result—with eerie foreshadowing of the global warming debate years later—all contrary science was pushed aside to ensure that the "right" message got out to the public. For want of better terms, "antifat/antimeat" studies received widespread praise and government funding, while "profat/promeat" conclusions and research did not. A significant and unconverted sector of researchers, nutritionists, and doctors who rejected the fat/meat/cholesterol hypothesis (which, by the way, was no longer treated by government officials as a hypothesis, but as a proven fact) were marginalized, isolated, and often ignored. Not until Dr. Robert Atkins's diet came out in 1992 did a major public figure challenge the fat/meat/cholesterol thesis.[71]

The Founders would have thought a federally endorsed and funded food pyramid was absurd—not because it was either correct or incorrect in its recommendations, but because the U.S. government should not have any role at all in telling people, even as a suggestion, what they should eat. Even in medicine, the Revolutionary doctor Benjamin Rush knew that one of his friends, Jacob Duche, died from having suffered from "a diabetes" for which he "took quack medicines constantly, by which means he probably shortened his life" (despite the fact that he lived to the incredibly old age, for that era, of sixty-two!), yet Rush did not recommend government involvement in medicine because such a role was not proper.[72]

What lies on the horizon for twenty-first-century America is truly chilling, for the 2010 health care reform promises to open doors that would have left the Founders dumbstruck. If a national public option becomes law in any form, it is unavoidable that the federal government will become the most powerful nanny in the world. President Barack Obama's comments in a town hall meeting that it was "unfair" for him to pay the health care of someone who "abused" his body meant that the only thing left to be determined is, what defines abuse? Certainly anything that causes obesity would count and would face the same public assault that the tobacco industry has witnessed for years.

But health care reform will prove to be far worse in terms of nannyism. Not only will the government tell people what to eat and drink but *neighbors* will be induced into ratting on neighbors, under the assumption that what one person eats affects everyone else. Imagine enjoying a grilled hot dog in your backyard one summer day and hearing your neighbor shout over the fence, "Hey, buddy! I don't want to pay for your hospital visit when you have a heart attack!"

Now that health care has become a matter of public policy, it is inevitable that it will pit the young against the old, the healthy against the unhealthy, and the lean against the obese. It also ensures government meddling in diets, as seen already in the bill introduced in the New York legislature to ban *all* salt from cooking in New York restaurants.[73] (Anyone who has *ever* cooked anything knows how ridiculous this is.) But as I repeatedly tell my students, "They're comin' for your Ho Hos." If Upton Sinclair fired the opening salvos in the "war on meat," and if Ike's heart attack led to early skirmishes, the health care reform act promises to lead to unprecedented invasions of private choices, activities, and even well-being, for one man's necessity will soon be another man's vice. The Founders knew this, and for that reason did not even entertain the notion that health care was a right, and certainly not a function of government. "Were we directed from Washington when to sow, and when to reap," Jefferson said, "we should soon want bread."[74] But today it would be worse: we should soon want for buttered popcorn and pepperoni pizza.

QUESTION #5

SHOULD THE GOVERNMENT STIMULATE THE ECONOMY AND OTHERWISE ENSURE FULL EMPLOYMENT?

Of all the Founders, few came up "through the ranks" in the world of work as impressively as Benjamin Franklin. He apprenticed in a print shop before opening his own, and later admonished people to "Work as if you were to live a hundred years." In 1753 he wrote to a friend arguing against a Pennsylvania welfare ("poor") law, noting that with its repeal, "industry will increase, and with it plenty among the lower people . . . and more will be done for their happiness by inuring them to provide for themselves than by dividing all your estates among them."[1] It is true that many of the Founders—the Virginians and South Carolinians most especially—owned slaves. But that did not mean they did not know the meaning of work. George Washington had toiled as a surveyor, and even on his plantation he engaged in physical labor.

Like so many other issues that modern Americans have come to see as the responsibility of government, jobs and all aspects of human labor were viewed by the Founders as so entirely *outside* the proper role of government that they generally did not offer any opinions as to what government "should" do to promote employment. Virtually all their ideas and programs involved, to one degree or another, getting government *out* of markets so that the private sector could create jobs. Many of them had developed these ideas well before Adam Smith had detailed them in *Wealth of Nations* and outlined the theory of capitalism.

In one of the first tests of the Founders' views of "job creation," the small financial panic of 1792, we have a clear demonstration of their reaction to unemployment. Then Treasury Secretary Alexander Hamilton, upon learning that the machinations of New York businessman William Duer had provoked a crash in March of that year, adopted a two-track strategy that modern politicians would be wise to copy. First, working behind the scenes with *private* banks, he negotiated a series of agreements that they would not allow the Bank of New York—which was under pressure—to fail. (As we will see in the banking chapter, it is true he used some leverage involving government money to entice them, but in fact he did not have to use much government funds at all to actually stymie the panic, instead relying on the mostly private lending of the Bank of the United States—an institution 80 percent privately owned and entirely privately controlled.) The second, and more important, indicator of the Founders' views of government-supported jobs came when Hamilton allowed Duer to fail, thus stating unequivocally that the government would not intervene with private individuals or companies merely to prop up the employment numbers.[2]

There will be more to say on this in a later chapter, but the immediate lesson was that Hamilton did not so much as even *mention* the desirability of adding jobs or curbing unemployment as a condition for any of his actions.

Thomas Jefferson, faced with a languishing economy in his second term as trade with Britain and France withered, did not even contemplate government action to "stimulate" the economy, nor were there calls for him to do so. His Embargo Act of 1807, which for national security purposes prevented any trade to European ports, brought on an economic depression. Jefferson's Treasury secretary, Albert Gallatin, argued against it.[3] Protests against the act occurred all along the eastern coast, and most merchants ignored the law. Thus—again, for national security reasons—not only did Jefferson *not* employ an "economic stimulus" or "jobs bill," he threatened to enforce every aspect of the law and to request another. Congress finally ended the matter with the Non-Intercourse Act of 1808, which allowed the president to declare the nation safe and to resume trade. Less than a year later, Jefferson lifted all embargoes except those on England and France, and in 1810 Macon's Bill No. 2 lifted all remaining embargoes.

Nevertheless, it was not long before some began to make arguments for government intervention in employment markets. Perhaps the first widespread calls for this came with the Panic of 1819, when hundreds of textile mills closed and thousands of workers were on the street. A memo to Governor Ethan Brown of Ohio in April 1820 noted, "One thing seems to be universally conceded, that the greater part of our mercantile citizens are in a state of bankruptcy . . . [and] that the citizens of every class are uniformly delinquent in discharging even the most trifling of debts."[4] In Pennsylvania, wages fell by two-thirds in some categories, including woodcutting. Industrial America, still young, suffered greatly.

Many called for government action, and the camel's nose in the tent came in the form of debts owed to the U.S. government for federal lands. Debtors had incurred their obligations when prices for farm goods were high, yet with the collapse in wages and prices, they now had to repay them when prices were low. One of the first relief proposals was not a jobs bill, but it did involve federal action. Senator Richard M. Johnson of Kentucky presented a resolution to allow land debtors to cede back a quarter of the purchaser's land to the government in return for clear title to the rest. Well intended though it may have been, this constituted a kind of reverse fire sale, a Carnegie-esque move in which the government would reacquire millions of acres at low prices to sell again at high prices when the market returned. But Treasury Secretary William Crawford worried about the implication for sanctity of contracts and watered down the measure with a proportional relinquishment of unpaid portions of the land. Proponents, sounding much like legislators discussing the twenty-first-century AIG bailout, noted that "artificial and fictitious prosperity" had placed the debtors in their positions.[5] Johnson claimed that unforeseen changes in the economy had slammed the debtors, not their "own imprudence."[6] Relief advocates in Congress, as legislators usually do, began to add amendments that expanded federal aid, including a provision to grant special, additional relief to debtors who had actually settled the land already, forgiving them an additional 25 percent of their unpaid debt. Once the government handout ball got rolling, it was difficult to stop.

Yet from President James Monroe on down, many officials viewed the panic as something outside the purview of government to address. Monroe insisted that the government hew to principles of restrained spending and balanced budgets, and in his second inaugural address (March 5, 1821), he applied a solution that seemed to come right out of the "supply-side" playbook: "Anxious to relieve my fellow-citizens in 1817 from every burden which could be dispensed with, and the State of the Treasury permitting it, I recommended the repeal of the internal taxes, knowing that such relief was then peculiarly necessary in consequence of the great exertions made in the late war."[7] A year later, he vetoed an appropriation for repairs in the Cumberland Road Bill, saying, "congress does not possess the power under the constitution to pass such a law."[8] The Detroit *Gazette* inferred that unemployment stemmed mostly from the laziness of laborers.[9] Others, such as young lawyer Willard Phillips, a leading Federalist, insisted that the economy "is a question which the merchants alone are acquainted with, and capable of deciding; and as the public interest coincides directly with theirs, there is no danger of its being neglected."[10] Or, it could be said that no one knew the economy better than those *in* the economy. The *New York Evening Post* observed, "Time and the laws of trade will restore things to an equilibrium, if legislatures do not rashly interfere to the natural course of events," and Virginia congressman James Johnson added, "let the people manage their own affairs . . . the people of this country understand their own interests and will pursue them to advantage."[11]

As often happens, however, not only did the western legislators vote for the bill (pleasing their debt-burdened constituents), but so did representatives from places such as New York City (where virtually no one benefited). Why? The answer lies in the fact that eastern bankers had engaged in considerable speculation, and would lose some of their profits. It seems that Bear Stearns was not the first to seek a bank bailout, even if indirectly in this case. Congressmen rationalized their votes on the grounds that *private* contracts were not at stake, only government contracts. Soon after passage of the federal law, states began to target banks, debating measures giving debtors relief from *bank loans* (keeping in mind that the original rationale for the federal relief was that it was "only" the federal government that was involved and thus no private citizens would be harmed by the relief). Most "stay" laws stalled, but Maryland passed a stay law on a two to one majority vote, exempting household articles worth up to fifty dollars from sales at execution (i.e., a form of repossession), which constituted a significant dollar amount for that day.[12] Other states changed their bankruptcy laws to make them more advantageous to debtors.

Instead of a jobs bill, Congress in the early 1800s sought to achieve the same results through modifications in the tariff. Through the newly established American Society for the Encouragement of Domestic Manufactures, protectionists tried to make high duties on cotton and wool permanent, require that government officials clothe themselves in domestic fabrics, and prohibit the importation of cotton from India. Worried that Americans were "buying Indian," the high-tariff forces (led by Philadelphia printer Matthew Carey) complained that the depression was caused by free trade. Reverend Lyman Beecher called the tariff the chief "means to national prosperity [and] recovery."[13] One writer, under the pseudonym "A Manufacturer," claimed that the government had the duty under the general welfare clause to ensure trade and commerce: the government "is the national physician," he wrote.[14]

Twenty years later, when the deep Panic of 1837 swept the United

States, there was even more dissatisfaction, but due to Andrew Jackson's "war" on the Bank of the United States, most of the public's focus was on banks, not on jobs creation. Ironically, it was the fairly mild Panic of 1857 that brought some of the loudest howls for the government to act, although even then few expected the government to provide jobs directly. When New York City saw the number of unemployed range from 30,000 to 100,000 (out of a population of just over 800,000, for a rate of up to 11 to 12 percent), the mayor, Fernando Wood, proposed one of the first public works programs in American history. He suggested paying men in "cornmeal, potatoes, and flour" for working on Central Park, paying for the scheme with new bonds redeemable in fifty years and bearing 7 percent interest.[15] In days of "general depression," he said, the poor "are the first to feel the change, without the means to avoid or endure reverses."[16] Unemployment rallies took place at Tompkins Square, which quickly spun out of control in a steal-the-wealth frenzy, and despite Wood's attempts to calm one of the gatherings, crowds marched on city hall, forcing Wood to surround municipal buildings with police and militia. Perhaps fittingly, Wood himself became a target of the mobs' ire: "Who is this Fernando Wood to whom we are told to put our trust?" said one ringleader, George Camphill. "He is a politician—he is a selfish, scheming politician."[17] Eventually, some public jobs were offered for Central Park work and for the Croton aqueduct, and the show of strength by the city government caused the demonstrations to dissipate.

New York was not alone in the Panic of 1857: between one-third and one-half of Pennsylvania's furnaces and iron operations shut down, coal operators were laid off, and shoe industries experienced a slowdown. Typically, most critics blamed the bankers, when in fact the cause of the panic (as I discussed in *Seven Events That Made America America*) was the *government*, specifically the United States Supreme Court, which handed down the infamous *Dred Scott* decision and triggered a crash in western railroad bonds. Nevertheless, the newspapers almost universally blamed the "vast expansion of currency" and financial speculations for the downturn.[18]

Perhaps it is helpful for us to review the Founders' own experiences when it came to work, achievement, and ambition. Patrick Henry, whose father's large family taxed his earning capabilities, was sent to work at age fifteen as a clerk in a general store.[19] A year later, Patrick and his brother William started a merchant trade of their own, where Patrick learned bookkeeping and sales while William managed the operations. Biographer George Willison concluded that the Henrys lacked capital to carry the planters through the dry spells, although some evidence suggests that the young man—as many young men do—spent much of his work time on pleasurable pursuits.[20] The business failed after a year and Patrick wound up the firm's affairs, whereupon he got married and began growing tobacco, and at that job he labored diligently and intensely. To no avail, it appeared, as Henry struggled, but he also took over management of his father-in-law's tavern and finally achieved some degree of financial success. In sum, Patrick Henry had experienced many aspects of employment, from apprentice to employee to owner to manager, and knew business from each end.

Alexander Hamilton, having worked hard as a clerk at the age of nine in the Virgin Islands, wrote: "my ambition is [so] prevalent that I contemn [sic] the grovelling and conditions of a clerk . . . to which my fortune &c. condemns me and would willingly risk my life, tho' not my character, to exalt my station."[21] At the same time, he personally witnessed the horrors of slavery on St. Croix, including castration of slaves and slaves being prodded with red-hot pokers. In Hamilton's mind, there was a clear separation of free labor (i.e., labor by contract, based on ambition and talent) and slave labor (work forced by the hands of others). James Madison "worked himself into a state of nervous exhaustion" by completing the Princeton requirements for a bachelor's degree in two years instead of three, and Aaron Burr not only tried to enter Princeton at age eleven—only to be rejected—but then studied so hard he applied for admission as a junior at age thirteen and was admitted . . . as a sophomore![22]

George Washington entered the workforce at age eleven when his father died, and later he was hired by his in-laws to survey their property. Washington worked diligently as a surveyor, laying out the town of Belhaven (Alexandria) in 1749, and was appointed official surveyor for Culpeper County, Virginia. He conducted more than 190 surveys and used the earnings to purchase a fourteen-hundred-acre plot of land in the Shenandoah Valley.[23] Like Hamilton, Washington observed a close connection between work, entrepreneurship, and success: "A people . . . who are possessed of the spirit of commerce, who see and who will pursue their advantages may achieve almost anything."[24] He saw the presidency as a "work assigned me," and praised those "who have contributed any thing, who have performed the meanest office in erecting this stupendous fabrick of Freedom and Empire on the broad basis of Independency."[25]

Washington was, as biographer Richard Brookheiser noted, an "exacting employer" because he expected others to work as hard as he did, even if the employees were relatives or friends. "As you are now receiving my money," he wrote a manager, "your time is not your own; [since] every hour or day misapplied is a loss to me, do not therefore [be] under a belief that, as a friendship has long subsisted between us, many things may be overlooked in you."[26] Yet it was troubling to Washington—who conducted a time-motion study of two men cutting wood and concluded that even after allowing for two hours for meals, the men could improve their efficiency many times over—that most slaves could not be motivated by their own ambition. Put another way, Washington internalized the reality that any labor not directly undertaken for the benefit of one's personal improvement was likely to be less useful, if useful at all. In 1797, in a letter to William Gordon, he disparaged workmen in "most Countries" as "necessary plagues," and "in this [country] where entreaties as well as money must be used to obtain their work and keep them to their duty they baffle all calculation in the accomplishment of any plan or repairs they are engaged in;—and require more attention to and looking after than can be well conceived."[27]

Henry Knox dropped out of school at about the same age that both Hamilton and Washington joined the workforce (age twelve) and supported his family by working for a bookseller and eventually opening his own bookshop. (It was from the books he sold, particularly those on military history, which he read constantly, that Knox got his knowledge of the military, even though he had never fired a gun until the Battle of Bunker Hill.)[28] James Monroe, who literally walked five miles through the snow to school each day, worked every summer beginning at age fourteen on building jobs when suddenly his father died and he had to run the entire estate.[29] Before he could delve deeply into that work, an uncle took over running the family plantation and, before the revolution and military service intervened, enrolled Monroe in the College of William and Mary.

Benjamin Rush attended school, then college, and upon graduation immediately began an apprenticeship in medicine, where he proved a diligent learner.[30] Lest someone think that a doctor does not know what work is, Rush described his chores: "In addition to preparing and compounding medicines, visiting the sick and performing many little offices of a nurse to [patients], I took the exclusive charge of [the physician's] books and accompts [sic]."[31] In between all his medical chores, Rush studied "all the books on medicine that were put into my hands by my master, or that I could borrow from other students of medicine in the city."[32] Once he received his license to practice medicine, he found steady employment in Philadelphia, and then, hired at the institute of medicine associated with the University of Pennsylvania, embarked on a rigorous schedule of preparing lectures on all aspects of medicine, including many that he had never explored. (He had witnessed a business downturn in 1792–1793, yet never opined that government should involve itself in any remedies.) In writing reforms for education, Rush insisted that students should be taught to work with their own hands, and, as well, taught the study of commerce, which could check the rise of landed aristocracies, and "as the means of uniting the different nations of the world together by the ties of mutual wants and understandings."[33]

Ironically, of all the Founders, it was Rush—a doctor—who experienced a severe slump in his business. In 1797, he found that he had few new patients and some of his old families had "deserted [him]," as he said, leading him to lobby for a job in government! President John Adams put him in charge of the U.S. mint. John Adams himself had a truncated work career, performing chores on the family farm but otherwise starting school early, before becoming a schoolmaster in Worcester. It was not a career that brought out the entrepreneurial spirit or exposed Adams to the normal vicissitudes of the market, but he did work, and, some might joke, then became a lawyer.[34]

Virtually all the Founders, it should be noted, served in the Continental Army or a militia, and while the military is not private-sector work, it is work nonetheless. All experienced the necessity of discipline, of achieving objectives, of managing time, of advancing in rank. Most were personally ambitious, as well as enthusiastic for the cause of their country. Put another way, none sponged off the government or the taxpayers in the slightest. Occasional unemployment was common in the American colonies and in the young republic, but some sort of work was almost always available—often hard, occasionally disgusting, but work nonetheless.

It was assumed from English heritage that joblessness and its often attendant poverty was a natural and tragic occurrence but not necessarily degrading or inherently immoral.[35] It was, in essence, an unfortunate fact of life, not a "social issue." As early as 1563, English law authorized justices of the peace to raise funds for poor relief based on three categories of poor: those who would work but could not (the "deserving poor" or "able-bodied poor"), for whom the townships provided work that came with a wage; the "idle poor," who could work but would not (and who were whipped); and the indigent or sick. The latter were cared for through almshouses, hospitals, and orphanages. England's Poor Law of 1601 put all men of the first category to work, and collected a tax from property owners, all administered by "overseers" of relief. Only the truly infirmed or aged escaped work. This would be modified, again on the same principles, in 1834 with Lord Earl Grey, whose revision included making the conditions of the public workhouses extremely harsh so as to discourage people from wanting to end up there.

Of course, by the 1780s, many Founders had become familiar with Adam Smith's *Wealth of Nations,* in which he noted that "the liberal reward of labour, as it encourages the propagation[,] so it increases the industry of the common people."[36] How much the Founders internalized, or accepted, Smith remains in dispute. Like notions of "free trade," which Walter Bagehot described as "in the air," it was a "tenet against which a respectable parent would probably caution his son."[37] Nevertheless, as an idea, capitalism replaced mercantilism rather rapidly, and soon it constituted the "respectable tenet." Smith's book said little specifically about the poor—after all, the purpose was to raise people *out* of poverty, not figure out how they got there—but it did observe that the largest number of society (then) were "poor" and "what improves the circumstances of the greater part can never be regarded as an inconveniency to the whole," who should "have such a share of the produce of their own labour as to be themselves tolerably well fed, clothed, and lodged."[38] The division of labor was essential to this end, increasing wealth to the "lowest ranks of the people."[39] For this, free trade was essential because only through free trade could prices be brought down (raising the poor's standard of living) while wages would rise (through competitive bidding for talent and skill). Yet one sees in Smith the essential philosophies of the Founders (stretching all the way to Abraham Lincoln): "The patrimony which every man has in his own labor, *as it is the original foundation of all other property* [emphasis mine], so it is the most sacred and inviolable."[40] Any hindrance of a man from using what Smith called the "strength and dexterity" of his hands was "a plain violation of this most sacred property."[41]

Labor unions, therefore, to the extent that they ever interceded between a man's "patrimony" over his labor and the employer, constituted an evil. While Smith allowed for the indolent, the ignorant, and the corrupt to pervert the process on a micro level, overall he presented an optimistic view of labor that treated people as intelligent, industrious, ambitious, and constantly seeking to better themselves. (Only later did leftist interpreters try to inculcate *Wealth of Nations* with negative, pessimistic overtones.)[42] But Smith also introduced an element that, as we have already seen, permeated the thinking of the Founders, namely, that productive members of society had to be educated, and that the common people needed to be taught reading, writing, and arithmetic, even at state expense. Smith's political economy sought to make freedom possible and, more important, to make it a form of virtue, turning the average laborer into a complete participant in society. He strongly opposed taxes, even for poor relief, if they exceeded the ability of people to pay for necessities. On the other end of the spectrum, Smith intended that only the "sober and industrious" poor would receive aid, not the "dissolute and disorderly."[43]

The Founders were also aware of efforts in England to alleviate hardships caused by the bad harvest of 1795 and the Napoleonic Wars, most notably the "Speenhamland system." An arrangement that arose out of a meeting of Berkshire justices of the peace at Speenhamland, the decree established that "every poor and industrious man" whose earnings fell below certain levels would receive money from the parish to push the family up to a predetermined income.[44] Historian Gertrude Himmelfarb wrote that few seemed to appreciate the significance of subsidizing both the unemployed and the employed until years later, but the significance of Speenhamland lay in the urgency with which government officials thought they had to deal with poverty across the board, not on an individual basis.[45] Likewise, the Founders, who kept up with parliamentary debates and with important thinkers in England, doubtless knew of Edmund Burke, whose treatise "Thoughts and Details on Scarcity" (1795) rejected the rationale used for the Speenhamland ordinance. Burke insisted that the rules of commerce and laws of trade were not subjects for government regulation, but rather workers in dire straits fell under the "jurisdiction of mercy," or charity.[46] He argued against "all meddling on the part of authority; the meddling with the subsistence of people."[47]

One of the most powerful condemnations of Burke's ideas came from the Revolution's voice, Thomas Paine, the perpetual revolutionary who has been labeled the originator of the welfare state.[48] His 1791 book, *Rights of Man,* was foremost an attack on Burke's criticisms of the French Revolution, but further, he offered a view of society so idealist with its "reciprocal aid" that no government would be necessary. In the process, he offered a defense of progressive taxation based on property ownership, once again with the proceeds going to help the unemployed and the poor.[49]

Based on their noninterventionist policies, their view that taxes should be kept low, and their distaste for widespread tariffs, there can be little conclusion other than that the Founders read and internalized Smith and Burke directly. Having inherited the English categories of able-bodied poor and malingerers, the American colonists balanced charity and concern for the disabled, elderly, or children with the reality that work was necessary in the difficult, and often deadly, Colonial setting. Generations later, students learned in their lessons that John Smith had saved

Jamestown by the "He who will not work will not eat" doctrine. Benjamin Franklin wrote in *Poor Richard's Almanac*, "O Lazy-bones! Dost think God would have given thee arms and legs if he had not designed thou shouldst use them."[50] "Determine never to be idle," Jefferson once wrote his wife.[51] Again he wrote in *Notes on the State of Virginia* that "our greatest happiness . . . does not depend on the condition of life in which chance has placed us, but is always the result of a good conscience, good health, occupation and freedom in all just pursuits."[52] Franklin likewise believed that "when men are employed they are best contented."[53]

French writer Michel Guillaume Jean de Crevecoeur, who was naturalized an American, published his *Letters from an American Farmer* in 1782, in which he observed, "It is here then that the idle may be employed, the useless become useful, and the poor become rich."[54] Much later, Daniel Webster noted, "Labor in this country is independent and proud. It has not to ask the patronage of capital, but capital solicits the aid of labor. . . . Labor is the great producer of wealth; it moves all other causes."[55]

While the Founders had significantly different views about how one became "self sufficient" and "free"—and certainly the definitions of, say, Jefferson would have differed from those of a mechanic in 1780 Philadelphia—there is little question that freedom to choose one's own work, and to engage in that labor without the interference (or support) of government, lay at the heart of the American work ethic. Thomas Doerflinger's study of Revolutionary Philadelphia, for example, found that "opportunity, enterprise, and adversity reinforced each other. A young businessman could borrow money and move into trade, challenging the commercial position of older, more established merchants. His opportunity was, in effect, their adversity."[56] While Doerflinger found what might be interpreted as large concentrations of wealth (10 percent of the landholders held perhaps 65 percent of the wealth),* he also found that a vigorous middle class existed, even in Revolutionary times, in which me-

---

* This statistic, often abused in a variety of circumstances, always fails to capture *age*. It is irrelevant what percentage of wealth a given segment of the population has: given that fifty-year-olds are more likely to be wealthy than twenty-year-olds, the only relevant statistic is the share of all fifty-year-old wealth owned by a given percentage of the fifty-year-old population.

chanics, merchants, inventors, shopkeepers, and craftsmen moved up and down the "ladder of wealth" with regularity. He found substantial satisfaction revealed in their letters and journals, mostly, it seems, because they were their "own bosses" and government had little control over their lives. Thus, what one lacked in pure capital, the freedom one gained in America more than made up for it.

Yet someone like the Colonial planter William Byrd II in an earlier time would have looked with scorn on the poor city shopkeepers and merchants. After all, Byrd acquired more than 20,000 acres in North Carolina alone before acquiring 105,000 acres in a deal with government that required him to supply each family who wanted 1,000 acres with land.[57] To a planter such as Byrd, it was essential to have large tracts of land to "pursue happiness," while to a city candler or leathersmith, a shop proved just fine. Byrd was no mere slothful slave owner, watching as his chattel performed his work. He actively managed his estates, surveyed constantly, explored, tested his soil and experimented with new crops, all with an eye toward finding "every thing [that] will grow plentifully here to supply either the Wants or Wantonness of Man."[58]

No American of the era better exemplifies the attitude toward jobs and work than the patriot hero Paul Revere (1735–1818). Revere made himself into the top silversmith and goldsmith in the colonies. His hardware store not only dealt in English and American goods, but he manufactured iron, "hinges of Brass," "Sley Bells," and "Truck Bells," as well as other products.[59] After the Revolution, at age sixty-five (when modern Americans think about retirement), Revere embarked on a new, extremely risky venture, building a rolling mill to produce sheet copper to produce plates for the U.S.S. *Constitution* ("Old Ironsides"). Using twenty-five thousand dollars of his own savings and a small loan from the U.S. government, along with copper from the government, he undertook fabrication of the rolling mill, calling it "a great undertaking [that] will require every farthing which I can rake or scrape."[60]

Like most Americans, Revere did not ever see his station in life as static, a trait he shared with Colonial bookseller Thomas Hancock (1703–1764), who learned book binding and printing as an apprentice, then went on to start his own shop. He acquired books, purchased and resold maritime products (particularly whale oil and bone), and steadily expanded his business. Ultimately, he not only became one of the premier booksellers in the American colonies but dealt in a wide variety of other products, pioneering the early use of credit in his shop. As business historian John Dobson concluded, "Although Thomas Hancock appears to have been a remarkably successful merchant, his story is by no means unique. Many other colonists rose from humble origins to positions of wealth and influence."[61] Studies of the wills of numerous Charleston, South Carolina, coopers, tanners, shoemakers, and other early "mechanics" or artisans revealed that they attained substantial wealth from their enterprises.[62] "Whether cabinet-makers or silversmiths, the careers of the mechanics were characterized by a high level of mobility—both upward and downward—on the ladder of wealth," I noted in *Entrepreneurial Adventure*.[63]

Whether it was Hamilton's willingness to let William Duer fail in 1792 or James Monroe's small-government noninvolvement in the Panic of 1819, the actions of the Founders demonstrate that they rejected the proposition that government should somehow create jobs or be responsible for full employment. Moreover, their attitudes toward work and, conversely, charity for those who could not work also reveal their views that government did not exist to create jobs. Thomas Jefferson, confronted with a stagnant economy in his second term, never once thought it proper for government to "stimulate" the job market.

Indeed, what stands out is that the Founders came from a generation of people who worked, often at a variety of jobs or professions. Their work ethic was powerful, and they shrugged off setbacks as part of life. Most important of all, none saw any connection between the government and their work, except that—in the case of taxes—the government could stand in their way of pursuing happiness. To the notion that government needed to guarantee someone a job, the Founders' response likely would have been, "Try the want ads."

QUESTION #6

DOES THE GOVERNMENT HAVE A RESPONSIBILITY TO KEEP LARGE BUSINESSES SOLVENT IN ORDER TO PROTECT AMERICAN INDUSTRY?

When the CEO offered his testimony before Congress, his goal was simple: to get the government to bail out his flagging company. Despite promises of improvement in efficiencies, lower costs, and profits just around the corner, the company was in fact no better off than before the government had stepped in the last time, and probably in most ways worse. And, despite his pleas to the contrary, the chairman knew it when he asked Congress for taxpayer money.

This is not a scene from 2008, but rather 1847. The CEO was not Rick Waggoner but Edward Knight Collins, and the company in question was not General Motors but the United States Mail Steamship Company, which built transatlantic ships to deliver the mail. Like the auto giant, however, the United States Mail Steamship Company begged Congress for a bailout. In the past, Collins had gotten one every time he asked, and once again he got a government subsidy to save his company. Yet that didn't save the United States Steamship Company, and he kept coming back, asking for another, then another—each one larger than the last, and each accompanied with promises of greater efficiency and growth. Instead, Collins found himself in a losing battle with the private, unsubsidized sector, led by Cornelius Vanderbilt.

If we were to ask the question Does government have a responsibility to bail out large companies that are in danger of going under? in 1789, the Founders' answer would largely depend on another question: What is the business and what does it do? Two things the Founders kept at the forefront of their approaches to public policy were national defense and national security. To the framers of the Constitution, these remained the primary functions of government, and only the preservation of liberty took precedence over them. Thomas Jefferson's phrase in the Declaration, "life, liberty, and the pursuit of happiness," reflected the order in which things should be protected, for only if one has security can one enjoy liberty, then acquire possessions and pursue happiness. Reaffirming this in the Constitution, Congress was given the power to raise armies and declare war against any enemy who posed a threat to life.

At the time of the Constitution's ratification, the concern for the survivability and viability of the young United States against foreign powers (including our former Colonial master) permeated almost every program by the Founders. Washington insisted, "A free people ought not only to be armed, but disciplined; to which end a uniform and well-digested plan is requisite; and their safety and interest require that they should promote such manufactories as tend to render them independent on others for essential, particularly for military, supplies."[1] Alexander Hamilton has long been criticized by conservatives for his "big government" approach to the economy, in which he sought to establish a system of protective tariffs for "infant industries" that the government deemed important to economic health.[2] However, it is worth examining the two industries that Hamilton cited as worthy of federal support—textiles and iron. Hamilton viewed government support for those two industries as grounded on the necessities of those products for war. He had painful memories of the Continental Army's shortages of guns, food, uniforms, and boots in the Revolutionary War, and concluded that the best way to ensure a strong military was to develop a set of domestic industries that could supply the armed forces when necessary.

That philosophical underpinning had shaped George Washington's "Farewell Address" (written by Hamilton), in which he proclaimed that the "period is not far off when we may defy material injury from external annoyance; when we may take such an attitude as will cause the neutrality we may at any time resolve upon to be scrupulously respected . . . [and] when we shall choose peace or war, as our interest guided by our justice shall Counsel."[3] Instead, if the United States were "preserved in tranquility twenty years longer, it may bid defiance, in a just cause, to any power whatever, such, in that time will be its population, wealth, and resource."[4]

Hamilton, more so than Washington—who never fancied himself a deep thinker about economic issues—came from the mercantilist tradition in which the government played an active role in the economy. Under this tradition, businesses existed only to advance the state, and those attitudes were only beginning to change as the United States was born. Adam Smith's *Wealth of Nations* was published in 1776, and concepts of free-market economics still percolated only into the business thinking of the young republic—but, noticeably, the notion that businesses existed to serve the state had already been discarded. Moreover, Hamilton, who had a sponge for a mind, willingly examined all alternatives. While writing the *Report on Manufactures* (1791), he immersed himself in the practices and processes of manufacturing. According to his biographer, Ron Chernow, Hamilton "canvassed manufacturers and revenue collectors, quizzing them in detail about the state of production in their districts. . . . He aspired to know everything: the number of factories in each district, the volume of goods produced, their prices and quality, the spurs and checks to production provided by state governments."[5] He requested samples of the textiles to touch and feel, accumulated swatches of cloth from Connecticut and Massachusetts, even putting them on display in Congress's committee rooms.

Having written many of Washington's wartime orders, Hamilton remembered the scarcities that the general had begged the Continental Congress to address, and knew that reliance on foreign manufacturers in strategic items could be devastating in time of war. In his *Report,* he said, "the extreme embarrassments of the United States during the late war, from an incapacity of supplying themselves, are still a matter of keen recollection." He insisted the protections given American industries would be temporary measures, withdrawn as soon as American companies were competitive. Throughout, he cited constitutional authority in the preamble clause that gave Congress the power to "provide for the common defence," and while tenuous in some respects, he never lost sight of the original goal to make the United States self-sufficient in arms and to support "an annual purchase of military weapons" and to aid "the formation of arsenals."[6]

It must be emphasized that although *Wealth of Nations* appeared in 1776 and its principles soon took root in the United States, the idea of capitalism as an economic framework remained something new and foreign in America. Everyone understood that people did better when they owned their own land—John Smith had proved this at Jamestown, and few debated the advantages of private property over communal property. And almost everyone accepted that the butcher, the baker, and the candlestick maker all had to earn a living through profits. The young republic had a small iron, textile, and publishing industry, but beyond that, virtually all of the nation's businesses consisted of farms or artisans known as mechanics.[7] Moreover, the *only* working economic models the newly independent Americans could observe were mercantilist or semimercantilist models in England and France. To have expected Hamilton or John Adams or James Madison to leap full bloom into the capitalist mind-set as we know it today would have been ahistorical and unrealistic.

What is remarkable, therefore, is that they intuitively understood so much about the necessity for private markets and noninterference by government *without* two hundred years of experience or data to back them up. Yes, Hamilton (as I discussed in the previous chapter) quelled the panic of 1792 by having the Bank of the United States provide loans behind the scenes to banks that were experiencing runs, but he publicly allowed William Duer, the culprit in the speculations, to bear the full penalty of his activities. Duer ended up broke, and in a debtor's prison.[8] In this case, Hamilton shrewdly distinguished between bailing out the *markets* to protect the U.S. economy and bailing out individuals, which he refused to do. To take it a step further, even the Bank of the United States, despite its name, was designed to be essentially a private institution and was 80 percent privately owned and nearly entirely controlled by its private investors. Thus, government involvement was minimal in the extreme.

Most of the Founders remained skeptical about supporting private businesses, and certainly rejected the notion that one should bail out an established company. Criticisms of the First Bank of the United States came mainly from those who feared that *specific* investors, namely, British investors, wielded too much influence within the institution.[9] Public funding for large-scale *projects,* as opposed to specific businesses, however, did catch the fancy of some Founders. Thomas Jefferson tasked his Treasury secretary to come up with a massive roads program that dwarfed any other expenditures, again under the auspices of national defense.[10] At no time did the governments headed by any of the Founders bail out or rescue an individual enterprise, even one that made weapons. (As late as 1840, Samuel Colt's arms company in Paterson, New Jersey, went belly up without so much as a "Look out below" from the federal government.) More telling, businesses did not even bother begging Congress for funds, fully aware that it was not the government's job to save them.

That trend was broken in the 1840s when Congress grew concerned about Britain's control of passenger service across the Atlantic. Samuel Cunard had convinced the British government to supply him with $257,000 a year to conduct mail and passenger service to America, whereupon he charged $2 per person and $.24 per letter, which he claimed was insufficient to cover the cost of delivering the mail.[11] It didn't take long for an American, Edward K. Collins, to approach the U.S. government with a similar plan, asking for $3 million and $385,000 per year in subsidies. Upon receiving federal money, he promised to "drive the Cunarders off the seas."[12] In fact, Collins promised neither to deliver mail cheaper than the British nor to open different routes only to establish American routes. With his taxpayer funds, Collins built "luxurious ships," and each of his four enormous vessels had "elegant saloons, ladies' drawing rooms, and wedding berths. He covered the ships with plush carpet and brought aboard exotic rose, satin, and olive-wood furniture, marble tables, exotic mirrors, flexible barber chairs, and French chefs."[13] He even had electric bells installed in the state rooms to summon the stewards.

What Collins could not do was reduce his costs and come up with better service. Quite to the contrary, he spent an inordinate amount of time wining and dining Washington bigwigs, intent on getting larger and larger subsidies. He succeeded. That is, until a competitor decided to enter the market—Cornelius Vanderbilt. Like most businessmen, Vanderbilt hoped to get government favors if he could, but in this case, even though he informed Congress that he would build and run an Atlantic mail service for $15,000 per trip, much cheaper than either Cunard or Collins, Congress refused. Some, such as Senator William Seward of New York, reasoned that the government had already invested heavily in Collins, and even if he couldn't perform, the United States couldn't abandon him. Collins gleefully accepted his *increased* subsidy of $858,000 per year, at which point Vanderbilt challenged the Collins monopoly, with no government support at all, by slashing the cost of letters and passenger fares. He also introduced a "steerage" class—the equivalent of modern-day "coach" class—at extremely low rates. Through a variety of innovative tactics, Vanderbilt cut his expenses even further so as to make his line profitable (all the while complaining that "it is utterly impossible for a private individual to stand in competition with a line drawing nearly one million dollars per annum from the national treasury," a point that Ford Motor Company no doubt echoed when General Motors and Chrysler received massive bailouts in 2009–2010).[14]

Predictably in this case, Collins's reliance on subsidies retarded technological applications in his fleet. He was slower to use iron construction, even though John Ericsson, later of *Monitor* fame, had been experimenting with iron hulls since 1843. Vanderbilt, of course, had looked at iron hulls, and the irony of Congress's recurring gifts to Collins was that the nation would use his fleet in time of war! On both sides of the Atlantic, subsidizing mail shipping proved a drag on innovation. Cunard actually interfered with attempts by competitors to introduce steam power, clinging to obsolete wooden hulls and paddle wheels long after they were proven out of date. Vanderbilt, meanwhile, introduced steam-hulled ships on his California mail routes, while in England, William Inman—Cunard's opponent—introduced twin screws and other innovations that Cunard resisted. Thus on both sides of the Atlantic, far from making either nation stronger militarily or more advanced technologically, government involvement had held both England and America back, and only the private sector had provided the necessary advances. And despite Collins's continued failures, Congress poured money into the Collins line right up to the time he went under, figuratively and literally when one of his mammoth ships sank, accounting for one-half of his fleet and killing five hundred passengers. For what it's worth, not one of Vanderbilt's ships ever sank.

Indeed, the early history of the United States is the story of the repeated triumph of private entrepreneurs over a host of government-supported enterprises. John Jacob Astor, for example, challenged the government fur trade monopoly in Michigan. Once again, the nation had inherited some of the mercantilist policies of the British and supported a series of fur factories to compete with the British trading posts that President George Washington thought constituted a menace to the United States. A series of government posts would "fix [the Indians] strongly in our Interest," he argued.[15] Congress allocated a subsidy in 1795 for the fur posts and raised it to $300,000, a substantial amount, but justified in Washington's mind by national defense. Regardless of the efforts of the Office of Indian Affairs, which supervised the fur posts, the exchanges failed to produce alliances with the Indians. But the director of the fur program, Thomas McKenney, misread the Indians and misunderstood what products they craved at the forts. Meanwhile, Astor founded the American Fur Company in 1808 and had heeded what he was told by his agents about Indian needs of food, blankets, iron tools, and muskets. More important, his traders, rather than holing up in posts, as McKenney's men did, lived with the Indians and gained their trust. And he offered credit, something the government did not do. Whereas McKenney attempted to turn the Indians into farmers, Astor supplied them with axes, kettles, muskets—whatever they wanted. Above all, Astor set up a marketing system for the furs, top to bottom, that whipped the government operations.

Within a year of creating the American Fur Company, he surpassed the government as the leading exporter of American furs, developing one of the largest companies in America. Briefly, the government posts were being beaten so badly that McKenney sought to ban private competition, and he dreamed up a national security excuse for doing so, claiming that Astor was defrauding the Indians. When he failed to ban private competitors, McKenney tried another government trick, requiring expensive licenses. That too failed. Finally, Astor went to Congress to urge the members to abolish the *government* system, and after an independent report on the government factory system and the American Fur Company, the author of the report, Jedidiah Morse, concluded that the private traders far outperformed the government, and in 1822, Congress finally ended the subsidized fur factories.

Ironically, despite a decline in the fur trade, Astor continued to remain competitive until the government helped kill his business. First, Congress passed a new tariff on English textiles, which raised the prices on the blankets Astor sold to the Indians. Second, Congress cut off the flow of liquor into Indian territory, removing another commodity that the natives wanted. Finally, Congress moved the Indians farther west, eliminating Astor's labor supply. In doing so, the government agitated the native population and removed a steady form of work that had continually brought whites and Indians together—thus enhancing national defense—but also slowly bringing the Indians into the market economy.[16]

Invoking national security constituted a surefire way to get Congress to turn on the money spigots, and everyone from John Fitch to Samuel Colt to Samuel F. B. Morse knew which buttons to push. Fitch, whose idea for a steam-powered ship promised to bring cheap goods upriver, wowed several members of the Constitutional Convention in 1787, but came away with no funds. He did acquire a charter to conduct a monopoly business on the Delaware River—a mistake, as it turned out, for the Delaware was not a difficult river to navigate and had good coach paths and roads on the banks. Fitch never made a profit from his breakthrough, leaving that to Robert Fulton, who perceived that the correct river to traverse was the Hudson.[17] Both Eli Whitney and, later, Samuel Colt sought arms contracts from the U.S. government, and because the need was pressing and genuine (because so few arms dealers were capable of their mass production techniques), both ended up with federal money. Morse got Congress to give him thirty thousand dollars to hook up a telegraph between Washington, D.C., and Baltimore, and, predictably, Congress yanked away his money at the moment he successfully proved his concept in practice, showing that even when the government makes a sound investment in a technology or process, it seldom capitalizes as fully as it should.

Of course the Great Depression provided a prime example of a national bailout of firms, first through Herbert Hoover's Reconstruction Finance Corporation (RFC), then through Franklin Roosevelt's National Industrial Recovery Act (NIRA). The RFC provided loans to "troubled" businesses and banks, attempting to stabilize them and (in the case of the banks) end runs. It did just the opposite: ultimately, the government prohibited nearly five thousand business practices and churned out nearly ten thousand pages of regulation. Worse, the RFC involved political decisions about business health, and "inevitably, the decisions were political, and those who were close to the Hoover administration were often first in line for taxpayer dollars."[18] But Hoover was a child in a sandbox compared to the ruthless and wily Roosevelt, who wielded state bailout money like a political battle-ax. Consider Pennsylvania, a critical swing state, which received only $12 million from the government in Hoover's term (having paid only $297,000 in taxes). Compare that with Democrat campaign literature that touted more than $678 million "contributed to Pennsylvania by the Roosevelt Democratic administration."[19] Roosevelt put a twist on the entire concept of bailouts, moving from individual companies to counties, districts, and regions. *Washington Post* columnist Raymond

Clapper likened it to governors wanting "to keep on the good side of Santa Claus."[20] The NIRA, with its 557 basic and 189 supplemental industry codes put into place in a two-year period, constituted nothing less than an attempt at Democratic fascism. Companies that complied sported the infamous "Blue Eagle," a quasi-fascist symbol indicating that the company had submitted to government supervision. The NIRA "provided a legal framework under which both government and business acted together to raise prices without fear of anti-trust punishment," and it ensured that new firms did not enter the marketplace.[21]

Nevertheless, until World War II, none of the bailouts under the New Deal could be said to have "worked," save for the bank holiday—which will be dealt with in a separate entry. (It is worth noting that in fact the New Deal was bad for your health, as average life expectancy dropped from an average of 63.3 years in 1933 to 62.9 years in 1940, after eight years of FDR's policies.)[22] Nor did the policies "bail out" laborers. Despite the myth that FDR was good for labor, the share of wages going to labor had risen from 55 percent to 60 percent in the 1920s, even as the share of corporate profits remained unmoved at 8.2 percent throughout the decade![23] Of course, when he delivered his acceptance speech at the Democrat Convention in 1932, Roosevelt simply lied, stating that "corporate profit resulting from [the 1920s] was enormous. . . . Very little of it went into increased wages."[24] Consumer prices fell throughout the decade, and with a larger share of profits eaten up by labor, it was simply untrue that workers were not better off. Indeed, the bailout of labor by the minimum-wage law ensured a permanent state of high unemployment, for a boss can employ twenty people at two dollars an hour, but only ten at four dollars an hour. The math was inescapable, as were the unemployment numbers.

Almost every New Deal program in itself was a bailout. The Agricultural Adjustment Act of 1933 bailed out struggling farmers—or at least promised to—by attempting to reduce production. But this resulted only in continued production at previous levels while farmers enthusiastically claimed government checks. The Federal Deposit Insurance Corporation (FDIC) provided a means to bail out depositors who had, or would in the future, lose their deposits because they put their money in failed banks.

(Later, the sister of FDIC, the Federal Savings and Loan Insurance Corporation, or FSLIC, would play a prominent role in encouraging the "moral hazard" by savings and loan operators to engage in increasingly risky behavior, knowing their customers were "protected.") Labor got the Wagner Act, which threw the weight of the federal government onto the side of labor in negotiations, while the investors, through the Securities and Exchange Commission (SEC), could exclude smaller companies from the capital markets by claiming they didn't meet SEC standards. And, tough as it may be to say, Social Security was a bailout to virtually all retirees who had chosen to spend their money on other things during their careers instead of saving for retirement. Government directly bailed out the railroads in the 1930s, attempting to maintain the value of their bonds. As one analysis of modern government bailouts notes,

> Here's a fun trick: Take any Depression-era railroad lending legislation, and place it into a document. Now do a "find & replace," substituting the words "home mortgages" for "railroad bonds." You very nearly end up with what became known as the Emergency Economic Stabilization Act, also known as the Troubled Assets Relief Program (TARP) passed on . . . October 3, 2008.[25]

Hamilton, Washington, and certainly Jefferson would have recoiled at—perhaps even revolted against—such abuses, maintaining that the only time government should involve itself in the economy was in cases of national defense. But even then, it was conducted in such a way as to keep the process in the hands of the private sector as much as possible. Eli Whitney, Samuel Colt, and dozens of other manufacturers of firearms received government contracts to make muskets and, later, revolvers. It is true that there were government armories and U.S. Navy shipyards over time, yet whenever practical, the government purchased weapons from private suppliers. More important, as Donald Hoke points out in his book *Ingenious Yankees,* virtually all the innovations long credited to government armories first appeared in private armories and in other parts of the private sector.[26] Samuel Colt's arms company went bankrupt and he nearly vanished from the face of history until, with the help of a Texas Ranger, he made some improvements to his revolving pistol that made it safer and more reliable.[27] Perhaps the most amazing part of Colt's story is that the government did *not* bail him out—and at the time, it would have been a mistake, for his design was not ready. Yet by persevering on his own, Colt came up with one of the most advanced weapons in the world, generally considered the "gun that won the West." What would have happened if Uncle Sam had subsidized the poorer design?

In their understanding of war, with the finality of its consequences and the depth of its damage, the Founders knew that if any sector had to be protected by the federal government, it was the so-called military-industrial complex. Yet from the early 1800s through the Civil War, while the army and navy had to acquire certain weapons, they did so whenever possible from a private source. We see in the American Civil War the best and worst of government support of business—in this case, arms manufacturers or other critical industries—on both sides. By and large, the Union government allowed the free market to supply the military with the needed weapons, which produced two desired effects. First, the government always had a number of suppliers that it could pit against each other, and thus competition was fierce, while at the same time the government never had to worry about running out of guns, ammunition, cannons, or other supplies. A second result of the Union policies of relying largely on private suppliers was that a steady stream of military breakthroughs unfolded, virtually none of them originating with the government. Dr. Richard Gatling introduced a rotating-barrel, rapid-fire early machine gun; John Ericsson designed the rotating-turret, steam-powered *Monitor*; before the war, Christopher Sharps had invented a breach-loading rifle; then in 1862, Christopher Spencer stunned the arms community with his rapid-fire repeating rifle. Many of these inventors, such as Spencer, had to struggle to persuade the army to purchase their (superior) weapons, so dense was the government bureaucracy. Even in the Confederacy, when the government allowed them to, inventors proved their worth, as when a Louisiana designer, Horace Hunley, designed and tested submarines at private expense. It is true that many of the larger cannons, such as the Parrott Gun, the Dahlgren Gun, and others, came from military foundries. But the Confederacy had its own foundries and failed to adopt the hollow casting techniques that made the Rodman guns superior.[28]

Meanwhile, in the Confederacy, a state-run approach to arms manufacture developed, leaving the Confederate government in charge of almost every aspect of supplying the war effort at the expense of the private sector. As I noted in *The Entrepreneurial Adventure* (2000), "the surprising fact of the Civil War was not that the Union did not use statist policies to direct the business community but that the Confederacy *did*."[29] Political scientist Richard Bensel, who contrasted the two systems, concluded, "the northern war effort left the industrial and agricultural sectors almost untouched by central state controls and only skimmed the surface of the northern labor pools."[30] Libertarians rightly carp about Abraham Lincoln's "big government" policies, but Lincoln knew not to slay the golden goose, and the ill-fated transcontinental railroad subsidies yielded completed railroad lines only in 1869, long after the wartime need for them was over. Wisely, however, when the transcontinental railroads all went belly up in the Panic of 1873, the government stayed out of the issue and allowed the railroads to be reorganized by the private sector under J. P. Morgan. Ironically, the *only* transcontinental railroad that did not go bankrupt during that time belonged to James J. Hill, who did not receive any federal subsidies at all![31]

The cold war brought new concerns, and would have caused the Founders to reassess their practices, but not their principles, when it came to bailouts. In that context, Dwight Eisenhower's concerns about a military-industrial complex demanded investigation, but in the end, the nature of weaponry had changed so much that the nation had no cushion, as it had in World War II, where distance and time allowed for the margin needed to rebuild our military. A missile fired from the Soviet Union had a thirty-minute flight time, and if fired from a Russian submarine not far from American shores, half that. Most analysts believed that if the USSR had chosen to invade Germany, the combined forces of the North Atlantic

Treaty Organization (NATO) would have been swept away in less than six weeks—before a single relief ship with additional troops or weapons could have arrived from the United States. Therefore, the concept of national defense took on an immediacy that the Founders had not faced. To that end, not only could the nation not afford to allow a critical arms manufacturer to fail but it had to ensure that *production lines* remained viable, even in peacetime and even if specific weapons of that type were not instantly needed.

The first genuine test of this evolution of national security involved Lockheed Aircraft. By 1971, the company had been posting losses for three years, in no small part because of management miscalculations on programs such as the C-5, whose contract it won from Boeing by underbidding. Its civilian airliner, the L-1011, also had military overtones, as all airline transports did, for in emergencies the U.S. government had to enlist the airlines as private troop delivery vendors. What made Lockheed so special, however, was its ability to supply cutting-edge fighter planes, such as the P-38 Lightning in World War II, the F-104 Starfighter, and radical reconnaissance aircraft, such as the U2 and the SR-71 Blackbird. Over time, Lockheed's famed "Skunk Works" operated well outside the traditional air force bureaucracy to unveil one advanced airplane after another, including the F-117 "Stealth" fighter, then the F-22 Raptor.

But in 1970, Lockheed was broke, and formally petitioned the U.S. government for help in March of that year, asking for $600 million (a modern-day equivalent of more than $3 billion). Attacked by Senator William Proxmire (D-WI), who coined the term "corporate welfare," Lockheed nevertheless provided products that the United States desperately needed, and which apparently no other aircraft manufacturers could match. A similar but less critical argument was made for another bankrupt firm, the Penn Central Railroad, for which President Richard Nixon attempted to invoke national security as an excuse to bail out the line by allowing the Defense Department to provide some $200 million in loans. Congress did not agree, but eventually passed the Rail Passenger Service Act in 1971 to create a National Railroad Passenger Corporation, later called Amtrak, which had no national security justification. Ultimately, though, Congress did provide $125 million in loan guarantees to Penn Central's creditors, and spent still more in general on railroads.

Chrysler Corporation became the next failing corporation to require a bailout. By 1978, the corporation was losing money, and after the oil embargo of 1978, it suffered a loss of a billion dollars. Its only money-making division at the time was the tank division, which had fought a half-decade battle with auto competitor General Motors over the M-1 Abrams tank contract. At the time, GM fared well, and while government officials denied that the health of Chrysler influenced the tank decision, certainly the automaker counted on its government business, which accounted for 5 percent of all its income (versus about only 1 percent for GM). Complaints about the M-1—especially its turbine engines—were, in fact, common for virtually all new weapons systems, and by the 1990s, in operation Desert Storm, the Abrams proved itself by far the most advanced tank in the world. Concerns that the larger gun would cause tanks to run out of ammunition on the battlefield turned out to be inconsequential when the Abrams could count on "one-shot-one-kill" capability.

Chrysler, meanwhile, received $1.2 billion in loan guarantees from the federal government, creating the myth that only the government funds had saved the auto giant. In fact, a clause in the Chrysler Corporation Loan Guarantee Act stipulated that the creditor make concessions to the company that allowed Chrysler to pay off its debts at thirty cents on the dollar.[32] More important, what saved Chrysler was the tank program itself—not the income, but the sale of the tank business to General Dynamics in 1982 for $336 million, giving the company the liquidity it needed to (temporarily) turn itself around. Nevertheless, the case for Chrysler or Lockheed from the Founders' perspective would have been stronger than that of the Penn Central.[33]

Even though Chrysler represented 123,000 jobs at the time, it is doubtful that the Founders would have seen that as sufficient grounds for keeping the company afloat. Alexander Hamilton justified all his arguments for textile and iron tariffs on the grounds of uniforms, cannons, and bayonets, and never argued for non-defense-related companies. Neither he nor any of the other Founders ever suggested saving a farm or a firm, a baker or a banker, simply because the entity had grown insolvent and risked bankruptcy. But the Chrysler bailout did have other, crucial long-term implications, most notably because the deal failed to provide for guaranteed pensions and health care costs for employees. The contract ended up costing the Big Three automakers billions of dollars until, in 2008, both Chrysler and GM collapsed.[34] Even so, it is not accurate to argue, as does Barry Ritholtz in *Bailout Nation,* that "we can trace Lockheed's $250 million bailout to the potential $34 billion . . . bailout of General Motors, Ford, and Chrysler in 2008 and 2009."[35] While the outcome of the first Chrysler deal, in particular, was problematic, the principles on which that bailout and that of Lockheed were made differed significantly from the auto bailout of the twenty-first century, when *no* national security rationale was even offered. In the former cases, the Founders well may have agreed that as distasteful as bailouts were, the nation's security may have rested on rescuing Lockheed and Chrysler; but in the latter case, no such justification was possible.

Whereas bailouts were scarcely even conceived by the Founders, subsidies brought a somewhat different attitude, particularly when it came to transportation. Direct government aid in the 1790s did not exist— the U.S. government had little money for such luxuries. States, however, did partially subsidize road building through the charter process, which gave private road builders monopolies over a stretch of land. The battle over charters—and exactly what legislators intended charters to include— came before the U.S. Supreme Court in 1824 in the *Gibbons v. Ogden* case, which involved future capitalist icon Cornelius Vanderbilt. Known as the Commodore, Vanderbilt had operated a steamship ferry service across the Hudson in competition with Robert Fulton's partner, Thomas Gibbons, and undercut the Fulton prices. Gibbons sued, claiming his charter constituted a monopoly over Hudson River traffic. The Supreme Court declined to rule on the specific nature of a charter, but instead returned an opinion that Gibbons had no monopoly because the Hudson was an interstate waterway, which belonged to neither New York or New Jersey but to the federal government. Only in 1837, in the *Charles River Bridge v. Warren Bridge* case, did the Supreme Court finally rule that a charter by itself did not constitute a monopoly for the company receiving it. Only if the charter expressly granted a monopoly did such a power exist.

A much different approach to government subsidies of private businesses appeared in the "Canal Era," from about 1820 to 1840, wherein *state* governments (but not the federal government), still hesitant to invest directly in private enterprise, nevertheless guaranteed the bonds of various canal companies. If the enterprise went belly up, the state paid off the bondholders. This is a form of government and private partnership known to economists as "mixed enterprise." Its benefits included a rash of canals that spread across the young nation—but many were unprofitable (with a major exception in the Erie Canal, completed in 1825) and few failed outright. Disadvantages, however, remained (as always) hidden, namely, the incentive for subsidized canal builders to put their efforts into those projects as opposed to, say, the burgeoning railroad industry. Would railroads in America have advanced even quicker without the canal bond guarantees? Perhaps. But it's also worth noting that states experimented with a variety of aid packages for railroads as well.

The point is, by the 1840s, when it came to discussing subsidies, bond guarantees, or any other sort of state or federal assistance to private enterprise, the national security justification had long been abandoned, and only the economic justification remained. Moreover, even when widespread subsidies were proposed with the canal bond guarantees (and later, in the case of the railroad land grants in the 1860s), these were industry-wide, across-the-board offers that in theory could apply to everyone, not firm-specific bailouts such as was later seen with AIG. In short, two characteristics described early government support of any type: it was reasonably fair and open to all competitors (textiles, iron, canals), and in most cases a case for national security could be made. The Penn Central bailout, therefore, perhaps was the first truly modern bailout in that it was firm-specific and had no noticeable national security justification. Even more remarkable, whereas Chrysler's bailout *did* have quite important national security implications, *those were not the justifications* given for a federal rescue package: instead, the company pleaded for help from Uncle Sam to "save jobs." Thus, by the 1970s at the earliest and the 1980s at the latest, activists lobbied for government interference in the fortunes of individual firms based on a strictly economic basis, and did not even invoke national security when it was entirely appropriate. Alexander Hamilton would have gagged.

Matters took an even darker turn in 1994 when the Clinton administration permitted a bailout of Mexico on the grounds that it could disrupt world financial networks. Soon, though, bailouts of Russia, Asia, and parts of South America followed. In no case was it ever demonstrated that the *United States* would be harmed; rather, the rationale was that some American *banks* or *financial institutions* would suffer, and that such a "hit" on the large banks *might* produce a panic. (These claims were never quantified or supported, let alone proven.) Yet the question of why American taxpayers should save banks that engaged in risky lending merely so they could boost profits remains unaddressed and unanswered. It came to a head with a vengeance from 2005 to 2008 when the mortgage-lending industry— largely through "minority-friendly" lending policies—caused a mortgage bubble that collapsed. This was then followed by the bankruptcy of Bear Stearns and other large investment banks, culminating with the events of September 18, 2008, when the chairman of the Federal Reserve, Ben Bernanke, and the secretary of the Treasury, Hank Paulsen, told Congress that the nation's financial markets were on the edge of Armageddon. Without immediate support, they argued, the investment banks would collapse and bring down the entire U.S. banking system. In fact, even *with* a $700 billion bailout, most of these big banks went under, while few banks on "Main Street" felt the impact. But a fascist premise that government and large corporations needed to "work together" took root as the U.S. government took over a large part of the banking industry for any banks that received government TARP money. Many bankers were forced to take TARP whether they wanted the money or not, and the government has made it extremely difficult for banks that received TARP funds to pay them off, specifically (many think) to ensure that the banks remain under the heel of Uncle Sam. In the end, the bailouts merely bailed out the officials of the large banks, while the taxpayers got the shaft. A more pernicious and despicable alliance of big business and government could not be imagined, and the Founders would have applied the brakes long before such nonsense even got rolling.

Nowhere did the Founders show any concern about the success or failure of individual businesses. Quite to the contrary, they focused on the tendencies of governments to use any occasion, any event, as a "necessity" to expand its own power. By any comparison, individuals were more to be trusted with business and finances than government was. "We are all liable to error, and those who are engaged in the management of public affairs are more subject to excitement and to be led astray by their particular interests and passions than the great body of constituents," warned James Monroe in 1823.[36] Adam Smith wrote in *Wealth of Nations* that kings and ministers "are themselves always, and without any exception, the greatest spendthrifts in society."[37] "A fondness for power is implanted," wrote Hamilton, "in most men, and it is natural to abuse it, when acquired."[38] Certainly we have seen that abuse since 2008 at the federal level, and under the Obama administration it has only grown. Mussolini would have beamed at what he would have seen in America since 2009. Washington would have wept.

DOESN'T THE GOVERNMENT HAVE A SPECIFIC STAKE
IN PROTECTING THE MONEY SUPPLY
AND THE BANKING SYSTEM?

Even though they weren't around to witness the recent financial crisis and watch Americans cry "foul" against Citigroup, Merrill Lynch, Goldman Sachs, and a slew of other major financial institutions, the Founders could well understand the modern contempt for banks. Andrew Jackson hated them and in 1832 declared a "war" on the Second Bank of the United States. In the late 1800s, the Populists, then later, the Progressives, both railed against the power of "New York banks." Today, "Wall Street" (in part, thanks to the Michael Douglas movie of the same name) connotes rich white men conniving to steal from ordinary people through financial deals that no one understands.

But this is nothing new. Even among the Founders—and even among those who saw the need for sound finances and a source of loans—the pejorative term "monied men," or "men of money," was employed. Part of the hostility to banks lies in the very essence of their operation: they rely on trust, in which they lend out the majority of the deposits, which they are supposedly keeping safe, to people who need it. Even though they pay interest on the deposits, and collect interest on the loans, in troubled times it is difficult and sometimes impossible for banks to get the money back from the borrowers in time to repay the depositors. In such cases, bank "runs" ensue, where the essential bond of trust is broken. In the last twenty years, the links between depositors, banks, and borrowers were stretched even thinner by the appearance of "derivatives," in which, essentially, brokers gambled on the upward or downward value of packages of loans and sold *those*. This completely severed the connection between the actual properties or collateral backing loans and the loans themselves, or, put another way, it broke the tie between the asset and the liability. In short, derivatives opened up a massive opportunity for risk—on the positive side, for massive profits, but on the negative side, for phenomenal collapses.

Yet for all their faults, banks were—and are—necessary intermediaries that accumulate unemployed capital and move it to the people who can and will employ it. This simple explanation accounts for the creation of national banks in almost every country dating back several hundred years. Nations have needed banks, often for ready funds in time of war, and thus created national institutions whose first obligation was to lend money to the state. Only later did advocates tout other advantages of national banks (though certainly not necessarily advantages *only* offered by national banks), such as a uniform currency or the ability to minimize economic cycles. Again, it must be emphasized that while national banks could perform some of these tasks, other private banks could as well, and therein lay the source of many conflicts in American financial history.

So what is the role, if any, of the federal government in the banking system? Did the Founders think some financial institutions were "too big to fail"? The answer to this question was clear: no. We know this because the first central bank that had a stake in a currency that affected multiple states, the Bank of North America, which had problems with corruption and foreign influence, lost its national standing and was rechartered by the state of Pennsylvania after it faced severe debts. Its successor, the (First) Bank of the United States, likewise saw its charter lapse with little concern on the part of Congress, mainly because it was mostly *privately owned* and therefore Congress feared undue influence by foreign investors. (This later proved an ungrounded fear.) Its successor, the Second Bank of the United States, had its recharter bill vetoed twice by President Andrew Jackson, who similarly cited the excessive power wielded by the bank (which again proved a mistaken view). Neither BUS actually went bankrupt—both were victims of their charters expiring. Nor did the Bank of North America fail while acting in the capacity of a "national" bank with a federal charter. Nevertheless, all three disappeared, and it is apparent that the Founders had no problem with a national or very large banking institution vanishing from the scene, no matter how important its operations seemed. And certainly no one prophesied the end of the republic if a major bank did collapse.

It is important to state again that Hamilton, and most of the other Founders, were products of the mercantilist system, in which business existed to advance the status of the state. By the mid-1770s, they had known something was amiss with mercantilism, but the ink was scarcely dry on Adam Smith's *Wealth of Nations,* and capitalism as he outlined it was little known as a theory (though it was already a widespread practice). Moreover, the Founders' experience with banks and banking mostly involved knowledge of the Bank of England (established in 1694), which was the banker to the English government. Throughout the 1700s, the bank had loaned money to the government and handled its debt. It is also worth recalling that England had sought to restrain American issues of paper money with the Paper Bills of Credit Act of 1763 (usually called the Currency Act), which could have potentially provided an independent source of money to the colonists—but one subject to severe inflation, as it was no longer tied to English gold reserves. In 1770, New York was permitted by the Crown to issue paper money, but otherwise such activities were discouraged both as a means to control prices and, more important, as an attempt to foster total dependence of the colonies on the mother country.

Hamilton apparently came across versions of *Wealth of Nations* not long after it was published, adopting similar wording and reasoning. He had also already pored over David Hume's 1752 essays on economics, and from those he gleaned an early version of what might be called a loanable funds theory of interest, claiming that renewed confidence in the government's credit rating would stimulate trade, and thus, by slightly increasing the money supply through loans, the nation would generate production. Whatever "enhances the quantity of circulating money adds to the ease with which every industrious member of the community may acquire that portion of it which he stands in need," he wrote.[1] Strangely—given the recent state-level struggles with overissues of money—he did not address the likelihood of inflation. But he did seek to draw gold and silver into circulation instead of remaining squirreled away in unproductive and non-interest-bearing caches.[2] Hamilton also understood (in the 1780s and 1790s context) the concept of a money multiplier, arguing that banks would circulate greater amounts than their paid-in silver and gold capital. To criticize Hamilton in the late 1700s for failing to flesh out a theory of commercial banking that had yet to be established anywhere would be misguided. Neither monetarist nor Keynesian nor laissez-faire Libertarian, Hamilton worked his way through the financial doctrines of the time by trial and error.

In 1779, Alexander Hamilton, concerned about the finances of the union under the Articles of Confederation, contacted Robert Morris (the so-called financier of the Revolution) about establishing a bank. Hamilton suggested land as security, though he later decided such an institution would need more liquid assets. Under the Articles, the states had issued paper money, which had depreciated rapidly (just as the Continental had during the war). Hamilton envisioned a quasi-national bank that would maintain a sound currency and thus, in essence, regulate state currencies.[3] The future Treasury secretary, however, had another motive in persuading Morris to found a bank. He had developed the theory that a nation's survival depended on an alliance of the wealthy with the government, in the form of creditors to the nation. In 1780, he wrote, "The only plan that can preserve the currency is one that will make it to the *immediate* interest of the monied men to cooperate with the government in its support. . . . No plan could succeed which does not unite the interest and credit of rich individuals with that of the state"[4]

When Congress approved the Bank of North America, issuing its corporate charter in 1781, it had essentially created the first American "national" bank, but because so few "monied men" stepped forward, the Bank of North America had to rely on a foreign loan from France to supply most of the capital. Thus, far from Hamilton's ideal of tying the monied men to the young republic, the first national bank was immediately tied to foreign interests. There was one hitch: when the Constitution was adopted, the Bank of North America did not receive a charter from the United States Congress but rather from the government of the Confederation.

The directors and president of the Bank of North America, who had founded the bank at the City Tavern and named Thomas Willing as the president, began with only $70,000 capital in domestic gold and silver. Some questioned the legality of the Confederation Congress chartering a bank; others fretted about the possible fracturing of the Confederation wherein the states would be left on their own, and therefore appealed to the Assembly of Pennsylvania for a state charter, which it received in 1782. Congress immediately applied for a $400,000 loan from the bank, and repaid the debt in 1784. Morris insisted, "the bank shall be well supported, until it can support itself, then it will support us."[5] In fact, the bank quickly proved profitable, generating 12 to 16 percent returns, and the government offered shares to the general public, which were snapped up. Its notes, including a one-penny note, circulated throughout Pennsylvania, New York, and Massachusetts.

But in the meantime, Alexander Hamilton became suspicious of the state charter, arguing that it put the institution in the "ambiguous situation" of serving both Pennsylvania and the United States, and was no longer acceptable as a national bank.[6] Worse, the combination of favoritism to foreign interests and "unfair competition" from other banks forced the Pennsylvania assembly to repeal the state charter in 1785. It received a new charter two years later, and continued in business from that point on. Other banks, such as the Bank of New York and Bank of Massachusetts, had started operations in 1784 as state-chartered banks, with no help from the Bank of North America, which used its once-monopoly status to retard the awarding of charters. This, in turn, provided a steady stream of criticism against the bank. Although it continued to operate into the twentieth century, the Bank of North America never became the national bank its advocates had intended.

Undaunted, Hamilton continued to press for a true national bank equivalent to the Bank of England. By that time, the Bank of Spain had also been founded (1782) for the same purpose of lending to the nation. Hamilton saw such a "central bank" (i.e., a bank that directs national monetary policy through its purchases or sales of government securities and its lending to private banks) as essential to providing credit to the government and, secondarily, to commerce as a whole. Only later did anyone claim that the national bank exerted a restraining power on the note issue of state-chartered banks—and that claim remains in dispute among economic historians. When combined with other elements of Hamilton's fiscal policies (a national mint, a "protective tariff," and assuming the Revolutionary War debts of the states), the Bank of the United States, chartered in 1791, grounded the new nation on a solid financial footing.

Economic historian Richard Sylla argues that Hamilton's financial system resulted in six major changes between 1788 and 1795, the most significant of which were that state "fiat" money (i.e., paper money with no gold backing) gave way to convertible U.S. dollars and that the three banks that existed in 1788 grew to twenty in number, including five BUS branches.[7]

Yet what provided stability to the nation was Hamilton's debt reduction plan, in which he offered a menu of options to attract the widest possible pool of lenders by establishing a number of different investments at different risk and reward levels. For example, longer-term bonds paid higher interest rates; short-term bonds, lower. This encouraged people to participate in their own risk comfort level. His "sinking fund" plan to retire old debt before new debt was assumed, sort of an early "American Express" form of debt—in which one is required to pay off the entire balance of the debt at the end of every month—as opposed to other nations'

"MasterCard" revolving repayment plans (that the United States has sub-sequently adopted), in which unpaid balances roll over to the next month on top of new purchases and stack up more interest owed to the bank. Perhaps not surprisingly, as soon as Hamilton left his post as secretary of the Treasury, his successor, Oliver Wolcott Jr., urged the sale of some gov-ernment stock in the BUS to raise new money. Hamilton objected, noting that the dividends on the stock held by the government were pledged to pay down the debt—but his position was defeated.

Shrewdly, however, Hamilton employed the sinking fund, originally established to reduce the debt and reassure Americans that the reduc-tion would occur, instead of using the BUS itself to deal with financial crises.[8] This sinking-fund/automatic-debt-repayment feature allowed the commissioners of the sinking fund (the vice president, the secretaries of state and the treasury, the attorney general, and the chief justice of the Supreme Court) to borrow money for the purchase of public debt on the open market "while it continues below its true value."[9] Such a mechanism would allow the government to inject liquidity into struggling markets, and, Sylla argued, was the "true purpose of the sinking fund."[10]

Records indicate that thirty-six hundred economic entities (includ-ing individuals, partnerships, municipal governments, and corporations) owned $12 million in federal bonds as of January 1, 1795. When security prices started to fluctuate in the fall of 1791, Hamilton—after conferring with the committee on the sinking fund—purchased government bonds, and the news that he had acted immediately quelled the markets. A sec-ond wave of speculation set in from January through March 1792, during which wild price swings in the bonds were followed by a crash. These were mostly traceable to the speculations of William Duer, a New York busi-nessman. Hamilton described the effects as "pernicious" and as "disgust-ing all sober Citizens and giving a wild air to everything."[11]

Using today's rationale, Duer was eligible for a bailout. After all, he was a major financial player: his undoing had a critical impact on markets. But, as I showed in previous chapters, instead of bailing out Duer, Hamil-ton allowed him to fail. In the short term this provoked other defaults, but Hamilton privately assured the Bank of New York that he would not let it fail, though he did not tell the public. He also extended extreme flexibility to those owing the government money. For example, the commissioners, despite Jefferson's objections, authorized the Bank of the United States (BUS) to purchase bonds. But Hamilton did not merely throw money at the panic: he loaned at a penalty rate to the Bank of New York while offering a repurchase feature that allowed the U.S. government to take half of the collateral of failed borrowers at prices Hamilton fixed. In short order, the New York branch of the BUS began lending "pretty liberally," and the panic was over.[12] Because Hamilton kept most of his maneuvers out of the public eye, the moral hazard of his intervention was minimal. The United States did not experience another panic until 1819. Duer, on the other hand, lost everything and ended up in a debtor's prison.

Hamilton, however, wisely encouraged the First Bank of the United States to engage in commercial and private lending and not solely act as a government lender, and its government business became secondary. Indeed, as part of its charter, the First BUS could not purchase government bonds and (in stark contrast to the modern Federal Reserve) could not issue notes or incur debts beyond its actual capitalization. More surprisingly, the bank was four-fifths private, with only 20 percent of the stock owned by the U.S. government. To further safeguard against "outside interests," foreign stockholders could not vote, thus they could not inordinately influence American financial decisions. The Treasury secretary could remove government deposits at will and inspect the books as often as *weekly* (again, in shocking contrast to the current Federal Reserve system). But the BUS was the nation's largest corporation and benefited from the huge government deposits that no other bank could tap. Its directors and officers kept its money sound (i.e., kept enough gold and silver specie on hand to ensure the notes' value), and made loans to state banks.[13]

Thus, while Hamilton is disparaged by modern-day radical Libertarians as "a protectionist" and a man who "fathered the idea of a central bank," he in fact stood out in the context of his time as a radical *non*-statist. At a time when two of the three other major powers had adopted true government centralized banking (France would follow in 1800), Hamilton introduced a largely non-government-controlled institution.[14] At a time when *every* nation in the world accepted, practiced, and revered mercantilism, Hamilton applied protectionism only to the most narrowly defined areas of national defense. And at a time when Britain and France repeatedly ran up massive debts, only Hamilton specifically introduced processes to ensure that the nation was debt-free. In such a context, Hamilton was something of a laissez-faire wonder; in practice, an early free-market Milton Friedman. Not until 1800 did a substantially different model of banking emerge in the so-called Scottish free banking system, which has been mostly praised by free-market advocates for its extra liability provisions for directors (if the bank went under, the owners and directors could be liable for up to double the bank's assets).[15]

Most observers agreed that the BUS was conservatively managed, earning 8 to 10 percent annually and maintaining solid specie reserves. An 1809 balance sheet, for example, revealed that it had $5 million in specie, $2.2 million in government securities, and $1.5 million in private individuals.[16] However, the First BUS generated considerable opposition, particularly from Thomas Jefferson, James Madison, and the newly emerging Republican Party. First, they questioned the constitutionality of the bank, which had been enabled by the "elastic clause," allowing Congress to pass all measures "necessary and proper" to carrying out its constitutional duties. (Jefferson despised banks, calling them "more dangerous to our liberties than standing armies.")[17] "The incorporation of a bank and the powers assumed [by legislation doing so]," he wrote, "have not, in my opinion, been delegated to the United States by the Constitution. They are not among the powers specifically enumerated." But Jefferson and Madison had already engaged in horse-trading when the BUS was created, exchanging their votes for the bank in return for a plan to move the capital of the United States to a federal district in Virginia. Republicans also feared the consolidation of power in the hands of the federal government that they thought such a bank would bring. In that regard, they were prescient, as by the 1820s, with the Second Bank of the United States under Nicholas Biddle, the institution became a powerful engine of patronage and a political entity all its own.

Meanwhile, the South continued to oppose the First Bank of the

United States, and in 1811, despite support from President James Madison, the recharter bill failed by one vote. Suspicion of Britain—with hostilities about to erupt at any time—further fueled the anti-BUS policies. At the same time, the Federalist supporters of the bank had decreased in number, while the Republican opponents had increased.[18] In no sense could it be claimed that the BUS failed, or that it needed a bailout. Nevertheless, the Congress at the time did not hesitate to allow it to die.

After the War of 1812, concerns about privately owned, state-chartered banks overinflating their currencies led Congress to create a Second Bank of the United States. Chartered in 1816, the Second BUS had a twenty-year charter and a capital stock of $35 million, again with the U.S. government owning 20 percent. The bank's charter explicitly designated it as the U.S. federal government depository, meaning that its resources would necessarily dwarf those of many other banks combined, and its assets by 1818 had grown to more than $40 million. Historians debate how much the BUS aided the note expansion of the decade, but when drains of specie started in 1818, the bank called in its loans, prompting calls for a new bank president. In fact, Langdon Cheves, the new president, contracted credit even more ruthlessly. In the process, the bank obtained title to large tracts of land. Nicholas Biddle, a Philadelphia banker, replaced Cheves in 1823 and a credit expansion followed. For many years, historians claimed that the BUS throttled credit by the state-chartered banks, making many enemies. Recent scholarship shows this to be in error as the BUS had little impact on lending. But the bank made an enemy of President Andrew Jackson. When Biddle (with the support of some of Jackson's political opponents, such as Henry Clay) tried to recharter the bank four years early, in 1832, Jackson vetoed the bill and essentially killed the bank by withdrawing all the government's deposits the following year.

Although the Panic of 1837, which ensued, was *not* related in any way to the demise of the Second BUS, a generation of historians viewed it as such, solidifying the case for a central bank that could restrain the greedy private bankers. Subsequent research has shown that the panic derived from the drying up of Mexican silver inflows and the subsequent automatic reduction in currency that produced. The perception, however, was perpetuated that if the BUS had survived, it would have minimized the panic. That view survived until 1969—often repeated by such historians as Bray Hammond, who had worked for the Federal Reserve and who had a strong "central bank" bias—and was first squelched by Peter Temin, who used previously unavailable computer models of international silver flows to reveal the actual cause of the panic.[19] What is most significant about the BUS saga is that not once but twice the U.S. government wasted no time in passively permitting or actively accelerating the end of its national banking system. Far from bailing out the "big bank," the U.S. government either acquiesced in its termination or administered the coup de grâce itself. Jackson flatly described the bank as a "monster" and a "hydra" and enthusiastically killed it, handing out its deposits to all of his political cronies. Thus, in the first three instances of a national bank that could have been deemed too big to fail, the government willingly accepted failure. In no case did a major financial panic or depression directly ensue, and one could argue that even in 1818, the Second BUS exacerbated the economic situation more than corrected it.[20]

During the interim between the age of "free banking" (i.e., with no government bank and with charters being issued through general incorporation laws) and the creation of the Federal Reserve System, or the period from 1860 to 1913, the nation's finances operated through the dual system of state-chartered banks (which could no longer issue money) and national banks (which could). Soon, the state-chartered banks outnumbered the national banks, as the restrictions on the national banks and the capital requirements made it disadvantageous to own. Three major panics occurred during this time—the Panic of 1873, the Panic of 1893, and the Panic of 1907. Each had a different cause, and each saw significant numbers of banks fail with no attempt by the government to bail any of them out. What the government *did* do, ironically twice with the direct intervention of the "biggest" banker of all, J. P. Morgan, was maintain its own solvency. When government gold reserves fell to dangerously low levels in the Panic of 1893, Morgan organized a syndicate that provided a $480 million gold loan to the United States. After the Panic of 1907, however, Morgan made it clear that he could not rescue the nation again, even with the help of syndicate members. A *system* was needed. But because the government had eradicated private notes and competitive money, which previously acted as a check on inflation by any one bank, no counterbalance to the national banks existed.

But let's reiterate this critical point: twice in the period from 1890 to 1910, the private sector bailed out the government. This merely repeated what had happened in the Civil War, when Jay Cooke had introduced the practice of selling bonds to average people, raising millions for the Union government at a time when the Confederacy—strapped to a socialist government-driven model—had trouble raising any money at all. It would not be unreasonable to suggest that, like J. P. Morgan later, Cooke "saved the government."[21]

Calls for reform led to a number of plans, most of them backed by the American Bankers Association, which in various ways addressed the three central financial issues of the day: (1) to provide a "lender of last resort" (because no one person could do it anymore), (2) to provide for a "more elastic" money supply that could expand and contract with business needs, and (3) to reduce the financial power of New York. The Federal Reserve System, which emerged from these plans, provided for a diversified network of "district" banks (nine of the twelve located outside the urban East), and set up a reserve process that would, in theory, prevent the failure of a large bank that would trigger a run, and, through the discount window and other tools, make the money supply more elastic. Inherent in the new system was a mandate to intervene by bailing out a bank in trouble, based on the philosophy that the failure of a single bank—or few banks— would trigger a financial panic.

What emerged, the Federal Reserve Act, seemed to create a nongovernment, private system that addressed all three concerns. Passed in 1913, the act, according to the proponents, set up a federal system of "autonomous, regional, reserve-holding, supercommercial banks."[22] Its creators deliberately avoided the structure and language of a central bank, and its twelve district banks seemed to convey that sense of decentralization. Each district bank was a corporation owned by the member banks in its district, which deposited 6 percent of its paid-up capital and surplus, and in return received a 6 percent annual dividend. In essence, the "Fed's" district banks provided regional pools of cash that could be transferred in case of emergency from the pool to a troubled bank. The intent was *not* to bail out a particular bank per se, but to prevent a panic that started with one (bad) bank from spreading to solvent institutions. Overseeing the entire structure, the Federal Reserve's board of governors was a separate organization located within the U.S. Treasury Building in Washington, D.C., and was intended as an oversight body to "coordinate the operations of the Federal Reserve as a whole."[23]

For an institution supposedly insulated from government influence, there was a troubling element to the board of governors: both the secretary of the Treasury and the comptroller of the currency served as ex officio members of the board, with the former serving as the chairman. The system's location in Washington was also problematic for an "independent" and "nonpartisan" organization.

Although the 1920s witnessed a massacre of rural state banks— almost entirely related to weaknesses in the farm sector—there was virtually no talk of bailing out or rescuing any of them. Even the Fed mostly ignored the plight of the farm banks, despite the fact that their demise slowly contributed to the shrinking money supply. But another troubling (to the government) pattern appeared in the 1920s, namely, the steady decline in the number of national banks relative to state banks. By law, national banks had to belong to the Federal Reserve System, but state banks could opt out. Thus, the Fed witnessed its member base shrink until passage of the McFadden Act of 1927, which allowed national banks to branch if state laws also permitted branching. Previously, if a state bank joined the national system, it could keep what branches it already had, but could not add more. The act did more to provide solvency and stability than all the state deposit insurance schemes already in place, but stopped short of permitting branching across state lines.

Following the stock market crash of 1929, a series of bank failures tested the powers of the Fed. From August 1931 to January 1932, more than eighteen hundred banks suspended or closed, tying up $1.4 billion in deposits. Bank loans contracted by more than 44 percent. Herbert

Hoover, concerned about banks that were not members of the Federal Reserve System, and thus unable to get sweeter loan rates, created the Reconstruction Finance Corporation, which promptly pumped out $1 billion in new loans to some four thousand troubled banks. Instead of saving the banks, the RFC made matters worse. Its interest rates were relatively high, and most important, because it was a government agency, the RFC had to publish the names of recipient institutions. Upon reading in the papers that their local bank was on the RFC list, anxious depositors raced to the bank to take out their money—making it *less* solvent and *more* likely to fail. The RFC ultimately loaned $80 million to banks and paid depositors of failed banks another $900 million, but neither action stopped the runs nor restored confidence. Indeed, like all government institutions, the RFC under Jesse Jones quickly aggrandized power and carved out its own empire. Another Hoover quasi-bailout consisted of the creation of the Federal Home Loan Bank Board (FHLBB), which provided short-term emergency credit to thrifts and savings and loan institutions. The runs continued, and in 1930, the Bank of United States in New York—the largest bank to that date to fail—was closed.

Desperate states began to invoke their own "bank holidays" to stem the runs, beginning with Nevada in 1932. Since gold remained the reserve currency, worried customers withdrew gold in significant amounts, and over a nine-day period in late February to early March 1933, the twelve Federal Reserve Banks lost $425 million in gold. Suddenly, the metal that went unmentioned in the Federal Reserve Act now threatened to bring down the entire system. New York, then Illinois, ordered bank holidays. Franklin Roosevelt, fresh in office, instituted a national Bank Holiday on March 6, 1933, and cut off all withdrawals of depositor funds. He ordered the comptroller of the currency and the Federal Reserve to perform emergency examinations of all national banks, and if they were declared solvent, they could reopen.

While it was never admitted by Fed officials themselves, many economists, including Milton Friedman, blamed the Fed for the severity of the monetary contraction following the Great Crash.[24] Friedman also more specifically claimed that the Fed gave legs to the financial panic of 1930 by permitting the Bank of United States (no relation to the old BUS) to fail. Not only did this violate the Fed's raison d'être but it signaled to the market that the system was unstable. While other economists have challenged this aspect of Friedman's analysis—some arguing that, in fact, the bank that the Fed *should* have bailed out was Caldwell & Company—the upshot remains the same.[25] Friedman's coauthor in *A Monetary History of the United States* pointed out that the "monetary character" of the Depression changed from that point on.[26] From the mid-1920s on, whether in terms of maintaining a money supply commensurate with the productivity growth or in terms of acting as a lender of last resort, the Fed failed miserably. From 1929 to 1932, as Friedman showed, the money supply fell by one-third, taking the economy down with it. A similar carnage was seen among the banks, where nearly six thousand that had existed in January 1933 were gone after the bank holiday.

Immediately the New Deal legislators attacked what they saw as weaknesses in the banking system, particularly what they saw as the cause of the speculation and the stock market boom, namely, associations between commercial banks and securities brokers (called securities affiliates). Enacting the Glass-Steagall Act, Congress demonstrated its flawed understanding of the stock market boom, in which it was thought the affiliates siphoned depositor money from their partner banks to "play the market." In fact, as bank historian Eugene N. White has demonstrated, it was exactly the opposite: banks were *less likely to fail* if they had a securities affiliate with which to defer risk.[27] Fearing that the Fed had been too influenced by the government, the Banking Act of 1935 removed the comptroller and the Treasury secretary from the board of governors (although the Treasury secretary continued to attend meetings until 1951), and the Fed soon also had its own building outside of the Treasury Building.[28] Yet the fundamental weaknesses that had afflicted Fed policy making were not addressed, except by accident: the gold standard no longer was a factor, having been abandoned by almost all the developed nations.[29] There still remained, however, the issue of whether or not to bail out large banks if they teetered on the edge of collapse, and FDR's "bank holiday" had temporarily taken that decision out of the hands of the Federal Reserve.

It was only later, in the 1970s, that the Fed began to rescue individual institutions on the grounds that the failure of a large bank might trigger across-the-board panics that would bring the entire system to a collapse. The trouble stemmed from rising energy prices following the Arab oil embargo of 1973 that led Congress to change drilling laws to encourage new oil-drilling operations. A burst of new oil exploration and drilling followed, with a great deal of financing provided by a small bank in Oklahoma City, Penn Square National Bank. Money from other large banks had flowed through Penn Square on its way to the drillers, but as the loans became more risky, the bank's vice president in charge of energy loans, Bill Patterson, began to repackage the loans (known as participations) and sell them to out-of-state banks. Penn Square grew from $62 million in 1977 to more than $250 million five years later, as the bank stacked one participation on top of another in an endless chain. Both the structure and the market were unsound—soon the energy market plunged, and the authorities moved in to close the bank in 1982. The Federal Deposit Insurance Corporation covered all deposits (not just insured deposits), making it the first bailout of a bank in excess of $100 million.

One of Penn Square's correspondents, Continental Illinois Bank, held $1.1 billion of the participations, which constituted almost 17 percent of Continental's energy loans. Ironically, in 1978, *Dun's Review* had named the bank one of the five best-managed banks in America, and as late as 1983 the bank had a $25 million profit. In May 1984, however, a critical run started, and within ten days the bank suffered $6 billion in outflows. Despite a credit line that included sixteen other banks supplying $4.5 billion, the bank drifted into an untenable position. The Fed justified its bailout on the grounds that some 175 banks had at least half their capital in Continental Illinois's correspondent deposit account, and two-thirds had 100 percent of their capital in the correspondent accounts. In a complex deal, the FDIC took over $4.5 billion in bad loans, giving the bank only $3.5 billion and requiring Continental Illinois to write off $1 billion. It constituted the largest bank bailout ever.[30]

But the fact that the government, through the FDIC and the Fed, bailed out Continental Illinois did not make it appropriate or constitutional. While Continental's failure might have been uncomfortable, even difficult, for hundreds of banks, in no way did it threaten the national security of the United States—always the overriding criteria of the Founders (including Hamilton) for aid to any private organization. And while the Federal Reserve System may at one time have maintained independence from the government, by the mid-twentieth century it had become little more than another national bank. While an argument could be made that the Founders might have accepted a structure similar to that of the original Fed in 1913, albeit without the secretary of the Treasury and the comptroller of the currency maintaining a seat on the board of governors, it is hard to imagine any of them having any favorable comments about the current structure and operations.

Certainly few of the Founders saw much good coming from debt. Washington warned, "There is no practice more dangerous than that of lending money."[31] Madison suggested it was "a question whether Banks, when restricted to spheres in which temporary loans only are made to persons in active business promising quick returns, do not as much harm to imprudent, as good to prudent borrowers."[32] Yet no one could doubt, he claimed, "that loan offices, carrying to every man's door, and even courting his acceptance of the monied means of gratifying his present wishes under a prospect or hope of procrastinated repayment, must, of all devices, be the one most fatal to a general frugality."[33] Whether there were banks or no banks, the issue was always confidence in the nation that drove the economy. James Monroe warned, "let the influx of money be ever so great, if there be no confidence, property will sink in value. . . . The circulation of confidence is better than the circulation of money."[34]

Yet for the past few decades, Congresses and presidents have disregarded this advice, with the first blow coming in the savings and loan (S&L) industry in the 1970s, when rising inflation forced banks to pay more to attract deposits. S&Ls, restrained by law as to what interest they could offer, found their income (mostly long-term mortgages) fixed at a fatally low level with interest rates that could not be changed, while inflation meant that attracting new money to lend demanded much higher savings deposit interest. Congress intervened to change the restriction it had put on the S&Ls when they were created during the New Deal, but the "disinter-mediation" effect of low-interest payments in and high-interest payments out destabilized the entire industry. Worse, another government institu-tion, the Federal Savings and Loan Insurance Corporation (FSLIC), which was the S&L version of the FDIC, actually encouraged risky lending poli-cies by desperate S&L owners and managers. For example, if, as an S&L president, you knew that the long-term disintermediation would cause your institution's collapse, and you also knew that the FSLIC would protect your customers from losses, wouldn't you have an incentive to "roll the dice" and put the S&L's money into questionable ventures that might pay off big and save the S&L? Of course you would, and so did thousands of S&L of-ficers. Most of the "investments" went into land (not "junk bonds," as was commonly claimed) and most of the land was the proverbial "swampland in Florida," which offered extraordinary returns, but came with fantastic risks.[35] Liberals have crowed that the debacle that befell the S&L industry occurred because of "deregulation," without ever admitting that the very problems that doomed the S&Ls to begin with started with government regulations. More important still, one bumbling government intervention after another ensured that the S&L industry could never recover, most no-tably FIRREA (Financial Institutions Reform, Recovery and Enforcement Act of 1989), which "forced thrifts to liquidate their junk-bond portfolios whether they had profitable potential or not," and saddled the new Resolu-tion Trust Company (RTC) with a $5 to $6 billion junk-bond portfolio.[36] But the sudden liquidation of otherwise potentially healthy junk bonds sent the junk bond market into a tailspin, forcing a decline of 90 percent in value in some cases. Then the RTC foolishly sold its junk bonds at truly junk prices, fueling the collapse even further. Eventually the "junk" re-turned to previous values, but not before the S&Ls were already in the grave and the taxpayers looted. Less than half the S&Ls survived to 1989, thanks to the government, and at least one subsequent investigation (the California-based Lincoln Savings and Loan) revealed that five U.S. senators (four Democrats and one Republican) had met privately with the chairman of yet another government agency, the Federal Home Loan Bank Board, to persuade him to intervene favorably for Lincoln Savings.

Two truths should have been obvious to Congress and the regulators. First, government insurance schemes (including the FDIC) were disasters waiting to happen because, despite countless layers of regulation, insurance schemes inculcate "moral hazard." They encourage the very behavior they seek to prevent. As long as bank officers know that "their people" are protected by the government, there is always a small voice urging greater risk in lending, because, after all, "no one will get hurt, and everyone could get rich." With the FSLIC, which shut its doors in 1989, the principle seemed abundantly clear. Yet the FDIC continues to "protect" depositors up to the present. As long as a member bank fails alone, the FDIC can indeed cover the depositors, but should a massive, across-the-board failure occur, the FDIC would suddenly look very much like its defunct cousin, the FSLIC. Second, there should be little doubt that, as the Founders knew, regulations and laws always come with weaknesses and flaws, and fixing one mistake with yet another law only introduces two mistakes into the process. The best thing that happened to American finance in the course of the S&L debacle was that the FSLIC, with all its perverse incentives, disappeared, but the creature of government took down thousands of savings and loans with it.

Certainly the most egregious violation of the Founders' principles came in the form of the Troubled Asset Relief Program in 2008. Commonly called TARP, the program unfolded as a desperate attempt by Congress to undo the damage it had already done in the mortgage industry by insisting that banks lend to uncreditworthy customers. For years, it had been the policy of both Republican and Democrat administrations to encourage home ownership—even to those who obviously could not afford it. Interest rates had remained low and the appearance of adjustable rate mortgages, "interest only" loans, and "balloon payments" all combined to create the illusion of home affordability for millions of Americans who in reality did not qualify even for the safest of mortgage loans. Added to this, the government (particularly through the Federal National Mortgage Association, known as Fannie Mae, and the Federal Home Loan Mortgage Corporation, known as Freddie Mac) sought to expand the market for mortgages. Created in 1938 during the New Deal, Fannie Mae bought mortgages from savings and loan associations, thereby creating a second-ary market, eventually splitting into a "private" corporation (Fannie Mae) and a government institution, the Government National Mortgage Association (Ginnie Mae), then joined in 1970 by Freddie Mac. These institutions did not make loans directly, but rather purchased existing mortgages that were protected by the U.S. government (to the tune of financing about 40 percent of all U.S. mortgages) and an assumed guarantee, or what economist Vernon Smith called "implicitly taxpayer-backed guarantees."[37] Worse still, now that mortgage banks had a full-time government-sponsored "backstop," the U.S. Department of Housing and Urban Development (HUD) saw an opportunity to wield political power for minorities by re-quiring that Fannie Mae and Freddie Mac purchase more "affordable" loans that could be made to low-income families (i.e., to risky clients with a higher likelihood of default).[38]

While the intricacies of how HUD encouraged such flawed lending are not germane, the fact of HUD's policies—which saddled borrowers with mortgages they could not afford—allowed Fannie Mae and Freddie Mac to count billions of dollars in subprime loans as "a public good that would foster affordable housing."[39] Throughout the period 2004–2006, the two leading perpetrators were Congressman Barney Frank (D-MA) and Senator Chris Dodd (D-CT), who continually insisted that the poli-cies were sound and that the mortgages themselves were not at risk. (Not surprisingly, Frank received plenty of Fannie Mae–related campaign dona-tions.) Frank, serving on the House Banking Committee for several years, said in 2003 that problems facing Fannie Mae and Freddie Mac were "ex-aggerated" and that "These two entities . . . are not facing any kind of financial crisis."[40] That year, Treasury Secretary John Snow told the House Financial Services Committee, "There is a general recognition that the supervisory system for housing-related government-sponsored enterprises neither has the tools, nor the stature, to deal effectively with the current size, complexity and importance of these enterprises," as he recommended yet another agency to oversee the mortgage agencies' operations.[41]

As with most corrupt government-related institutions, the mortgage duo's weakness stemmed from yet earlier government interference in the market with the 1977 Community Reinvestment Act (CRA), introduced by the Democrats and signed by President Jimmy Carter. This act, intended to ensure that minorities would receive a fair shake in acquiring housing, in fact ensured that mortgages would be given to those most unable to repay them. Beginning with "directed" pressure on mortgage lenders, the CRA soon evolved into "quotas" that lowered standards. Thus, as the mortgage-lending banks toppled, and as their government backup faltered, inevitably the government stepped in yet again to "fix" the problems it caused, offering TARP. Little more than a rehash of the failed Reconstruction Finance Corporation under Herbert Hoover, TARP immediately demonstrated the dangers that led the Founders to resist such well-intentioned bailouts: designed to increase lending, the program resulted in few new loans (most banks did not cite lending as a priority); and many bank chairmen who received TARP money said they intended to use their TARP funds to expand strategically in the future, not to lend in the short term. "We're not going to change our business model or our credit policies to accommodate the needs of the public sector as they see it to have us make more loans," said one bank chairman.[42] Most sought to use federal TARP money to ride out the recession—itself largely caused by federal policies! And typically, the Treasury found it could not track the bailout money, and that measuring the impact was difficult if not impossible.[43]

The Founders' version of TARP would have been "Try to Avoid Repressive Policies." They knew that the federal government had a role to play in ensuring the *nation's* financial solvency and the *nation's* fiscal integrity. They knew that wars or other genuine emergencies might require quick cash that could be provided only by a national bank. They knew that one way to ensure that the "men of money" didn't control the government was to indebt the "monied men" *to* the government. But nowhere did they imply that the federal government should rescue any bank, or think that a bank—or *any* business, for that matter—was "too big to fail." Banks existed to make profits, and as such they involved risks just the same as any other enterprise. The only time the Founders would have bailed out a banker would have been through their own personal compassion—by bailing him out of debtor's prison.

QUESTION #8

SHOULD THE UNITED STATES TOLERATE HIGH
DEFICITS AND A LARGE NATIONAL DEBT?

Many of the Founders grappled with debt on a personal level before and during the Revolution and constitutional period. Alexander Hamilton, left fatherless and then, as a young teenager, motherless, experienced financial hardship throughout his youth (the probate court even seized the family's few pieces of silverware). Thomas Jefferson constantly struggled to make ends meet, even with slave labor, leaving many to conclude that the main reason he never freed his slaves was that his plantation would go under without them. Thus by the time they confronted the inflation of the American Revolution, and the challenges of the new republic, they knew firsthand the dangers of debt.

Moreover, none forgot that it was the debts and money pressures of the French and Indian War that had driven Great Britain to begin her ill-guided assault on the liberties of British Americans through higher taxes. In the minds of the Founders, war and debt went hand in glove, and both were to be avoided if possible. Only later did Alexander Hamilton—who began his life with mercantilist philosophies—start to show the influences of Adam Smith. But this is a critical point to keep in mind: the economic world in which the Founders lived had *never* operated on free-market principles per se because to that point none had been elaborated in a thorough-going manner. Smith, after all, was only the first of a number of thinkers who refined the concepts of capitalism. Until that time, the local-market guild system of the Middle Ages, which still retained a strong Bible-based cautionary attitude toward debt, had given way to the national states and a new economic doctrine of mercantilism. This appeared by the early 1500s, but was not outlined until 1620 by Thomas Mun. Mercantilist doctrine permitted, and even encouraged, larger private companies to operate as long as they served the interests of the monarch and the state. The London Company and Plymouth Company were first and foremost private extensions of state power—outposts of English economic outreach into the New World that were allowed to make a profit.[1]

Moreover, until the 1400s, debt instruments, such as the bill of exchange, scarcely existed, and these instruments, combined with double-entry book-keeping, made it easier to track loans and debts.[2] The joint-stock companies of the early 1600s further refined the concept of debt through the practice of limited liability, under which an investor stood to lose only what he put in. Thus, risk was spread among hundreds, or even thousands, of stockholders. Debt, therefore, became manageable because the company that contracted a debt had already invested capital and therefore was likely to be repaid. Better yet, because the joint-stock companies had permanence (i.e., the death of the president did not affect the life of the company, because it was a legal creation or a legal "individual"), people more willingly put money into them.

American Founders also knew their English history and that the civil war between the monarchists and the forces of Parliament had originated as a result of the king's need for cash. They also knew that early American labor needs had been served by another form of debt, indentured servitude, wherein a British subject allowed himself to become a servant for a period of time in return for passage to British America and its lands. Early tobacco planters also knew the role of debt—some more painfully than others—as a means to expand their plantations through advances on their crops.[3] Southern farmers, in particular, grew accustomed to acquiring more land (and, often, slaves) on credit, confident that the returns would cover their debts.

Thomas Jefferson, who had practiced law for a time, had turned to management of his plantation at Monticello, with its 10,000 acres of land (though only 2,000 acres were productive at the time). But Jefferson was often broke—"money bound," was his term—and once he had to ask a friend to lend him $100 to get by.[4] After one trip to Philadelphia, it took Jefferson several months before he could borrow money to buy a few dozen sheep.[5] Much of Jefferson's land consisted of little more than uncleared timber, and 2,000 acres for a Virginia gentleman was not all that much to support the immediate family, relatives, and the dozens of slaves (154 in the case of Monticello) needed to work it. A manager who approached agriculture scientifically, Jefferson finally made most of the land productive and profitable, achieving remarkable crop yields. (Like Washington, he had pioneered a new contoured plowing approach.)

Jefferson clearly saw the connection between potential indebtedness and slavery, for to free his slaves would have condemned himself and his family to poverty.[6] Taxation also led to a form of slavery, as virtually all of the Founders agreed. Hence, Jefferson noted to Samuel Kerchival, "If we run into such debts, as that we must be taxed in our meat and in our drink, in our necessities and our comforts . . . our people . . . must come to labor sixteen hours in the twenty-four, [and] give the earnings of fifteen of these to the government for the debts and daily expenses."[7] He wrote Alexander Donald in 1787,

> The maxim of buying nothing without the money in our pocket
> to pay for it, would make of our country one of the happiest on

earth. Experience during the war proved this; as I think every man will remember that under all the privations it obliged him to submit to during that period he slept sounder, and awakened happier than he can do now. Desperate of finding relief from a free course of justice, I look forward to the abolition of all credit as the only other remedy which can take place.[8]

Eleven years later he added, "I wish it were possible to obtain a single amendment to our constitution. I would be willing to depend on that alone for the reduction of the administration of our government to the genuine principles of the constitution; I mean an additional article, taking from the federal government the power of borrowing."[9]

As president, Jefferson would have his Treasury secretary, Albert Gallatin, change the method of budgeting by submitting to Congress a system detailing the appropriation bills (only as a suggestion, of course). "Would it not be useful," he asked, "also to oblige our successors, by setting the example ourselves, of laying annually before Congress a . . . calendar of the expenditures . . . ?"[10]

If Jefferson had stopped there, his position on debt as a concept would have been simple and nearly unanimously held by his fellow Founders. But Jefferson went further, which left him in a logical swamp. His famous letter of 1789 to James Madison, made public only after the Sage's death, states:

No man can, by natural right, oblige the lands he occupied, or the persons who succeed him in that occupation, to the paiment [sic] of debts contracted by him. For if he could, he might, during his own life, eat up the usufruct of the lands for several generations to come, and then the lands would belong to the dead and not the living, which would be the reverse of our principle.[11]

He concluded, "The earth belongs in usufruct to the living"; that is, in trust to the living. Jefferson saw a difference between government debts, which could possibly be shifted from one generation to the next (what he labeled "municipal debts") and "moral" debts of individuals: "I suppose . . . that the received notion, that the public debts of one generation devolve on the next, has been suggested by our seeing habitually in the private life that he who succeeds to land is required to pay the debts of his ancestor or testator [but] this requisition is municipal only, not moral . . . [and] by the law of nature, one generation is to another as one independent nation is to another."[12] Jefferson's concern was that the excess of one generation would be foisted on the next, preventing it from enjoying its natural liberties.

Many of Jefferson's observations in this regard came from his experiences in France, where the government of Louis XV, who borrowed from Genoese moneylenders, engaged in wonton self-indulgence.[13] Defining a generation as roughly twenty years, Jefferson insisted that even a nation could not validly extend a debt, and that "every constitution . . . every law naturally expires at the end of 19 years."[14] Jefferson's focus was on the construction of government in America, though, not France, and specifically to the contracting of debts. (It appears that Jefferson acquired these views in the context of discussions with the Marquis de Lafayette and a British physician, Dr. Richard Gem, who was attached to the British Embassy.) A certain element of Jefferson's concern over the independence of America from Europe also emerged from his letter.

One cannot separate the indebtedness of Jefferson the planter from Jefferson the thinker, and certainly his lifelong experiences as a marginal businessman when it came to running his affairs. More germane to this context, Jefferson's own debt problems weighed on him at the time of his writing. He owed British creditors considerable sums, and could have been forced to liquidate part of his estate to pay them. Worse still for Jefferson, the creation of the federal court system with the U.S. Constitution now removed the potential protection of Virginia laws and exposed him to federal courts. His debts stemmed from a gamble he took in 1773–1774 when he voluntarily assumed the debts of John Wayles to British merchants, along with Wayles's land and slaves. Perhaps Jefferson hoped the war would produce a different result, but ultimately he found himself in "exactly the situation he describes to Madison when he speaks in the letter of the heir who succeeds to land being responsible for the debts of the testator."[15] Instead, the Revolution's inflation wiped out much of his paper wealth and forced him to repay in depreciated dollars, made worse by the terms of the Treaty of Paris, which required that American debtors repay their British creditors. It is more than speculation that these genuine, real debts consumed Jefferson's thought at the time: "The torment of mind I endure till the moment shall rive when I owe not a shilling on earth," he wrote in 1787, "is such really as to render life of little value." He described the future reduction of his personal debt as "a person on shore, escaped from shipwreck."[16]

While it is always possible to read too much into the motivations of persons in the past, in this case Jefferson seemed clear about hereditary debt, writing that Virginians experienced burdens "hereditary from father to son for many generations" to the British bankers.[17] (In this, he differed little from jurist William Blackstone.) He even likened debt to slavery—the basest of comparisons. He deemed public debts that leverage society's wealth a "heresy" (a common word for him) and warned that debt could not be passed from one generation to the next. Debt in the hands of legislators not only produced corruption and favoritism, but in the hands of someone like Alexander Hamilton could lead to outright tyranny. Even Jefferson's colleague James Madison in February 1790 explained that generational obligations could not be avoided. Using the term "improvements," Madison stated that some exertions were significant enough to justify a burden on those not yet born. No greater example could be found than the Revolution itself, with its debt that "posterity" would repay.[18] Logic, of course, suggests that if such "future debts" were not incurred, Jefferson's "usufruct" letter itself could never have been written! The notion that debts—or constitutions, as Jefferson suggested—had to be rewritten or adopted anew every generation was also rejected by Madison, who politely explained to the Sage that such a system would produce radical uncertainty in property, and thus, in the future. If society dissolved every nineteen years, there would be no guarantee of civil rights for anyone, let alone property rights.

That is not to say that Jefferson did not attempt, during his administrations, to live up to his rhetoric. As noted earlier, he strove to eliminate the national debt. In his second inaugural address he argued that the United States should "meet within the year all the expenses of the year, without encroaching on the rights of future generations, by burdening them with the debts of the past."[19] He and his Treasury secretary Albert Gallatin did in fact pay down the national debt during his two terms, even after shelling out $15 million for the Louisiana Purchase. Yet he did so without having to fight a war, and the nation paid in blood for Jefferson's unwillingness to prepare the military, particularly a deep-sea navy, for the coming confrontation with Britain. Ironically, perhaps, it would be the cautionary Madison whose administration would bear the financial cost of Jefferson's lack of vision. And, as I have written elsewhere, Jefferson did seek to saddle the nation with the largest public works project ever seen up to that time—a network of "internal improvements" whose cost would have equaled that of the entire federal budget. Congress did not pass Gallatin's plan as proposed, leaving it instead to the private sector, which funded it over the next twenty years without government aid.[20] Later, Jeffersonian Republicans would attempt to pass a bill containing many of Gallatin's internal improvements in the form of the Bonus Bill of 1817, only to see it vetoed by President James Madison on the grounds that it was not government's concern.[21] John C. Calhoun, then a Republican, saw the internal improvements as the solution to potential disunion, and hoped to "bind the republic together with a perfect system of roads and canals."[22]

Many other Founders shared a suspicion of personal debt. Benjamin Franklin wrote in *Poor Richard's Almanac,* "If you know how to spend less than you get, you have the philosopher's stone."[23] (Franklin also quipped in *Poor Richard's,* "If you would know the value of money, go and try to borrow some.") But many also harbored concerns about a public debt, most notably Madison. "I go on the principle," he wrote to Henry Lee, "that a public debt is a public curse."[24] Other Founders disagreed, however, including Thomas Paine, who wrote in *Common Sense,* "No nation ought to be without a debt. A national debt is a national bond."[25]

Hamilton is often held up as the early republic's "debt pimp," and receives unwarranted criticism as some sort of rampant inflationist. Like Jefferson, Hamilton had experienced financial distress, though under different circumstances. Whereas Jefferson struggled as a grown man with money issues, Hamilton had seen poverty and uncertainty as a child. His biographer, Ron Chernow, recounts a daunting catalog of disasters that Hamilton and his brother experienced as young teens:

> their father had vanished, their mother had died, their cousin and supposed protector had committed bloody suicide, and their aunt, uncle, and grandmother had all died. James, sixteen, and Alexander, fourteen, were now left alone, largely friendless and penniless. At every step in their rootless, topsy-turvy existence, they had been surrounded by failed, broken, embittered people. Their short lives had been shadowed by a stupefying sequence of bankruptcies, marital separations, deaths, scandals, and disinheritance.[26]

Such experiences seemed tailor-made to groom a person to reject the subservience of debt, and indeed Hamilton viewed credit and debt as opposite sides of the same coin, one favorable, one unfavorable. The uncertainty of a debtor—whose creditor can sweep the world from under his feet—was to be avoided by ensuring that a near-automatic payment system, with funding from growing enterprise, was always in place. More important, Hamilton had absorbed a considerable amount of Adam Smith by the time he became Treasury secretary. Smith's dictum in *Wealth of Nations* was that it was "the highest impertinence and presumption . . . [for] kings and ministers to pretend to watch over the economy of private people, and to restrain their expense. . . . They themselves always, and without any exception, [are] the greatest spendthrifts in society."[27]

Yet Hamilton did not see debt merely as a means to allow government its whims. Rather, he viewed it as a necessary relationship between wealthy individuals and the state. Hamilton's goal was to place in debt the *wealthy to the government,* not the other way around: "The only plan that can preserve the currency is one that will make it the *immediate* interest of the monied men to cooperate with the government in its support."[28] This was his mercantilist upbringing coming out. "If all the public creditors receive their dues from one source," he wrote, "distributed with an equal hand, their interest will be the same. And having the same interests, they will unite in the support of the fiscal arrangements of the government."[29] Too many competing systems with their "different provisions," he warned, would create "distinct interests, drawing different ways."[30] The federal government, he further reasoned, should neither be independent nor too much dependent. It should neither be "raised above responsibility or control, nor should it want the means of maintaining its own weight, authority, dignity, and credit."[31] Permanent funds were therefore indispensable, but "they ought to be of such a nature and so moderate in their amount *as to never be inconvenient* [emphasis mine]."[32] Hamilton therefore seems to have made a case in 1782 for maintaining a very light national debt, accompanied by extremely low taxes.

In the second place, Hamilton's comments on debt have been wildly misconstrued. He *never* called debt in general a "national blessing." Rather, context, as always, is essential:

> Persuaded as the Secretary is [i.e., Hamilton, speaking of himself], that the *proper funding of the present debt,* will render it a national blessing: Yet he is so far from acceding to the position, in the latitude in which it is sometimes laid down, that "public debts are public benefits."[33]

It is entirely clear that Hamilton rejected the concept that "public debts are public benefits," and that it was the funding of the debt, i.e., the system *he devised to pay it off,* that would provide the "national blessing." Indeed, he went on to insist that the view that "public debts are public benefits" was "a position inviting to prodigality, and liable to dangerous abuse." Moreover still, while Hamilton wanted the United States to "commence their measures for the establishment of credit, with the observance [i.e., payment] of it," the system of public credit which he intended to create contained a key condition: "that the creation of debt should always be accompanied with the means of extinguishment."[34]

Having placed the monied men in subservience to government, and having set up a self-paying system of credit, Hamilton then tied debt retirement to taxes. In many ways, the Treasury secretary sounded much like future Treasury Secretary Andrew Mellon when he derided the ill effects of high taxes. Writing in *Federalist No. 21,* he observed, "if duties are too high, they lessen the consumption: the collection is eluded; and the product to the treasury is not so great as when they are confined within proper and moderate bounds. This forms a complete barrier against any material oppression of the citizens by taxes of this class, and is itself a natural limitation of the power of imposing them."[35] Taxes, he noted, were "evidently inseparable from the Government," and without them "it is impossible . . . to pay the debts of the nation, to protect it from foreign danger, or to secure individuals from lawless violence and rapine."[36] Hamilton's order is worth noting: debt will accompany almost any nation, and taxes are required to keep the debt low.

Some two hundred years later, "supply-side" economists would argue that the tendency of government to grow would always outstrip the ability of taxes to pay for that growth, and as a result the only feasible response was to instead keep taxes extremely low and broad in order to generate so much economic growth that it would proportionally outstrip government growth. At the same time, however, there is little doubt that Hamilton—for all the bad press he gets on debt—failed to appreciate the acquisitiveness of government and the inherent inability of tax revenues to stay apace. Jefferson absolutely had that aspect of the equation right. But neither could Hamilton have then known the work of French economist Jean Baptiste Say, whose theories produced the concept of supply creating its own demand. In such a system, a broad-based low-tax system oriented toward entrepreneurial growth would always create more revenue to pay off debts than a static system that assumed tax revenues would simply pay off debts.[37]

This blind spot of Hamilton's constituted a narrow element of his general philosophy. He knew, as did all the Founders, that "a fondness for power is implanted, in most men, and it is natural to abuse it, when acquired."[38] "Men," he observed, "always love power."[39] So it bears reiterating that Hamilton's entire credit and banking structure was oriented toward *reducing* the power of the monied men and subjugating them to the interests of the state, lest they control the government at the expense of the people. Hamilton's support of a national bank included many of the traditional rationales for advocating banks—increasing productive capital, improving circulation through bank notes, making loans for industry and trade. "The tendency of a national bank," he wrote to Robert Morris, "is to increase public and private credit. The former gives power to the state for the protection of its rights and interests, and the latter facilitates and extends the operations of commerce among individuals." Industry, he told Morris, "is increased, commodities are multiplied, agriculture and manufacturers flourish, and *herein consist the true wealth and prosperity of a state* [emphasis mine]."[40] But he also noted that a national bank would "facilitate the payment of taxes by keeping circulation more full and active, and by direct loans to the Merchants to pay their duties."[41] Again, the merchant class would be beholden to the government, even to the extent of borrowing money to pay their taxes. Yet the proper order of Hamilton's financial universe remained unmistakable. When in 1796 Congress sought to authorize the sale of Bank of the United States stock to pay off a sum due the bank itself, it constituted an abrogation of Hamilton's design whereby "dividends of the Bank Stock are appropriated to the Sinking Fund," meant to retire the national debt. Such a move, Hamilton wrote to Washington, would "subvert the system of the Sinking Fund and with it all the security which is meant to be given to the people for the Redemption of the Public Debt." Hamilton was aware that Washington's prestige, in part, might have suffered from a defeat of the bill, but the consequences of the bill becoming law would have rendered the nation's creditworthiness "prostrate at a single blow."[42] Nothing took precedence over the elimination of debt, so that the United States could *if necessary* acquire credit again easily in the future.

Of course, George Washington agreed with these principles, saying in 1793, "No pecuniary consideration is more urgent, than the regular redemption and discharge of the public debt: on none can delay be more injurious, or an economy of time more valuable."[43] The Revolution had left the young republic seriously indebted: America had borrowed more than $75 million from individuals and foreign lenders, which was one reason he supported Hamilton's program to pay off the debt with revenues from a tariff and the whiskey tax. As a rule, Washington thought that "to contract new debts is not the way to pay old ones," and he supported Hamilton's plan precisely because the sinking fund promised to pay off the "old ones."[44] Washington believed Hamilton had put the nation on the proper path to financial freedom when he gave his Farewell Address in 1796, where he urged, "as a very important source of strength and security, cherish public credit." One means of preserving it, he observed, "is to use it as sparingly as possible, avoiding occasions of expense by cultivating peace, but remembering also that timely disbursements to prepare for danger frequently prevent much greater disbursements to repel it."[45] (One wonders if this was a veiled reference to the fact that Washington's administration, lacking a "blue-water" navy, had been forced to pay tribute to the Barbary pirates.) He further urged "vigorous exertion in time of peace to discharge the debts which unavoidable wars have occasioned, not ungenerously throwing upon posterity the burden which we ourselves ought to bear."[46]

This reasoning greatly colored Washington's concerns over permanent treaties, for it was war, more than any other government activity, that drove up debt. Indeed, across the board—from Hamilton to Jefferson to Washington—their views on finance were as much shaped by the Revolutionary War and its ill effects on finances as they were from their own personal circumstances. Understanding their thought processes is important, particularly in that they did not believe it was tolerable to lose a war, and that once in, the nation had a moral and financial duty to see the cause through to victory. Thus, no expenditure was too much in such a case. Of course, all three men (but Jefferson and Washington especially) wrote and spoke at length about the necessity of avoiding wars at all costs, and certainly the financial burdens of conflict shaped their attitudes. That led Washington in the same inaugural to warn against "a passionate attachment of one nation for another [which] produces a variety of evils." Rather, he urged (back to money!) that "the great rule of conduct for us in regard to foreign nations is in extending our commercial relations, to have with them as little political connection as possible."[47]

The purpose of this essay is not to debate whether Washington or Jefferson was "isolationist," and yet much in Washington's tone suggests that his recommendations were intensely time-specific. He urged honoring "already formed engagements," but not to seek new ones *with Europe,* for Europe "has a set of primary interests which to us have none; or a very remote relation."[48] It is not unreasonable to suggest that if Washington thought that indeed there was a "set of primary interests" Europe and America shared, alliances would be welcome until they had achieved their goals.

At any rate, realizing that war tended to throw budgets out of kilter, Adams, Jefferson, and, for a time, Madison were able to steer clear of war. One could argue that at sea the nation possibly paid a higher price for this neutrality when war finally did come, and that the utter destruction of Jefferson's cheap-but-ineffective gunboats was an object lesson in unwise expenditures. Nothing is as expensive as a military defeat. Fortunately, the nation had the frigates built by the Federalists (accounting for part of the debt) and those ships acquitted themselves well. Also, the nation's acquisition of Louisiana, even beyond the vast natural, mineral, and agricultural resources it added to the United States, accounted for one of America's greatest military victories of the War of 1812 at New Orleans. Certainly the Founders, with their willingness to spend federal money on armories, textiles for uniforms, and iron, understood that the United States could not lose a war once it started one.

The easiest way to avoid debt and financial difficulties, as the drafters of the Constitution concluded, involved making it difficult for the government to spend money and, whenever possible, placing the authorization of those expenditures directly with the people's representatives in the House. Thus all spending and taxation measures had to originate with the House of Representatives, whose two-year terms made them more likely to be influenced by irate taxpayers than the senators, who owed their positions to the state legislatures. The Founders also hoped, though, that the Senate would slow down unnecessary expenditures because of the pressure from the states to restrain the federal government. And, given that the entire workforce of the United States government in the early 1800s (aside from the army) consisted of a few thousand (mostly) men—postal employees, customs agents, and a handful of bureaucrats—virtually no one ever dreamed that the office of the president would include much in the way of patronage. After all, Jefferson answered the White House door himself, an astonishing far cry from Michelle Obama's staff of twenty-two personal assistants.

With all their foresightedness, none envisioned the formation of a political party system almost entirely oiled with the award of government jobs. Martin Van Buren's creation of a national political party, which I detailed in *Seven Events That Made America America,* established a system that subjugated principle to patronage. From then on, it didn't matter what causes or initiatives one supported but rather what *candidate* he did. More than any other single change in the American political landscape, and more than even wars, the impact of the refounding of the political parties with the "spoils system" ensured that every election, for every office, would result in the growth of government. To get elected, a candidate simply had to promise more jobs than his opponent. While wars produced more marked upticks in spending, the consistent peacetime growth of the government inevitably marched on—though at a much slower pace before the Civil War. What caused the most radical change of all was not the Civil War itself, at least not directly. Instead, the explosion in the number of veterans who received benefits led to predictable calls for "reform," a word from which Americans should always flee. Predictably, the reform made things far worse. With passage of the Pendleton Civil Service Act in 1883, the issue of handing out jobs to political supporters supposedly was solved. In fact, government had only begun to grow, and with it, pressure to establish perpetual jobs that would never come up for review.

Nevertheless, the Founders, including Hamilton, all knew that a symbiotic relationship existed between debt, taxes, and government power. The more any one point expanded, it pulled the other two out along with it. Imagine a pyramid with government power at one corner, taxes at another, and debt at another. If any one corner gets out of line, it begins to distort the other two. But by reducing any one, the other two are also minimized. Their reasoning was sound, and it is why today, in virtually every country in the world, we still see this relationship. Some government power is necessary—of course the Founders knew that, and sought to instill the U.S. government with the powers needed to defend the people and keep public order. Some taxes are required to fund the government. None—not Jefferson or George Mason or Thomas Paine, some of the more "liberal" Founders— disagreed. A few disagreed that the government would have some debt, but even those who advocated some debt, such as Hamilton, demanded it be kept small and employed for the purposes for which it was intended, namely, a thriving economy, abundant lubrication for commerce, and as a tool to be used in a national emergency. Hamilton noted, arguing for a national bank, "it will be our wisdom to select what is good in this plan and in any others that have gone before us, avoiding their defects and excesses."[49]

But wasn't this what the Founders did each time? They did not entirely discard the governmental structure from England, but learned from it and built upon it, improving the parliamentary system to include still more checks and balances. They did not abandon the idea of a chief executive, but stripped away the Crown and the office's perpetuity and substituted humility, accountability, and regular elections. And with the Bank of the United States, Hamilton removed as much as possible from the hands of government, placing it under the control of private investors. While still in the midst of revolution, Hamilton asked,

> Are our monied men less enlightened to their own interest or less enterprising in the pursuit? Let the government endeavor to inspire confidence. . . . Let it exert itself to procure a solid confederation, to establish a good plan of executive administration, to form a permanent military force, to obtain at all events a foreign loan. If these things were in a train of vigorous execution, it would give a new spring to our affairs.[50]

Tom Paine wrote in *The Crisis*, "If we believe the power of hell to be limited, we must likewise believe that their agents are under some providential control." For men such as Paine, not only could the agents of hell be contained—with God's help—but so too could any government man had devised. The trick, as Hamilton observed, was to learn from others' mistakes. "Governments," wrote William Penn, "like clocks go from the motion men give them, and as governments are made and moved by men, so by them they are ruined too."[51] One could say the same for finances and debt: some men and some nations were ruined by it; for others, it became a tool. Modern American governments have forgotten what Washington, Jefferson, Madison, and Hamilton all knew, that there existed a rigid association of debt, taxes, and government power.

By the second year of the Barack Obama administration, the United States marched into unprecedented and reckless levels of national debt totaling $12 trillion by May 2010, with unfunded obligations (Medicare, Social Security) adding an estimated $88 trillion. The "official" debt as a percentage of output stood at close to 80 percent, a level exceeded only once in our history, during World War II, and even then lasting only a few years. That debt plunged steadily after the war, to about 35 percent in 1986. Even under Franklin Roosevelt's New Deal, the level of debt to output did not exceed 40 percent until war approached.[52] And what was the level of debt in the time of the Founders? Washington inherited a debt-per-output level of 31.4 percent; by John Adams's term, it stood at about 18 percent, and continued dropping until the War of 1812, getting into the single digits during the Jefferson administration. More astounding, debt per capita from 1790 to 1818 hovered at about ten dollars! Even measuring in the currency of the day, that was phenomenally low, and meant that the average American's share of the national debt could be paid off with a few weeks' wages.

Compare that to modern Americans' *public* debt per capita of nearly $50,000, or more than most Americans make in a year. Remember, however, that is only the "official," acknowledged debt, and does not count the "unfunded obligations," of which the Founders had none. If individual Americans had to pay for all the promised spending of Congress, the amount would come to at least $150,000 per person and perhaps as high as $250,000.

These staggering debt levels suggest that Jefferson's concerns were valid and that Hamilton's design has been stymied by clever and profligate Congresses over the years. But the Founders were not without hope, nor should we be, for if the power of hell is limited, restricting the abilities and proclivities of Congress to drown us in debt must ultimately face a reckoning of its own. We must face it, and the sooner the better, for if we do not control our own excesses, someone else will. Better at our own hands than at those of malevolent others.

QUESTION #9

WHAT IS THE PURPOSE OF WAR AND
SHOULD IT BE AVOIDED?

As anyone who has spoken with veterans knows, the last thing they want to see is another war. So too the Founders had fought the Revolution so that their children would not have to fight; and their approach to the Constitution and toward government actions and attitudes reinforced this philosophy.

Let's begin with the obvious: many of the Founders were veterans. Alexander Hamilton began his career as a New York artillery officer, and eventually came to Washington's attention because of his actions at the battles of Trenton and Princeton. (At Trenton, he attacked one of the Hessian guardhouses with one other soldier, killing four enemies.) But even before that, in July 1776, he had confronted two British warships near southern Manhattan with his battery of four cannons. No sooner had he begun returning British fire than his gun exploded. It is uncertain whether he took part in the Battle of Brooklyn Heights in August, although his biographer Ron Chernow suspects Hamilton authored an anonymous account of the fight.[1]

Hamilton served as Washington's aide-de-camp through much of the Revolutionary War, and chafed at missing any combat for administrative duties.[2] He joined Washington's staff in March 1777 and became the best of the general's aides in communicating his commander's wishes and ideas.[3] (Nathaniel Greene is thought to have touted Hamilton to Washington.) When Hamilton left Washington's staff in July 1781, it was so he could acquire a combat command, whereupon he led the successful assault on the British Redoubt Number 10 at Yorktown.[4] That he was willing to put his life before dishonor is evidenced by his duel with Aaron Burr, in which he was mortally wounded. He was willing to repel all threats to his country through military action, and supported the undeclared war with France from 1798 to 1800.

Repeatedly during the war Hamilton demonstrated heroism—at the retreat from New York, at Trenton, at Monmouth. After the war, he pushed for a national military academy, then in 1798 became the inspector general of the army under President John Adams (whereupon he was addressed as General Hamilton). He enthusiastically wore (and was painted in) his "dazzling military dress, braided with epaulettes."[5] As inspector general, Hamilton laid out comprehensive charts for the military's line and staff command, noting how many men were in a company, a platoon, a squad, and a file. He also stocked the nation's arsenals with ammunition, set up recruitment centers, and drafted operational regulations. With his eye for detail and his near-obsessive mastery of the smallest matter, Hamilton designed different huts for each rank, drafted training manuals, and even conducted experiments to determine the most effective marching step.

Of course, unlike Jefferson, Hamilton intended that the army be a permanent fixture in America. He considered a strong national army necessary for the safety of the nation, and thought the central government's weakness had nearly lost the Revolution. In his battle to establish a large Continental Army, he lost to Elbridge Gerry.[6] With Washington, he conceived the idea of a national military academy that would come to fruition in Jefferson's administration. Indeed, Hamilton envisioned five military schools, one each for military science, cavalry, engineering, infantry, and the navy. With James McHenry, he got legislation introduced to build West Point (even though at the time Jefferson denounced it as unconstitutional).[7] Many were suspicious of Hamilton's ambitions—Abigail Adams nicknamed him "Little Mars"—but most of Hamilton's hypothetical targets were foreign, particularly the Spanish in Florida. Under his leadership, the army nevertheless remained extremely small due to lack of funding. John Adams later in life congratulated himself with characteristic hyperbole that "save for me [Hamilton] would have involved us in a foreign war with France and a civil war with ourselves."[8]

Nathaniel Greene, who, like Knox, had learned most of his strategy and tactics from books (he did have two years' militia duty), became one of the most effective military leaders of the Revolution. He was largely responsible for Lord Cornwallis departing the South, and he pushed the British back to the Carolina coast.[9] John Lamb was an artillery officer who rose to the rank of brigadier general during the Revolution. Initially a fervent supporter of the Sons of Liberty, Lamb had a distinguished career during the war. He took an active part as an Anti-Federalist and sought to defeat the ratification of the Constitution in New York, being allied with Patrick Henry and Richard Henry Lee of Virginia. He fought virtually throughout the war.

Thomas Mifflin, a Pennsylvania merchant, became a major general in the Continental Army, and often found himself at odds with Washington. As a member of the Continental Congress's Board of War dealing with the "Conway Cabal," he sought to replace Washington with General Horatio Gates (later denying he had engaged in such activities). Expelled from his Quaker Meeting for not holding to his pacifist beliefs, he continued to argue for strengthening the militia rather than building a national army. His patriotism was undoubted, and he became the fifth president under the Articles of Confederation, and actively participated in the Constitutional Convention. He supported the constitutionalists, became instrumental in securing Pennsylvania's ratification, and sided with Washington and his Federalists in the first years of the Republic.[10]

William Livingston, governor of New Jersey for most of the Revolution, served in 1775–1776 as general of the state militia. In that capacity, he understood better than most the risks of warfare, and barely missed being captured by the British, who sent a special unit to snatch him at his Elizabethtown home. A signer of the Constitution, Livingston, like Mifflin and Jefferson, favored a strong militia. The father-in-law of John Jay, Livingston endeavored to upgrade the militia, providing them with von Steuben's drill manuals and the best equipment he could obtain. But Livingston was not as committed to having only a militia as Jefferson was, and sought a compromise whereby a small national force could readily be augmented by a militia in emergencies. Eventually, this position carried the day in the formation of the United States.[11] Henry Knox, a bookseller, taught himself military tactics and strategies through his stock of books, then by hard experience. A large man with a strong constitution and a gift for artillery, Knox became George Washington's chief artillerist, and he treated his cannons like his children. He transported the guns seized at Ticonderoga to the Siege of Boston under extremely adverse conditions to drive the British out.[12] On the other hand, it was his insistence on attacking the Chew House that cost Washington a victory at Germantown.[13]

Knox was the originator of the Society of Cincinnati, named for the Roman farmer-general Cincinnatus and open to all officers who served in the Revolutionary War. Washington was the first president of the society, followed by Alexander Hamilton and Charles Cotesworth Pinckney. Qualifications were changed from time to time, and the organization survives to this day. Knox made valiant attempts to maintain a Continental Army between 1783 and Washington's inauguration, initially as the successor to Washington as commander in chief, but by 1784, the entire Continental Army consisted of only eighty men. Knox then was appointed secretary of war in 1785, and served in that capacity until the end of 1794. Scotch Irish and martial to the core, Knox was willing to resist British incursions and punish Indians at every opportunity.[14]

Edmund Randolph was another aide-de-camp to George Washington, although for only two months. He applied for that position possibly to prove his loyalty to the cause.[15] Randolph's father remained a Loyalist, while his uncle Peyton became a leading patriot. He initially refused to sign the Constitution because he believed it possessed insufficient checks and balances, but later voted for ratification by Virginia. He was the first attorney general, and a supporter of a strong national government.[16]

Some of the Founders, of course, were not veterans. Adams did not fight; Jefferson, then governor of Virginia, fled Monticello as redcoats approached. Elbridge Gerry of Massachusetts, a major force in maintaining a small national army, nevertheless opposed Hamilton at every turn. Marked for arrest on the British expedition to Lexington and Concord, Gerry narrowly escaped capture by running half-dressed into a nearby cornfield to hide. He served throughout the war in the Continental Congress, and became a member of the Constitutional Convention. Perhaps best known for the term "gerrymandering," or dividing up voting districts to favor a particular party, he was staunchly antinationalist, and thought a standing army inimical to the safety of a nation. The United States, he thought, could rely on a militia and three thousand miles of ocean to stop enemies. He was the only New Englander to refuse to sign the Constitution at the convention.[17]

Jefferson had little impact on the initial formation of the U.S. Army, but after he became president in 1800, his policies shaped the military preparedness, or lack thereof, for the next forty-five years. He favored the maintenance of a force sufficient to defend against Indian attacks, but failed to see the need for a military capable of meeting other European-style armies in the field. Regular troops were to be reduced to the bare minimum to garrison arsenals and coastal forts, but otherwise everything fell on the militia.[18] In 1802, he signed legislation establishing the United States Military Academy at West Point, representing the culmination of many of the Founders' views that the United States needed such an institution so as not to be reliant on foreign engineers, artillerists, or officers capable of training American soldiers. In 1814, he wrote, "To carry on our war with success, we want *able* officers, and a sufficient number of soldiers. The former, time and trial can alone give us; to procure the latter, we need only the tender of sufficient inducements and the assiduous pressure of them on the proper subjects."[19] Aware that the navy lacked such an institution, he wrote to John Adams in 1821, "There should be a school of instruction for our navy as well as our artillery; and I do not see why the same establishment might not suffice for both. Both require the same basis of general mathematics, adding projectiles and fortifications for the artillery exclusively, and astronomy and theory of navigation exclusively for the naval students."[20]

Jefferson's fear of a standing army was abundantly apparent, and it separated him from Washington and Hamilton, who understood from their field combat experience that militia had severe battlefield deficiencies. As early as 1775 he insisted, "standing armies [are] inconsistent with [a people's] freedom and subversive of their quiet," a point he reiterated in his first annual message in 1801: "Nor is it conceived needful or safe that a standing army should be kept up in time of peace for [defense against invasion]."[21] But Jefferson saw a standing army as an instrument of repression. Instead, the militia could protect the United States, at least until a regular army could be raised in time of war. In his first inaugural address, he said, "A well-disciplined militia, our best reliance in peace and for the first moments of war till regulars may relieve them, I deem [one of] the essential principles of our Government, and consequently [one of] those which ought to shape its administration."[22] Should an enemy attack, the militia "so organized that its effective portions can be called to any point in the Union" would suffice to maintain the public interests until "a more permanent force shall be in course of preparation."[23]

In his eighth message to Congress, he reiterated his view that "For a people who are free and who mean to remain so, a well-organized and armed militia is their best security. It is, therefore, incumbent on us at every meeting [of Congress] to revise the condition of the militia and to ask ourselves if it is prepared to repel a powerful enemy at every point of our territories exposed to invasion."[24]

While Jefferson rejected conscription, he did insist that every male citizen must be trained, and that the nation needed to "make military instruction a regular part of college education: "We can never be safe till this is done," he wrote to Monroe.[25] Yet despite his opposition to a draft, by 1810 he wrote, "[One measure] which I pressed on Congress repeatedly at their meetings . . . was to class the militia according to the years of their birth, and *make all those from twenty to twenty-five liable to be trained and called into service* [emphasis mine] at a moment's warning."[26] In 1814 he told Madison that he hoped to enforce universal militia training by abolishing through a "declaratory law the doubts which abstract scruples in some, and cowardice and treachery in others, have conjured up about passing imaginary lines, and limiting . . . their services to the *contiguous* provinces of the enemy."[27] By 1807, he had already come to the conclusion that a militia would be "entirely useless for distant service," and that "we never shall be safe until we have a selected corps for a year's distant service at least."[28] Jefferson thus grudgingly began to embrace the notion of a limited standing army. But even after the War of 1812, he refused to admit that regular soldiers were superior to militia for defending the homeland, despite the fact that regulars had won impressive battles, while the militia-dominated force outside Washington had fled in the "Bladensburg Races." Nevertheless, when he assumed office, Jefferson commanded approximately fifty-four hundred officers and men, and within a year he had eliminated the cavalry, reduced the number of artillerists and engineers, and cut the overall size by about 50 percent.[29]

Henry Dearborn, a Revolutionary War veteran who had served with distinction, became Jefferson's secretary of war and received almost no resources and little support from the president. While Dearborn has gone down in history as a disaster, the fault lay with Jefferson. Financial supervision in the administration was so close that an expenditure of only fifty dollars required Dearborn's personal approval.[30] While monetary values over time are always questionable, this amount was the equivalent of perhaps less than two to three thousand dollars today. One can scarcely envision Donald Rumsfeld or William Gates scrutinizing Pentagon expenses of such small amounts.

While Jefferson had a blind spot for the weakness of militias—after all, it was an ineffectual militia in 1781 that failed to hold up British troops under Benedict Arnold marching toward Monticello that forced his escape—he nevertheless consistently expressed concern about the need for the supremacy of civil over military authority. "The freest governments in the world have their army under absolute government," he noted in 1780.[31] "The spirit of this country is totally averse to a large military force," he wrote Chandler Price in 1807.[32] What Jefferson failed to understand was that an American standing army was distinctly patriotic, and took its constitutional oath seriously to protect against enemies foreign and domestic. Over the years—at least until the Civil War—American soldiers repeatedly put away their personal views and concerns when operating under the orders of the commander in chief. The exception was, of course, the Civil War, in which its sectional nature led to each side viewing itself as "patriotic" and in keeping with the Constitution. Yet even after that divisive war, not counting a short period of military occupation of the South, the army once again downsized and returned to its barracks, while one of the largest navies in the world (more than seven hundred ships) decommissioned most of its vessels.

Potentially worse than his attitude toward a standing army was Jefferson's policies concerning the navy. He allowed the frigate fleet, built up under Adams, to languish, and put his faith in a fleet of coastal gunboats. Each of these had a single cannon, which Jefferson rationalized could defend the United States against the Royal Navy. Ultimately, 278 of these gunboats were built, kept on land in times of peace, then run out and manned extemporaneously in times of war. (In the War of 1812, the United States was practically defenseless, and Jefferson's gunboats were casually blown out of the water by the British or scuttled by their own crews while British gunners laughed.)

Jefferson thought a standing navy did not constitute the same threat as a standing army: "Every rational citizen must wish to see an effective instrument of coercion, and should fear to see it on any other element than the water. A naval force can never endanger our liberties, nor occasion bloodshed; a land force would do both."[33] But a big, "blue-water" navy he also saw as a source of friction, writing to Elbridge Gerry in 1799, "I am for relying for internal defense on our militia solely till actual invasion, and for such a naval force only as may protect our coasts and harbors from such depredations as we have experienced; and not for . . . a navy which, by its own expenses and the eternal wars in which it will implicate us, will grind us with public burdens and sink us under them."[34] Typically, costs concerned Jefferson. He noted that a navy was expensive, and that during a long period of peace, the entire navy could either go "to entire decay" or could cost as much to maintain as to build a new one. Thus, if a nation could count on twelve to fifteen years of peace, it "would gain by burning its navy and building a new one in time."[35]

The Founders' hesitancy to involve the United States in new wars, especially as a bit-part ally to one of the earth's great powers, can be seen in the writings of both Thomas Jefferson and George Washington (many of whose speeches were written by Alexander Hamilton). "Entangling alliances," a phrase often wrongly attributed to Washington, actually belonged to Thomas Jefferson, although Washington's Farewell Address contained many similar sentiments. Moreover, iterations of Washington's Farewell Address all include phrases of this type, indicating it was a deep-seated belief of both his and Hamilton's that the United States needed to avoid aligning with any particular power.

That said, recall that *no American* had a problem with "entangling alliances" in 1776, when the United States desperately needed the help of France, Spain, and whoever else would lend it. We eagerly sought and received a promise of "armed neutrality" from one of the largest commercial shipping powers in the world, the Netherlands, and successfully negotiated treaties with most of the Indian tribes for neutrality. Context is essential when reading Washington's Farewell Address. As I pointed out in *48 Liberal Lies About American History,* he "urged his countrymen to 'observe good faith and justice towards all nations: cultivate peace and harmony with all. Religion and morality enjoin this conduct.'"[36] Washington sought "amicable feelings towards all," and warned against "permanent, inveterate antipathies against particular nations, and passionate attachments for others."[37] He expressed the concern that *unfounded* or *unchanging* attitudes—good or bad—would color interactions with other countries. Writing specifically of England, he warned that imagining unrealistically close friendship with a nation "where no real common interest exists . . . [risks] a participation in the quarrels and wars of the latter without adequate inducement or justification."[38] In other words, where such adequate inducement or justification for war existed, the United States would be ready and able to defend itself. Instead of military alliances, Washington wanted to extend "our commercial relations, to have with [foreign powers] as little political connection as possible." Europe, however, had "a set of primary interests which to us have none or a very remote relation."

Of all the Founders, only Washington was essentially a military man from the start. He had engaged in surveying work, and of course he ran his plantation. His dream, though, was to become an officer in the British Army; and once the American Revolution broke out, he fit into the seat of command as if it were designed for him.

Washington understood the maxim that amateurs talk tactics and professionals think logistics: he trained his men constantly. Indeed, contrary to the oft-claimed notion (made famous in the Mel Gibson film *The Patriot*) that "standing toe to toe with the Redcoats is madness," Washington knew that *only* when the American army could face the British in open field and defeat them would the nation have a chance at survival. He harangued and harassed the Continental Congress for more supplies, while never losing sight of that essential component of victory, courage. One of his most sterling addresses is contained in his general orders of July 2, 1776:

> The time is now near at hand which must probably determine, whether Americans are to be, Freemen, or Slaves; whether they are to have any property they can call their own; whether their Houses, and Farms, are to be pillaged and destroyed, and they consigned to a State of Wretchedness from which no human efforts will probably deliver them. The fate of unborn Millions will now depend, under God, on the Courage and Conduct of this army—Our cruel and unrelenting Enemy leaves us no choice but a brave resistance, or the most abject submission. . . . We have therefore to resolve to conquer or die; Our own Coun-

try's Honor, will call upon us for a vigorous and many exertion, and if we now shamefully fail, we shall become infamous to the whole world.[39]

Placing trust in the militia, he warned, was "resting on a broken staff," and men "dragged from the tender Scenes of domestick life; unaccustomed to the din of Arms; totally unacquainted with every kind of Military skill, which being followed by a want of confidence in themselves, when opposed to Troops regularly train'd, disciplined and appointed . . . makes them timid."[40]

During his tenure as commander of the Continental Army, Washington instituted Draconian, British-style discipline, carried out by a provost marshal and special detachments of what would be considered today as military police. American Colonial troops had been subjected to the British Rules and Articles of War since 1754, and the Virginia legislature had adopted various regulations following the British code in 1755. Congress adopted the Articles of War on June 30, 1775, copying much of the code and penalties from the Massachusetts military code of April 1775. Washington then proceeded to use the death penalty in example cases to instill fear in the troops. Other than the death penalty, punishments were severe: floggings were a daily occurrence, and the number of lashes ranged from 20 stripes to 150.[41] Sometimes this harsh punishment worked, sometimes it did not.

It wasn't until 1778 that Washington was able to establish effective drill regulations, and they came from the appointment of Baron Frederick von Steuben as inspector general. Von Steuben later produced his "Regulations for the Discipline of the Troops of the United States to which is added An Appendix containing the United States Militia Act."[42]

Washington's forces benefited from excellent drill sergeants from Europe, such as von Steuben. As a commander, Washington learned from his mistakes, and, above all, provided the personal glue that held together the Continental Army. On at least one occasion, before the Battle of Trenton, he personally appealed to the men whose recruitment papers were about to expire to stay longer; the first time, they rejected his plea, but they changed their minds after his second speech to them. (It didn't hurt that

General Thomas Mifflin agreed to offer a bonus to them for extending their enlistments!)

After the Revolution, Washington thought he had seen the last of his military days. He wrote,

> I never expect to draw my sword again: I can scarcely conceive the cause that would induce me to do it; but if, contrary to all expectation, such an event should take place, I should think it a fortunate circumstance, and myself highly honored, to have it supported by yours. My time is now occupied by rural amusements, in which I have great satisfaction; and my first wish is, altho' it is against the profession of arms and would clip the wings of some of you young soldiers who are soaring after glory, to see the whole world in peace, and the Inhabitants of it as one band of brothers, striving who should contribute most to the happiness of mankind.[43]

"How pitiful, in the eye of reason and religion," he wrote in 1788, "is that false ambition which desolates the world with fire and sword for the purposes of conquest and fame; when compared to the milder virtues of making our neighbours and our fellow men as happy to their frail conditions and perishable natures will permit *them to be*!"[44] As president, and afterward, Washington grew concerned about the possibility of violence in Europe once again touching North America. He advocated a third party negotiating a peace between Britain and France:

> A bystander sees more of the game, generally, than those who are playing it; so, Neutral Nations may be better enabled to draw a line between the contending Parties, than those who are Actors in the War. My own wish is, to see every thing settled upon the best and surest foundation for the Peace and happiness of mankind, without regard to this, that, or the other Nation. A more destructive Sword never was drawn (at least in modern times) than this war has produced. It is time to sheathe it, and give Peace to mankind.[45]

In 1797, he wrote to Benjamin Goodhue, "No man wishes more devoutly than I that a stop was put to the further effusion of blood; that harmony was restored to all nations; and that justice was done to ours."[46] After one of the brief periods of peace in the 1790s, Washington referred to it as the "all clearing Sunshine of peace," and wished to see "the blessings of it diffused through all countries, and among *all* ranks in every Country; and that we should consider ourselves as the children of a common parent."[47] When war broke out in Europe after the French Revolution, Washington wrote to his old acquaintance, the Count de Rochambeau, that he hoped for America's independence. War between France and her neighbors, he noted, "might probably, in a commercial view, be greatly for the advantage of America," but he rejected the notion that war anywhere was to be America's gain. Regardless of the commercial benefits to the United States, he told Rochambeau, "I shall never so far divest myself of the feelings of a man, interested in the happiness of his fellow-men, as to wish my country's prosperity might be built on the ruins of that of other nations."[48]

Other than Washington's Farewell Address, perhaps the most significant document Washington produced with respect to America's military establishment was his report to Hamilton's committee in 1783 entitled "Sentiments on a Peace Establishment."[49] Interestingly enough, he wrote "that the defense of the Empire" required a broadly based and strong military establishment. He envisioned three missions for the military: to defend the country, to protect trade and commerce, and to promote the opening of the West. Washington felt that preparation for war was the best way to ensure peace. He wanted promotions based on competence rather than seniority—an axiom regularly violated by American government and unions today. He proposed a standing regular army as the basis of the military establishment, and supplemented by a well-organized and well-trained militia, military depots maintaining weapons of war that would be kept up to date to meet changing conditions and new technology through "laboratories," military academies to produce military leaders, and a strong navy to protect commerce and the American coast.

But Washington understood that at times, both armies and alliances would be necessary. His concern was with "permanent alliances," but he also insisted that existing treaties be honored and that future treaties "for extraordinary emergencies" might be necessary. Under this guideline, certainly the alliance of World War II fits Washington's qualifications, and likely the alliance in the War on Terror. Most important, however, Washington sought this buffer with Europe because the United States military, particularly the navy, was in no shape to fight abroad. Such a condition would not last forever, he promised. The "period is not far off when we may *defy material injury from external annoyance* [emphasis mine]; when we may take such an attitude as will cause the neutrality we may at any time resolve upon to be scrupulously respected . . . [and] *when we shall choose peace or war* [emphasis mine], as our interests guided by our justice shall counsel." His next phrase placed all his thinking in context, for he said if the United States "is preserved in tranquility twenty years longer, it may *bid defiance, in a just cause, to any power whatever, such, in that time, will be its population, wealth, and resource* [emphasis mine]."[50] In short, when the military, economic, and commercial strength of the United States matured, we would proverbially "give the finger" to anyone who sought to impose their will on us.

Moreover, a draft version of the Farewell Address was worded quite closely to the final product, again with the twenty-year period mentioned. In 1796, the United States had virtually no navy and a tiny army, and was incapable of doing much except quelling Indian raids and small internal rebellions. But within twenty years, the U.S. Military Academy had been founded, John Adams and the Federalists had built a respectable navy, and the economic and commercial power of the United States was sufficient to support military action.

Thomas Jefferson had indeed used the phrase "entangling alliances." It is an irony, then, that in 1785, when Algerians captured two American ships and held their crews for ransom, Jefferson tried to form an alliance with many of the European powers (including Naples, Malta, Portugal, Venice, England, and France) to crush the Barbary pirates. He favored "peace thro' the medium of war," and, writing to James Monroe the following year, stated, "The [Barbary] states must see the rod; perhaps it must be felt by some of them."[51] In that, he failed: not a single European power, not even

England with her navy, would assist the United States in stopping the depredations of Tripoli, Algiers, and Tunis. Washington, lacking a navy, had in fact paid the ransoms and bribes to allow American shipping through the Mediterranean. Now Jefferson, armed with the blue-water navy that John Adams built (and which Jefferson systematically dismantled during much of his administration), sent American forces after the demands kept going up.

By the time Jefferson became president, the Barbary states were receiving up to one million dollars per year in ransoms, and every year hundreds of American sailors ended up in jails in Tunis, Morocco, Tripoli, and Algeria. To a considerable degree, Jefferson launched a preemptive strike much in the vein of George W. Bush with Iraq in 2003 when he, without a declaration of war from Congress, acted on a joint resolution to send American naval forces and marines to the Mediterranean. The specific act that precipitated Jefferson's action occurred when the bey of Tripoli cut down the U.S. flagpole (then considered an act of war). Sending the U.S.S. *Enterprise, Constellation, Argus, Intrepid, Chesapeake,* and *Philadelphia,* along with "Old Ironsides," the *Constitution,* to attack the Barbary states, Jefferson did not distinguish between what today would be called terrorists and those who harbored them. The U.S. Navy was to deal equally with Tunis and Algiers, even though *only* Tripoli had engaged in an act of war. Commander Edward Preble set up a blockade of all Barbary ports and began shelling Tripolitan cities. Morocco quit early, in 1803, but the *Philadelphia* ran aground outside Tripoli and was captured by Tripolitan forces, wherein Captain William Bainbridge and the entire crew became hostages.[52] Within three months, Lieutenant Stephen Decatur's crew from the *Intrepid* boarded the *Philadelphia* and burned it down to deny it to the Tripolitans, then in 1805, a tiny force of marines, led by ex-consul William Eaton and Marine Lieutenant Presley O'Bannon, backed by a mercenary force of Greeks, Turks, French, Egyptians, and others, stormed Tripoli from behind and the bey sued for peace.

When James Madison was president, the Barbary states engaged in more piracy, and he dispatched a similar force as Jefferson's, this time under Commodore Stephen Decatur and Commodore William Bainbridge. Decatur captured a pair of Algerian ships and forced the dey of Algiers to return all hostages and pay the United States ten thousand dollars, as well as pledge to end all seizure of hostages at sea.

Madison had agreed with Jefferson that a standing army was a threat. In the spring of 1783, before the peace treaty with Britain was concluded, he opposed the congressional committee report written by Hamilton concerning the establishment of an army for peacetime. Instead, at that time he supported Jefferson's frugal measures that eliminated any military preparedness, and also relied on militia in times of emergency. During the first two years of Madison's presidency, only a single law was passed affecting the military, and that was to cease recruiting for the eight additional regiments that had already been authorized in 1808.[53]

The United States also, of course, despite extreme and often burdensome measures domestically, struggled to stay out of the Napoleonic Wars under Adams and Jefferson. Adams had danced delicately in what has been labeled the "Quasi-War," avoiding either aligning fully with France or with England. His decision to nominate William Vans Murray as a plenipotentiary to France in hopes of ensuring peace at once made him an enemy in the eyes of the Federalists and gained him no accolades from the Republicans. The move not only short-circuited Hamilton's rebuilding of the army but led to the infamous "X, Y, Z Affair." Adams's Treasury secretary, Oliver Wolcott, was slow to provide money for the military, and a furious Hamilton had a grand spat with Adams that severed their working relationship. It also pushed Adams into the antiarmy camp with Jefferson, leading Adams to note that the army "was as unpopular as if it had been a ferocious wild beast let loose upon the nation to devour it."[54] Such invective was, of course, aimed almost entirely at Hamilton and not at the institution.

Meanwhile, Napoleon's ascension as emperor hardly calmed international matters, as Adams and others had hoped. As Adams left for Massachusetts and the pro-French Jefferson took the presidency, there was more reason than ever for the United States to avoid entangling alliances. Jefferson placed an embargo on American trade in Europe, which badly damaged American commerce, and after several years was eventually reversed in part by Macon's Bill No. 2. Under the new legislation, the

United States would trade with any European country that would lift its blockades across the ocean. Of course, such a policy constituted little more than an entangling alliance with England, because only England had a navy capable of denying trade to anyone else. The British opened their ports, while keeping the French ports sealed.

By 1812, the navy consisted of 9 frigates, 7 smaller ships, and 276 useless gunboats. The United States literally invited attack: 4,500 regular British troops were stationed in Canada, and Madison had only 6,744 regulars of all kinds stationed in penny packets throughout the land to oppose them. Only 89 men had graduated from the military academy, and the officer corps was made up of aging Revolutionary War veterans or untried (and untrained) volunteers. The militia had no training and no discipline, and could hardly be expected to stand up to British regulars. Fortunately, the war with Napoleon was still dragging on, but if that ceased, many thousands of battle-hardened veterans of the Napoleonic Wars could be made available for reconquering the United States. In many respects, declaring war on Great Britain in 1812 constituted an extraordinarily reckless act. Jefferson had maintained that officers above the rank of captain were not needed, and in 1812, only 29 field officers (with ranks of major and above) were in service. There were almost no manufacture of weaponry, no strategic stockpiles, and no logistical organization.

During the War of 1812, Madison and his secretaries of war micromanaged the deployment and supply of troops, and time and again brought the United States to the brink of disaster. Washington was attacked and burned in 1814 and the U.S. fleet was driven from the high seas. New England threatened to secede, northern New York actively aided the enemy, and the Canadians stood resolutely with their British overlords. Had the British general prevost been successful on Lake Champlain, Madison might well have lost Louisiana and the Northwest Territories to England. There is a lesson in Madison's folly: when one decides to go to war, one should have first prepared—a lesson reiterated by Ronald Reagan in his principles for going to war elaborated in the 1980s.

Nonetheless, it must be understood that these were all very brave men. They had risked their lives for principle and country on many occasions, and had been hardened by adversity. The Revolutionary War had been a long list of defeats, punctuated intermittently by victories, and the fact that the patriots had prevailed was due in large measure to their willingness to absorb great losses yet rebound and fight again like the hydra. The war had ruined the economy, impoverished the vast majority of Continental soldiers, and left the new country with a staggering debt. Yet the new nation survived. The Founders were willing to go to any lengths to accomplish their aims, as long as they could be attained with honor. And, of course, they had been blessed with a great leader, one who lost the majority of his battles but never lost heart. Not surprisingly, the one who had fought the most—George Washington—had the most sober assessments of the nature of combat, a standing army, and alliances.

The answers to the question What was the Founders' view of war? are relatively simple. They all abhorred it; they strove to avoid it; but when necessary, most embraced the methods needed to win. Sentiment for a militia-based system remained until the War of 1812, but the superiority of well-trained regulars was evident by that time, and *no* major American military leader who ever saw combat wished that he had a militia instead of regulars. The Founders, including Jefferson and Washington, did not refrain from preemptive war when it appeared that such an approach was the most certain to ensure victory. Jefferson might have feared a standing regular army, but a few years later, Madison was thankful he had one.

Of all the Founders, only Jefferson, Madison, and Gerry tended to disagree with Washington's analysis of the military and war. All three would see their theories be proven catastrophically wrong in the War of 1812, and Washington proved farsighted and correct. In fact, it would not be too much to say that Washington's analysis has stood the test of time to the present day. His advice for both avoiding—and winning—wars still rings as profound as when it was uttered.

SHOULD FEDERAL, STATE, OR LOCAL GOVERNMENTS
COLLECTIVELY OR INDIVIDUALLY HAVE THE
AUTHORITY TO REGULATE GUN OWNERSHIP?

Although not as hot a topic in the news today as, say, bank bailouts or health care, no issue in recent American history except abortion has produced such heated passions or inflammatory rhetoric as the gun control debate. Witness the claims of a recent compendium volume containing the documents of gun control in which the author states, "something is sorely amiss in the United States" when put in the context of other nations' gun laws, namely, that "the United States has a homicide rate that is six times higher."[1] Newspaper headlines routinely cite the presence of firearms when used in a crime, yet almost never mention them when used in successful defense against a crime.[2] Few, for example, ever heard that the Pearl High School shooting in Mississippi was ended by a school administrator who had a pistol in his car. Almost every American knows the phrase "Guns don't kill people, people kill people," and liberals cite it relentlessly.

This was an interesting comment, given the constant refrain from the Left that gun ownership was intended to be a "militia," not an "individual," right. Who, exactly, were these people arming against if not the government? They certainly were not expecting crack addicts or the KKK to suddenly threaten their lives. The obvious answer was that they feared their government, and that in the tradition dating back to their English heritage, they were arming themselves against incursions by the state on their other rights. These concerns were underscored by the steady erosion of the Second Amendment until recent court decisions.

Most modern gun laws stem from the so-called crime wave of the late 1920s and 1930s, usually associated with Prohibition. (It is worth noting that some historians have challenged the existence or the causes of this crime wave.)[3] The Franklin Roosevelt administration enacted the National Firearms Act of 1934, called the "first significant modern national gun control law."[4] That law taxed manufacturers, importers, and dealers in "certain firearms and machine guns," and defined a firearm as a "shotgun or rifle having a barrel of less than eighteen inches in length, or any other weapon, except a pistol or revolver . . . capable of being concealed on the person."[5] A second act followed in 1938 that established a gun licensing system. Then, in the wake of the John and Robert Kennedy and Martin Luther King assassinations, the Gun Control Act of 1968 restricted interstate gun shipments and expanded licensing. Stemming from the assassination attempt on Ronald Reagan, the so-called Brady Bill (passed in 1993) imposed national background checks for handgun purchasers and required a waiting period before a person could take ownership of a gun. A year later, so-called assault weapons were banned.

The tide began to shift in 2001 with the case of *United States v. Emerson,* in which Timothy Emerson, who, under a restraining order in 1998, was required to dispose of all of his firearms, even though the divorce court prohibited him from disposing of any marital property (including firearms). After a further confrontation with his ex-wife in his office, in which he allegedly pulled a gun, Emerson was arrested and later acquitted by a jury. Unsatisfied, the federal government brought a new case of aggravated assault. The district judge, Sam Cummings, dismissed the case on the grounds that the government had violated Emerson's Second Amendment rights and confirmed that the Second Amendment was an individual right. The Clinton justice department, under Janet Reno, appealed, and eventually a second federal trial was held and Emerson was convicted. Finally, in 2001, the U.S. Fifth Circuit Court held that the Second Amendment guaranteed individuals the right to bear arms, and after challenges in other cases, the U.S. Supreme Court, in *District of Columbia v. Heller* (554 U.S. 2008), reaffirmed the language of the Second Amendment that it "protects the individual right to keep and bear arms." Meanwhile, in 2005 the federal incursions into Second Amendment rights were curtailed, beginning with the Protection of Lawful Commerce in Arms Act, which protected gun manufacturers from lawsuits associated with gun crimes.[6] Although the court certainly did not hold that the Second Amendment was unlimited—arguing that state concealed-carry prohibitions, in which individuals with permits can carry concealed weapons in public, were legitimate—it nevertheless established once and for all a constitutional right to self-protection, and in the process defined the Second Amendment precisely as the Founders intended it.

What did the Founders mean by the language of the Second Amendment? Did they mean, as some antigun advocates began to argue in the twentieth century, that the preamble phrase "The right of the people to keep and bear arms shall not be infringed" was significantly modified by the clause that followed the semicolon, namely, "a well armed, and well regulated militia being the best security of a free country: but no person religiously scrupulous of bearing arms, shall be compelled to render military service in person"? In short, did the Founders insert the "well regulated militia" clause because of their intention to keep guns out of private hands? Did the militia constitute the "regulatory force" of 1700s-era "gun control"? Or did the individual operate within a sphere of rights that brought with them duties, one of which was to serve in the militia—a service for which gun ownership was necessary? Ronald Dworkin, a constitutional law scholar, once observed that taking rights seriously meant honoring them even when a significant social cost accompanied the preservation of those rights. In no case is this more appropriate than that of guns, where obviously every year the "social cost" of preserving gun rights involves, literally, the death of many innocent people.

Gun regulation did not start with the Founders. In Connecticut, a 1643 order *required* "on[e] in a Family to bring his Arms to the [church] meeting house every Sabb[a]th," and imposed a fine for not doing so.[7] Colonial South Carolina went further: not only did males of military age have to bring weapons to "church or any other public place of divine worship," but they had to carry on their person "a pair of horse-pistols" or "a gun" (i.e., musket or fowling rifle).[8] Still other colonies required deacons or church wardens to check to make sure that all congregants brought a weapon. Under early Virginia laws, all travelers had to be armed, and if found unarmed were to be punished by "community service," namely, cutting weeds at a local church![9] Clayton Cramer, in his response to the bogus "evidence" presented in the notorious book *Arming America* by Michael Bellesiles, detailed extensive early regulations in which the governments insisted that families be armed, and that whenever possible, lost or stolen weapons were to be returned to their rightful owners (early Americans often notched their names or initials into the stocks of their muskets).[10]

Either way, it is certain that the Founders, including both Federalists and Anti-Federalists, interpreted the "militia" as necessary to restrain *government,* and whatever *other* justifications might be found for personal gun ownership, the imperative to check government tyranny was supreme.[11] Put another way, as David Young, author of *The Founders' View of the Right to Bear Arms,* noted, the phrase "well regulated militia" had an "easily identifiable meaning" prior to 1774.[12] What that easily identifiable meaning was, and where it came from, bears investigating.

American law and political theory derived heavily from the English Whig tradition, which, in turn, constituted a compilation of the works of Aristotle, Cicero, Cato, John Locke, and Algernon Sidney. These were referred to as the "elementary books of public right," and often also included Niccolo Machiavelli and Cesare Beccaria. The Revolutionary-era Founders, in particular, studied the afflictions of the late Roman Republic, or what George Mason of Virginia called the "essential maxims" of the Roman commonwealth that were undermined to lead to tyranny.[13] John Adams and George Mason, in particular, relied on Machiavelli's analysis of the Roman militias, and on his model of Florence, in which "the sovereign power is lodged, both of right and in fact, in the citizens themselves."[14]

This tradition had existed for centuries in Western thought—Aristotle had insisted that the "polity," his ideal political state, consisted of those who bore arms. In Rome, after the standing army defeated essentially an armed citizenry in 43 B.C., the practice of maintaining defensive arms against enemies nevertheless persisted. With the spread of mercenary armies and invasions by barbarians and the fall of the Roman Empire, an interlude followed in which the Italian city-states revived the notion of an armed populace as the central component of defense. Machiavelli particularly described the difficulty in overcoming an armed population fighting close to their homes. Tyranny, he insisted, never came from arming the citizens, but from failing to arm them. He ended his analysis of Italy's problems with the famous maxim that states are founded on "good laws and good arms. . . . [And there] cannot be good laws where there are not good arms."[15]

Nor was this a new development, as it was entirely consistent with English tradition and practice. Henry II's Assize of Arms of 1181 divided English males by property, with each class assigned a certain level of armaments for which the free man and landholder had to provide. For example, anyone designated a knight had to provide armor, a shield, and a lance, while free men who did not hold a title had to provide either a hauberk (chain mail jacket) or, if possessing less land, a doublet (a quilted jacket worn over the hauberk). Under the Assize, town burgesses were to ensure that if someone had extra arms and another lacked arms, the weapons were properly distributed. In the 1200s, Henry III in various edicts continued the tradition of requiring English males to possess armor, horses, and a variety of arms based on their holdings of land, and to maintain them for the public defense. Even by Henry VIII's time, the king complained that archery practice had declined and he decreed that every man keep a bow and arrows and practice shooting. (Ironically, Thomas Esper later argued that it was the decline of archery practice that enabled the then-inferior musket to replace bows as the standard range weapon in English armies.)[16]

Later, those more closely associated with the American Revolution would further expand on the necessity of an armed population for protection against the monarch. John Locke warned about monarchs who achieved total power by disarming the population, writing, "by supposing they have given up themselves to the absolute power and will of a legislator, they have *disarmed themselves, and armed him, to make prey of them when he pleases.*"[17] Algernon Sidney, employing a phrase that would be found in the Virginia Declaration of Rights in 1776, wrote, "the body of the People is the public defense, and every man is armed and disciplined."[18] Perhaps the most influential English Whig writer on the subject of arms, however, was James Burgh, who in 1774 wrote, "Nothing will make a nation so unconquerable as a militia, or every man's being trained to arms."[19] Again, it was clear the militia was *not* a government body or organization, but an informal system of armed individuals, and in Burgh's mind, the citizen was distinctly different from the soldier: "A militia-man is a free citizen; a soldier, a slave for life."[20] In other words, that which made the citizen free—that which actually defined him as free—was the possession of arms outside the control of the government.

A further element of the Whig viewpoint, which surfaced again in parliamentary speeches about the American situation in 1775, was that Englishmen had always resisted tyranny. Parliamentary Whigs appealed to the history of opposition to Charles I and to the establishment of the English Bill of Rights in 1689 as examples of the foundation of sovereignty resting in the people, not the monarch. In America, James Wilson appealed to those very principles when he stated that it was the right of British subjects in America to resist the force of unjust authority. The source of that resistance had to come from the militia.

American Colonial militias typically consisted of all men between the ages of eighteen and fifty (but in some colonies they could be as young as sixteen or as old as sixty), who had to, by law, provide themselves with arms and to train for a specific number of days a year. Males were listed in militia muster rolls and were required to provide themselves with a specific armament (shotguns were not considered suitable, for example), and even the poor had to pay for their own arms. If a man failed to acquire arms the city would furnish him one, for which he had to sell property to repay the cost, and lacking property, he could be put out to labor until the cost was covered.[21] Few were exempted from militia laws, though clergymen, justices of the peace, physicians, lawyers, millers, or anyone physically infirm were usually excused. Some colonies also exempted ferrymen and schoolmasters, but often even they were required to maintain weapons. As a rule, colonies discouraged masters from arming slaves, but free blacks, while not required to participate in the militia, could voluntarily join.[22] On drill days, known as muster days, all armed men turned out and practiced forming lines, firing and reloading in order, advancing, and retreating. If a threat was near, the number of muster days increased. In short, Colonial America was armed to the teeth.

By the mid-1700s, the word *militia* had taken on a distinctly American flavor when *all* able-bodied males were to participate—not just what the English had come to call the "select militia," or those trained regularly. Moreover, by the time of the American Revolution, the British select militia was drawn from men with qualifications generally higher than those who served in Parliament! This often amounted to only four men per thousand people, while in America, the ratio could be one hundred times that or more. Further, when considering the phrase "well regulated militia," which antigun activists have grabbed hold of with such fervor, it is necessary to look at the intent and explicit requirements of the Colonial militias. In West Jersey in 1692, the proprietors issued instructions that the governor ensure that the militia practice routinely so that they would be experts in the use of their firearms.[23] Virginia offered a somewhat different story in its Militia Law of 1705, which revealed that the free Virginia males were already so skilled at hunting and shooting that they needed little muster and training. They needed no law to require them to have guns, or to shoot well.

One major exception, due to the heavy influence of Quakerism, was Pennsylvania, where Benjamin Franklin wrote in 1747 that the colony was in a "defenseless state" and lacked a militia.[24] Nevertheless, Pennsylvania sidestepped the Quakers (who controlled the assembly, despite being a minority) by creating "voluntary defensive associations." Modern leftists might label these "vigilante groups." In *Plain Truth* (1747), Franklin pointed out that all parts of the colonies were subject to attack and that it would likely come within a year. But the colony could call upon, in Franklin's estimation, up to sixty thousand men able to bear arms and who were experts in their use. A population comfortable with hunting and using muskets with rifled barrels developed good accuracy. Franklin then took the next step, publishing the "Form of Association" in December 1747, which outlined the procedures by which individuals would voluntarily band together for defense. Citizens signed the forms, wherein they promised to provide arms and ammunition, and the associations organized companies of fifty to one hundred men who elected officers and set training days—all without fines, punishments, or taxes.

This was free-market defense at its most pure, and, of course, it concerned the authorities because it took militia powers away from the government and put them in the hands of the people. Thomas Penn, the proprietor of the colony, therefore complained to the Pennsylvania Council (a body appointed by the legislature) in 1748 that the militia was an infringement of the king's power (though no less his own). In 1755 the council disapproved an updated voluntary association law, which would have made all military service voluntary, claiming it was invalid precisely because it did not force everyone (including Quakers) into the militia. But when armed Philadelphia rioters threatened public order in 1764, Franklin and more than one thousand other Philadelphians (including a substantial number of Quakers) took up arms in a new informal association to smash the uprising. The riots had been instigated by frontiersmen from the Paxon area concerned about the possible release of Indians who they asserted had committed atrocities. The fact that in Philadelphia alone more than one thousand inhabitants met the frontiersmen (whose numbers were put at fifteen hundred) suggested that many Pennsylvanians were armed. When the riots subsided, Pennsylvania still had no official militia law, but certainly had plenty of armed men willing to serve in voluntary organizations.

A decade later, in 1774, George Mason, George Washington, and Patrick Henry met at Mount Vernon to plan for a defense against the British, resulting in Mason's organization of the Fairfax County Militia Association. But they were only copying a more informal set of actions occurring across the Massachusetts countryside—General Thomas Gage, in charge of the British forces in Boston, wrote on September 1 of that year that the entire countryside had taken up arms following the so-called Powder Alarm earlier that day, in which British troops sailed to Charleston to remove gunpowder and two cannons from a local storehouse.

The presence of cannons reveals an interesting facet of the relationship between the individual's right to bear arms and the community's role in defense (i.e., to possess weapons that an individual could not "bear," but which collectively several people could). The rights of individuals, in part, were defined by their capacity to physically manage the weapon. Since no individual could "bear" a cannon, it was not considered a necessary right—although no laws prohibited individuals from owning such large weapons, and, indeed, over time many did. (As late as the 1840s, Jay Gould and Jim Fisk would outfit their "Fort Taylor" bastion at the Taylor Hotel in New Jersey with three twelve-pound cannons against the expected attack by the forces of Cornelius Vanderbilt, which never came.)[25] The Powder Alarm touched off meetings in Suffolk County, Massachusetts, resulting in the Suffolk Resolves and the formation of still more voluntary militia groups.

Fearing an armed population, the British instituted an import ban on firearms and powder, causing "shortages and scarcity" (the definition of which was one firearm for every two men) in places such as Brunswick.[26] Sam Adams had started writing to friends urging them to acquire firearms and quickly instruct themselves in military arts. George Washington provided interesting insight on the condition of the militia when he noted in 1756 as the French and Indian War approached that men of Culpeper County, in particular, had "odd behavior" and perhaps three-quarters were insufficiently armed.[27] Far from being evidence of a *lack* of guns, it constituted a testimony to the widespread presence of firearms in that every other county showed up appropriately armed.

British policies in the 1760s, and the pending arrival of redcoats in 1768, had prompted Bostonians to reaffirm their town ordinance that required people to have arms. While Parliament interpreted this as insurrection and insisted that the colonials' militia laws required them to fight *with* the government, such appeals were emphatically rejected in Massachusetts.[28] But despite such laws, Bostonians weren't wont to resort to violence. Even the famed Boston Tea Party of 1773 unfolded with no real violence—except to the tea—although the participants, disguised as Mohawk Indians, all carried pistols. Yet the retired Royal Governor Thomas Hutchinson warned in a manuscript history of Massachusetts that the colonists had learned military arts, but not from the British government! It was an insightful and serious comment that the king and Parliament ignored.

Throughout their preparations for defense against the anticipated redcoat invasion, Massachusetts citizens frequently invoked the phrase "well regulated militia" in Revolutionary tracts, always in conjunction with their defense *against* government troops.[29] Thus, there can be no doubt that the primary (and perhaps *only*) interpretation of the phrase "well regulated militia" involved individuals protecting themselves against both domestic (Indians) and foreign (British) threats. This interpretation found its greatest voice in Josiah Quincy, whose *Observations on the Boston Port Bill* (1774) differentiated the militia, which came from the people, from a standing army, which had a tendency to destroy liberty.[30] John Adams corresponded with the aforementioned James Burgh about the possibility of the militia resisting the Crown, and Adams told Burgh in 1774 that New England alone had 200,000 men under arms and that although the Massachusetts militia was established by law, it nevertheless would not obey officers appointed by the governor unless the units themselves had elected the men.[31] But this mentality also spread outside New England. Maryland delegates unanimously adopted the Resolve of December 12, 1774, that recommended communities form their armed militias into companies of 68 men and to train in defense. James Madison noted that upland Virginia riflemen possessed such accuracy that even poorer shots could hit a target the size of a man's head at one hundred yards and that he himself didn't often miss such a target.[32]

In each case, the concept of "well regulated militia" included a pledge of readiness and preparation, of prior acquisition of firearms and powder, and of sufficient training so as to be able to make formation, volley fire, and obey officers in an effective manner. These, by the way, were distinguishing characteristics of what Victor Davis Hanson has called the "Western Way of War," namely, the use of organization and drill to ensure that men fight in formation and that the formation retain its integrity over individual tendencies to one-on-one melee combat.[33] Furthermore, the well-regulated militia was *without exception* differentiated from the standing army of the king and indeed was posited as the counterbalance to that professional military. Again, one exception to the norm was Pennsylvania, which lacked a militia law, but which nevertheless saw an instantaneous gathering of armed men into militia units (later called the "Pennsylvania Associator") following the Battle of Lexington. Adams, in July 1775, noted the presence of all sorts of armed Philadelphians: "Rifle Men, Indians, Light Infantry, Light Horse, Highlanders, with their Plaid and Bag Pipes, and German Hussars."[34] Some Colonial governors fretted that their citizens possessed weapons of insufficient quality, making them inappropriate for military service. (In modern terms, this is the equivalent of New York City Mayor Michael Bloomberg walking up to someone and saying, "Here, bub. That snub-nosed isn't powerful enough. Take one of these AR-16s—and have a couple of clips on the city!")

Most colonies, at one time or another, passed some firearms restrictions, almost always disarming specific individuals for specific crimes. In Massachusetts Bay Colony, for example, records indicate that the government feared certain persons being "so hot headed [over religious issues] that they feared breach of peace," and that several towns disarmed those specific persons.[35] When a roundup of guns occurred, it was in the context of events that threatened to ignite violence, such as the death of the Protestant Queen Anne in 1714 and the expected disruption of "Publick Tranquillity" that might erupt from Catholics in case James III of Scotland sought the throne.[36]

In the 1600s, it was illegal in most colonies to sell firearms to Native Americans, though a few exceptions occurred. (In the Carolinas in the

1680s, the government sold muskets to Indian allies.) But by the turn of the century, thousands of firearms flowed into North America for sale to Indians. Even before then, however, some Indian tribes had almost entirely replaced bows and spears with guns for hunting.[37] If anything, the record of Indian gun ownership provides early evidence of the failure of "gun control," even in the 1600s.

General Gage responded to Colonial resistance on June 9, 1775, by issuing a proclamation directed at the citizens of Boston in which he noted that they had not turned in their firearms as ordered earlier, on April 19. Punishment for failing to turn in a weapon consisted of seventy-five days in jail. This resulted in only further insubordination by the British Americans: North Carolina delegates to the Continental Congress described Gage's actions as an invasion of the liberties of the people and again appealed to the rights of all Englishmen to own a weapon for self-defense. Wisely, the North Carolinians advised their brethren back in the colony to store up powder.

This raises an important point: if, as Michael Bellesiles argued in his fatally flawed book *Arming America,* all guns were "public property," then there would have been no need to confiscate such weapons from private hands. Indeed, as early as 1756, Maryland distinguished between publicly owned guns and those in private hands.[38] In the 1600s, Colonial governments even paid gunsmiths to repair *private* arms, later sending a bill to the owner.[39] Some colonies also required that militia officers do a house-to-house inventory, and if anyone had surplus guns when another man did not, the excess had to be redistributed to the unarmed man. Those rules were soon viewed as an infringement on the right to bear arms, and, moreover, on the private nature of gun ownership, and were repealed or modified.

The Continental Congress responded to the British version of "gun control" by recommending in July 1775 that all able-bodied men form into militia companies and train for defense. Not only should each man furnish musket, powder, and ball, Congress advised, but also a bayonet and other gear. This was a significant step, for the bayonet was the calling card of professional soldiers. Warfare at the time involved the "law of forbearance," in which the last unit to give fire usually prevailed. If an army could withstand the enemy's first volleys, then it had a clear shot at masses of soldiers reloading. The only way to overcome that disadvantage was to charge with the bayonet after a volley—but only disciplined troops, who possessed bayonets, could do so.

Congress *did* enact certain gun restrictions. In March 1776, fearing that Loyalists would support the British against the American colonists, the Continental Congress passed a resolution recommending that any individuals who did *not* associate with the militia or sign a written agreement to support the resistance were to be disarmed, the value of their weapons and powder assessed, and they were to be recompensed for their loss. Any who did not sign the statements were deemed "Tories." Two months later, General George Washington wrote Congress asking where those weapons had been stored and noted that he would send an agent to collect them. Congress never replied, and the record is unclear if any Tory weapons were ever confiscated. It's doubtful that Congress ever had sufficient funds to pay for them in any event.[40]

As combat between the patriots and the redcoats spread, the former colonies formed themselves into states and issued their own declarations of rights. Virginia led the way in June 1776, with the first American state Declaration of Rights, and followed a few weeks later with the first state constitution. Seven of the thirteen colonies prepared state constitutions that included a bill of rights. If, as some gun-control advocates argue, localities and states should prohibit guns, it is worth asking, what did the states *then* say? George Mason authored the Virginia Declaration of Rights, although Jefferson had submitted his own draft that stated, "No freeman shall ever be debarred the use of arms."[41] The final version that appeared in Section 13 of the Virginia Declaration of Rights read:

> [We resolve] That a well-regulated militia, composed of the
> body of the people, trained to arms, is the proper, natural, and
> safe defense of a free state; that standing armies, in time of
> peace, should be avoided, as dangerous to liberty; and that in all

cases the military should be under strict subordination to, and governed by the civil power.[42]

This triad developed by Mason—that there was a need for a militia composed of armed individuals, that standing armies constituted a threat to liberty, and that the military should be subjected to the civil authority—in some form or another appeared in the declarations of other states as well. Delaware's Declaration of Rights, issued in September 1776, for example, contained nearly identical language proclaiming, "a well regulated militia is the proper, natural and safe defence of a free government," as did Maryland's two months later. Pennsylvania modified the language slightly to read, "the people have a right to bear arms for the defence of themselves and the state," though North Carolina adopted identical wording. Massachusetts chose slightly different wording: that "the people have a right to keep and bear arms for the common defence." This was an important alteration of the notion that bearing arms was for both personal defense and protection of the state. These "Mason Triads" dovetailed closely with the actual events of the Revolution, in which Americans exercised their rights to bear arms and associated together for common defense. The British then used the standing army to either oppress or infringe upon other liberties, such as extracting higher taxes on the population, or stationing troops in people's homes. Finally, whether in the form of declarations of rights, documents of the Colonial governments, or the founding constitutions and bills of rights, power over the military was always placed in the hands of civilians.

By the time the Founders gathered to frame the federal Constitution, the right to bear arms was clearly understood and accepted by everyone as an individual right to self-defense as well as a communal right to resist authority by the national government. So why wasn't it in the Constitution itself? One obvious answer is that the views were so universal and commonplace, having already been outlined by individual states, that few at first thought it necessary to spell out the particulars.

Even at the Constitutional Convention, many delegates expressed concerns that the federal government had too much power and that a bill of rights was necessary to amend it. Charles Pinckney submitted seven amendments in 1787 (later expanded to ten) that included no quartering of troops and civilian authority over the military. Some Federalists argued that the state constitutions would prove sufficient to protect the rights, but many Founders anticipated that federal power would quickly eclipse state laws.[43] Specific protections, therefore, were needed.

During the ratification debates, two arguments surfaced, one by the Federalists and one by the Anti-Federalists. The former, which gun historian David Young calls the "Federalist Mantra," maintained that the people were de facto armed and thus tyranny could not take root. This soon became the central component of tracts by Noah Webster, Tench Coxe, Alexander Hamilton, and James Madison. It maintained that because the people were armed, their rights were, *de facto,* forever safe. The Anti-Federalists operated from the opposite perspective, namely, that under a strong central government the people could be disarmed and unable to resist tyranny, and that the Constitution needed to include specific protections for speech, firearms ownership, religious expression, and other civil rights. Pennsylvania, the first state to hold a ratifying convention, proposed amendments including one that provided for the right to bear arms and guaranteed that "no law shall be passed" infringing on such rights. After the initial rush to ratify the Constitution slowed and states began insisting on amendments, George Mason again played a key role in the Virginia Ratifying Convention by supplying the "keep and bear arms" phrase, followed by the "well regulated militia" phrase. During the debates, Patrick Henry in particular fretted that the new national government possessed enough power to disarm and destroy the militia with a standing army. New York's convention provided an amendment with similar language to Virginia's.

In sum, each iteration of the "keep and bear arms" language provided for in these amendments presumed that a large federal government would eventually attempt to disarm the population and establish a large standing army that would tyrannize the public. In a pair of letters dated December 20, 1787, and July 31, 1788, Thomas Jefferson wrote to James Madison that without a bill of rights, the Constitution was flawed, and that such a bill of rights would protect the people against the government.[44] Madison introduced the ten amendments proposed by the states to the House of Representatives in June 1789. These included a clause on keeping and bearing arms that was contained in a larger group of protections, and the wording was modified into what is now the Second Amendment.

The most thorough and detailed analysis of the evolution of the Second Amendment is provided by David Young's *The Founders' View of the Right to Bear Arms*. Young concludes:

> Those making modern assertions about the intent of the Second Amendment often assign meanings and intentions to period terms, phrases, and clauses that not only are inaccurate, but are in fact the exact opposite of the period understanding. It is often suggested that the well regulated militia language of the Second Amendment intended a government regulated militia. The language of the Second Amendment, its Bill of Rights nature and intent, and the history of the Second Amendment and its predecessors all directly contradict this interpretation.[45]

As we've seen, not only did the term *militia* refer to free men who possessed their own firearms, but the purpose of owning arms in the first place was to allow citizens to defend themselves against the government. Hence, the Second Amendment *restricted* the government instead of empowering it to regulate the possession of firearms. In the context of the day, these terms were never mistaken to provide for a national army or government force. This misinterpretation is most specifically contradicted by the example of Pennsylvania, where there was no *duty* to bear arms at all— since there was no militia—only a *right*. That has led James Lindgren, a law professor at Northwestern University, to conclude that "household gun ownership in early America was more widespread than today—in a much poorer world."[46]

Thanks to the Constitution of the United States, frontal assaults on gun ownership have largely been defeated. While the *Emerson* and

Heller cases established the individual right to own a firearm, therefore upholding the unequivocal original intent of the Second Amendment, big cities have continued to insist that they need to have gun control—this in the face of the worst violent crime rates on the planet in some of these metropolitan areas. How, exactly, violent crime could be so high where guns are essentially banned is a question sidestepped by most antigun advocates, and usually "solved" by claiming the guns are brought in from the outside, thereby requiring an *expansion* of gun control! Therefore, the personal defense ruling in *Heller* remains to be tested in courts as to its ultimate limits.

Meanwhile, the foundational question of this book, namely, What would the Founders say? has been answered beyond question in its most elementary basis, which is that virtually *none* of the Founders advocated government depriving the people of their right to bear arms. None. *All* of them maintained that a well-regulated militia was constituted of ordinary men trained in the use of firearms, which they themselves supplied. What debates existed involved whether individuals who lacked such weapons could be prosecuted, whether those who had extra firearms could be required to share with those who did not, and who constituted a male capable of "bearing arms." And the obvious bears mentioning: that almost all of the Founders at one time or another owned, and fired, pistols or muskets at other human beings. Most were in the Continental Army (Hamilton, Henry, Madison, Monroe, Washington—Tench Coxe fought on both sides!). Many were officers in the Colonial militias or the Continental Army. Thus, by their very actions, one can assume what they would say if asked their opinion on the matter today.

But the longer answer to, What did the Founders mean by a "well regulated militia"? rests on the underlying assumptions that the best defense of free people was the free people themselves . . . armed. By the time of the constitutional debates, the opposing sides differed only on whether specific protections to keep and bear arms were necessary to prevent *government* tyranny, or whether there would be no government tyranny *because* the people were already armed. Eventually, those insisting that specific protections were needed emerged victorious, and fortunately so, for it has been abundantly clear that governments—local, state, and federal—invoking the best of reasons and for the (supposedly) purest of intentions have over the past two hundred years consistently sought to "infringe" upon that very right that the Constitution explicitly states was not to be infringed upon!

Moreover, in 2008, after Barack Obama was elected president and the Democrats took control of the House and Senate, many Americans worried that the government would spin into an oppressive tyranny of regulations that would impinge on personal liberties. Gun sales had spiked after 9/11, but they absolutely skyrocketed after the election of Barack Obama as president. "I was here for Y2K, September 11, [and] Katrina," said one gun store owner in Manassas, Virginia, in November 2008, "and we did notice a spike in business, but nothing on the order of what we are seeing right now."[47] Many feared that a president who was viewed as antigun—and coming from "gun-free" Chicago—might use the government to seize all firearms. Thus a massive buying spree of guns took place.[48] While the press reported the phenomenon, it typically missed the causes, attributing the rise in sales to fears of "crime and terrorism." The United States, of course, had not had a successful domestic terror attack since 2001, and crime levels had dropped precipitously in the 1990s and remained low by traditional measures. Indeed, crime rates had gone up sharply in 2005 and 2006, but that did *not* correlate with increasing gun sales; then the rates fell in 2008.[49] The media had once again failed to understand how gun ownership, as provided by the Founders, was meant to protect Americans from *government,* not from foreign terrorism.

It was undeniable, however, that more guns meant less crime. Economist John R. Lott's extensive studies showed that concealed-carry laws in America consistently reduced crime; and subsequent worldwide studies have found that there is no particular correlation between high rates of gun ownership in a society and high murder rates. If anything, there is no pattern: gun restrictions in most, but not all, places increase crime (including homicides), and higher rates of gun ownership often correlate with lower homicide rates.[50]

Modern governments are well aware of the fact that guns are not used primarily for hunting, and that while most people who keep a weapon do so—at least in part—for self-defense, the fundamental argument for gun ownership is that an armed population cannot be controlled or tyrannized as easily as an unarmed population. It's no surprise, then, that the government has relentlessly sought to demonize guns, as with its antigun ad campaign from 1993 to 2000, where more than a dozen different antigun ads were run. Inaccurate statistics were deliberately circulated by the media, with the government's blessing, citing "ten deaths a day" that involved children and firearms.[51] This statistic implied that kids were dying routinely because of unlocked or available guns. In fact, the real record during the previous year had been 0.5 accidental deaths per day. What the media had done was to include murders, suicides, and accidental deaths to achieve its ten-deaths-per-day number.[52] Similarly, suicide "facts" about kids and guns were inaccurate—to the point of being off by a *factor of six*![53] ("A child between ten and nineteen commits suicide with a handgun every six hours," when the actual rate was one every forty-four hours). Yet the most violent act on American soil since the Civil War involved foreigners using box cutters, and not a shot was fired—as even leftist filmmaker Michael Moore admitted on his Web site.[54]

On the other hand, Israel, which suffers from relentless terror attempts, allows trained citizens to have concealed handguns—and more than 10 percent of Israeli adults do. The Israeli police inspector general, in a 1776-style proclamation, called on all handgun permit holders to keep their weapons on them at all times.[55] In the 1970s, when the United States experienced a rash of airline hijackings, the introduction and expansion of armed air marshals (combined with improved identification of hijackers) caused the number of hijackings to fall by one-third to one-half.[56] These statistics just go to show that an armed population is a free population, largely free from the "fear of violent death," as Thomas Hobbes put it, and also free from the fear of tyranny by its own government. Thomas Paine observed that "arms like laws discourage and keep the invader and the plunderer in awe, and preserve order in the world."[57] He wasn't talking about criminals; he was referring to the king of England! Alexander Hamilton said that a goal of the nation was to have the people "properly armed and equipped." So if the Founders were alive today and you wanted to ask them what they thought about gun control, you might have to head to the shooting range.

CONCLUSION

It should be apparent from what the Founders said and how they acted that such current practices as bailing out banks and auto companies, having the federal government dictate diet and health practices, requiring the government to provide jobs, and sending the nation spiraling into astronomical levels of debt would all be anathema to them. Many modern government "functions" are so outrageously outside the powers that the Founders permitted government to have that, faced with modern society, they would certainly be revolutionaries, burning the whole structure down to start anew. In such a case, a new bill of rights would likely be double its current size, and deeper in specificity, and the limitations on the powers of the federal government would almost certainly be vastly expanded.

Historical context is critical, and one cannot ask the equivalent of, Would Jesus have a Facebook page? or, What if Washington had possessed machine guns at Brooklyn Heights? and expect a sensible answer. The Founders did what they did in large part because of who they were and when they lived. *None* was born into a "capitalist" world. All of them lived under, for lesser or greater lengths of time, a mercantilist structure that saw businesses as an arm of state policy. That they changed those perceptions is itself a remarkable testimony. Many came from the ranks of planters, and, as such, had slaves. Slavery was so common as to go without comment in the 1700s—throughout the world. England and France and parts of Europe had few (if any) slaves on their European soil, but many practiced slavery in their colonies. While the European masses had gone from slavery in ancient times to a limited freedom under feudalism to increased civil and political rights in the 1700s, large parts of the rest of the world continued to practice slavery as a matter of course, especially in their colonial empires. Thus, concepts of freedom were always qualified with the unstated assumption that such rights belonged to Europeans. It differed little from the Japanese view that all foreigners were subhuman *gaijin*.

That said, the fact that the flexibility of the Declaration allowed for "all men" to indeed mean "all people" spoke to the genius and the divine inspiration of that document. Just as the economic structure that the Founders erected constituted a remarkable free-market system (despite the fact that it came from a state-controlled construct), so too did the assumption of political rights and human liberty come despite the widespread denial of such liberty to most people on earth. In short, while the Founders were definitely men of their time, at key moments, in transformative concepts, they stepped outside of it.

Above all, in everything they said and did, the Founders unceasingly displayed two characteristics. One was a devout patriotism, in which the United States was an exceptional nation, a "shining city on a hill," and a beacon to the world. America was *different* from, and, yes, *better than* the countries of the Old World in the eyes of the Founders. If they had thought otherwise, they wouldn't have fought the Revolution. Second, the Founders had a deep-seated and profound distrust of government—less so at the local and state level, but substantial at the national level. All of them railed at the powers of kings and princes, all of them warned about the lust for power that men naturally have, and all sought to limit the powers of government in all areas of life. That today a U.S. president would be seeking to dictate the salaries of *private* insurance company executives, or through his Health and Human Services secretary seek to shape in any way (let alone control) the diets and eating habits of the people, would have provoked them to violence, just as the abuses of King George provoked them. While not one for swearing, George Washington would have likely responded to Barack Obama's demands that bank officials reduce their pay with, "It's none of your damn business."

Jefferson wrote in the Declaration that "whenever any Form of Government becomes destructive of these ends, it is the Right of the People to alter or to abolish it, and to institute new Government." Opposing tyranny and despotism are not only man's right, Jefferson concluded, but it was "their duty, to throw off such Government, and to provide new Guards for their future security." The current administration and those in Congress today seldom refer to the Founders, and with good reason. The Founders would have utterly rejected their attitudes and direction.

Remarkably, there was almost no disagreement among the Founders—even among such polar opposites as Hamilton and Jefferson—that freedom was good and tyranny was bad. That seems an obvious statement on the surface, yet modern Americans daily are confronted by policies enacted by local, state, and federal *representatives* who see freedom as a threat and greater government control as desirable. We are not talking about tiny, incremental nibbling around the fringes of liberty, but instead about wholesale usurpation of individual choice. Can anyone build a structure on his property without a blizzard of paperwork from city or county officials? I recently met a gentleman who fought a two-year battle to install a wheelchair ramp on his house for his infirmed father, and gave up in the face of bureaucratic resistance and obstructionism. Ask western farmers about the "shoot and shovel" approach to animals or birds protected by the Endangered Species Act: federal authorities are so invested in protecting the kangaroo rat and the spotted owl that individuals have simply started to break the law and, literally, cover up the evidence. Some thirty years after seat belt laws were enacted, states (such as my own, Ohio) have to hold "Click it or ticket" rallies in public areas (attended entirely by union members, mostly police) to encourage people to buckle up. Didn't Ralph Nader argue that seat belts were so desired on the part of the driving public that people would gladly pay for their installation? And yet now states must *organize* public meetings to tout the blessings of seat belts.

Certainly the Founders disagreed on *which elements* in society posed the greatest threat to liberty—but none of them wished to limit freedom. Indeed, the debates were about which system protected individual liberties, one with strong state governments or one with a strong national government. Where Jefferson feared the monied men and aristocrats, Hamilton distrusted the masses. Yet neither envisioned government as the counterweight. Quite to the contrary, Hamilton, always viewed as "Mr. Big Government" among the Founders, sought to shackle the monied men by obligating them to the government, while James Madison and Thomas Jefferson sought to dilute political power through the largest number of hands.

Each step of the way in their design of the United States government, they labored to make tyranny by the many or the few impossible, to lay out what rights *must* be protected, and to erect as many obstacles as possible between the federal government's actions and the individual. John Adams, another "big government" Federalist, left the District of Columbia as quickly—and as often—as possible for his farm. Jefferson answered the White House door himself. These were clearly not men enamored of power or the trappings of authority. Perhaps our current occupant would consider Jefferson's example. These actions (or, more appropriately, "inactions") had another important effect: they kept the presidents busy with ordinary activities so that neither they, nor Congress, had time for mischief. When members spent months of their lives riding to and from Washington, D.C., it meant that they had less time to oppress the people.

What can we learn from the Founders, even when "our" problems weren't "their" problems? A great deal. They operated on a set of principles that, like mathematics, was applicable in almost any situation, and across time. It is the genius of the Constitution that it provided flexibility to adapt to almost any modern problem, while at the same time containing the overall imperative of reducing or limiting the power of the national government and placing power in the hands of the people. Not surprisingly, virtually none of the modern Left—save when it comes to *certain* types of free speech or *certain* civil rights—ever refers to the Constitution. To them, it is a stumbling block, an impediment. To the Left, the

Constitution must be overcome, flanked, or ignored. When Martin Luther King Jr. led civil rights marchers in singing "We Shall Overcome," he meant that they would overcome the barriers that denied them their constitutional rights. When modern leftists employ the phrase, they mean "We Shall Overcome the Constitution"! A better solution to the nation's problems would be overcoming the Left and its deviant, perverse, and, yes, sinister ideas, once and for all.

Finding out what the Founders thought is relatively simple, and generally clear. Like all men, they had disagreements on the proper approach to problems. But all loved America, most fought for her, and some died for her. It is worth remembering that all the signers of the Declaration of Independence became traitors in the eyes of the British government, subject to death. Many paid a heavy price for their courage. At the very least, we owe them the courtesy of a virtual consultation about every policy. They earned that much.

Acknowledgments

As with any of my works, this book was made possible only with an extensive support network that enabled me to focus on putting fingers to the keyboard. Most important, my wife, Dee, organized my daily existence and freed my time from important routine chores without which none of us could survive. Two researchers in particular assisted me, most notably my son, Adam, and my friend Brian Bennett. Clayton Cramer supplied important information and suggestions for the chapter on guns. Dave Dougherty was instrumental in improving the chapters on property and religion, and I'm grateful to them.

The University of Dayton has been most generous in supporting me in a variety of ways, particularly Dean Paul Benson and the chairman of the history department, Julius Amin. Ed Knappman and everyone at New England Publishing helped get this off the ground while Brooke Carey at Sentinel did her usual marvelous job of editing. Thanks also to Amanda Pritzker and Allison McClean for their work in publicizing this volume. And as with some of the previous titles we've done together, Sentinel's publisher, Adrian Zackheim, helped formulate the approach of this book. Most of all, however, we should thank the Founders, for it was their ideas—rejuvenated by the Tea Party movement—that provided the basic idea for a book on their thoughts about current issues.

NOTES

INTRODUCTION

1. "GM's Bailout Plan Includes Thousands of Job Cuts; Flint Will Not Be Unscathed," *Flint Journal,* December 2, 2008.
2. "Bush Says Sacrificed Free-Market Principles to Save Economy," http://www.breit bart.com/article.php?id=081216215816.8g97981o.
3. *A Few Good Men,* 1992, http://www.imdb.com/title/tt0104257/quotes.
4. See, for example, "The Myth of Second Hand Smoke," http://www.smokersinfo .net/the-myth-of-second-hand-smoke/; C. S. Redhead and R. E. Rowberg, *Congressional Research Service Report for Congress Environmental Tobacco Smoke and Lung Cancer Risk,* 1995, http://tobaccodocuments.org/pm/2048280251-0329 .html?zoom=750&ocr_position=above_foramatted&start_page=1&end_ page=79, found that "statistical evidence does not appear to support a conclusion that there are substantial health effects of passive smoking," and "it is possible that very few or even no deaths can be attributed to second hand smoke," and "the absolute risk, even to those with the greatest exposure levels, is uncertain"; Roger A. Jenkins and Richard W. Counts, "Personal Exposure to Environmental Tobacco Smoke: Salivary Cotinine, Airborne Nicotine, and Non-smoker Misclassification," *Journal of Exposure Analysis and Environmental Epidemiology* 9 (1999): 352–63; and the Congressional Research Service's own J. G. Gravelle and C. S. Redhead, Congressional Research Office Memorandum "Discussion of Source of Claims of 50,000 Deaths from Passive Smoking," March 23, 1994, http://www.nycclash.com/Cabinet/CRSDiscusses_50000_Deaths.html. For

those who insist that sidestream, or "passive," smoke is in fact dangerous, see *The Health Consequences of Involuntary Exposure to Tobacco Smoke: A Report of the Surgeon General,* June 27, 2006, http://www.surgeongeneral.gov/library/second handsmoke/; and Gina S. Lovasi et al., "Association of Environmental Tobacco Smoke Exposure in Childhood with Early Emphysema in Adulthood Among Nonsmokers," *American Journal of Epidemiology* 171 (2010): 54–62; among many others.

5. Buckner F. Melton Jr., ed., *The Quotable Founding Fathers* (New York: Fall River Press, 2004), 28.

6. "Obama Transportation Secretary: 'This Is the End of Favoring Motorized Transportation at the Expense of Non-Motorized,'" http://www.cnsnews.com/news/article/63290.

QUESTION #1: HOW IMPORTANT IS RELIGION, ESPECIALLY CHRISTIANITY, IN MATTERS OF STATE AND GOVERNMENT AND SHOULD THE TWO BE ENTIRELY SEPARATE?

1. Galileo Galilei, "Dialogue," 1623, cited in "The Trial of Galileo: Key Figures," http://www.law.umkc.edu/faculty/projects/ftrials/galileo/keyfigures.html.

2. The first article, dealing with the number of citizens per representative, was never ratified, and the second article was ratified in 1992 as Amendment XXVII; articles three through twelve became amendments one through ten as ratified.

3. Andrew Browning, ed., *English Historical Documents, 1660–1714* (London: Eyre & Spottiswoode, 1953), 122–28.

4. Ibid., 127.

5. Harry S. Cohn, *Connecticut Constitutional History, 1636–1776* (Hartford, CT: Connecticut State Library, August 1988), 3.

6. State of Connecticut, secretary of state, *1818 Constitution of the State of Connecticut,* from original in the Connecticut State Library, August 2007.

7. Wesley W. Horton, *Connecticut Constitutional History, 1776–1988* (Hartford, CT: Connecticut State Library, 1988), 19.

8. *Journals of the Provincial Congress, Provincial Convention Committee of Safety and Council of Safety of the State of New York, 1775, 1776, 1777,* 1 (Albany: Thurlow Weed, Printer to the State, 1842), 892–98.

9. Page Smith, *John Adams* (Garden City, NY: Doubleday & Company, 1962), 438–44.

10. Francis Newton Thorpe, *The Federal and State Constitutions, Colonial Charters, and Other Organic Laws of the States, Territories, and Colonies Now or Heretofore Forming the United States of America* (Washington, D.C.: Government Printing Office, 1909), as extracted and printed as *Constitution of Massachusetts, 1780,* National Humanities Institute, 1999, 1.

11. Ibid., 2.

12. Francis Newton Thorpe, *Constitution of Pennsylvania, September 28, 1776* (New Haven, CT: Avalon Project, Yale Law School, 2008).

13. Ibid.

14. Alexander James Dallas, *Laws of the Commonwealth of Pennsylvania* (Philadelphia: Hall and Sellers, 1795), 3:22–29.

15. *Constitution of Virginia, June 29, 1776* (Washington, D.C.: National Humanities Institute, 1999).

16. *Constitution of New Hampshire, June 2, 1784* (Novi, MI: Lonang Institute, 2003); *Acts and Laws of the State of New Hampshire in America* (Exeter, NH: General Assembly, 1780).

17. *New Jersey Constitution of 1776* (Trenton, NJ: The New Jersey State Library, State Government Information Office, 1997).

18. *Constitution of Maryland, 1776* (Bowie, MD: National Humanities Institute, 1999), in Thorpe.

19. *Constitution of North Carolina, 1776* (Bowie, MD: National Humanities Institute, 1999), in Thorpe.

20. Robert and George Watkins, *Digest of the Laws of the State of Georgia, from Its First Establishment as a British Province down to the Year 1798, Inclusive, and the Principal Acts of 1798: In Which Is Comprehended the Declaration of Independence* (Philadelphia: R. Aitken, 1800), 7–16.

21. *Constitution of Delaware, 1776* (New Haven, CT: Avalon Project, 2008).

22. Richard B. Morris, *John Jay, The Making of a Revolutionary, Unpublished Papers 1745–1780* (New York: Harper & Row, 1975), passim.

23. Ibid., 392.

24. Ibid.; *Constitution of New York, 1777* (Bowie, MD: National Humanities Institute, 1999).

25. Charles Francis Adams, ed., *The Works of John Adams, Second President of the United States,* vol. 9 (Boston: Little, Brown, 1854), 229.

26. Richard B. Morris, *Seven Who Shaped Our Destiny, The Founding Fathers as Revolutionaries* (New York: Harper Colophon, 1976), 190.

27. John Adams diary entry, August 14, 1796, in Buckner F. Melton Jr., *The Quotable Founding Fathers* (New York: Fall River Press, 2004), 311.

28. John Adams, "Proclamation for a National Fast," 1798, ibid., 313.

29. John Adams to Thomas Jefferson, July 16, 1814, ibid., 314.

30. John Adams to Thomas Jefferson, May 19, 1821, ibid., 314.

31. Michael Novak and Jana Novak, *Washington's God, Religion, Liberty, and the Father of Our Country* (New York: Basic Books, 2006), 243–45.

32. Ibid., 226.

33. William J. Johnson, *George Washington, the Christian* (New York: Abington Press, 1919), 24–35.

34. George Washington, "Farewell Address" (New Haven, CT: Avalon Project, 2008).

35. Hugh Heclo, *Christianity and American Democracy* (Cambridge, MA: Harvard University Press, 2007), 32–33.

36. *Everson v. Board of Education*, 330 U.S. 1, 1947.

37. Thomas Jefferson to the Danbury Baptists, January 1, 1802, http://www.loc.gov/loc/lcib/9806/danpre.html.

38. Thomas Jefferson to Thomas Cooper, November 2, 1822, in Andrew A. Bergh and Albert Ellery Lipscomb, eds., *The Writings of Thomas Jefferson,* Memorial Edition (Washington, D.C.: Thomas Jefferson Memorial Foundation, 1903), 15:405.

39. Morris, *Seven Who Shaped Our Destiny,* 190.

40. Melton, *Quotable Founding Fathers,* 316.

41. Ibid.

42. James Madison to Mordecai M. Nash, May 15, 1818, ibid., 316.

43. James Madison to Mordecai M. Nash, ibid., 316.

44. Jon Roland, ed., *Selected Works of James Madison.*

45. Robert S. Alley, ed., *James Madison on Religious Liberty* (New York: Prometheus Books, 1989), 86–88; Gaillard Hunt, ed., *The Writings of James Madison,* vol. 9 (New York: G. P. Putnam's Sons, 1910); James Madison to Edward Livingston, July 10, 1822, http://press-pubs.uchicago.edu/founders/documents/amendI_religions66.html.

46. Thomas Jefferson to James Madison, December 8, 1784, quoted in Morris, *Seven Who Shaped Our Destiny,* 203.

47. Elizabeth Fleet, ed., "James Madison, Detached Memoranda," *William and Mary Quarterly,* 3rd Series, no. 3, October 1946, 554–60.

48. Fleet, "James Madison, Detached Memoranda," passim.

49. Paine quoted in Melton, *Quotable Founding Fathers,* 300.

50. Paine, *Common Sense,* quoted in ibid., 301.

51. Ibid., 300.

52. Benjamin Franklin, *The Autobiography of Benjamin Franklin* (New York: The Modern Library, 1944), 65.

53. Benjamin Franklin to Messrs. The Abbes Chalut and Arnaud, April 17, 1787, in Jared Sparks, ed., *The Works of Benjamin Franklin* (Boston: Tappan, Whittemore and Mason, 1840), 10:297.

54. Benjamin Franklin, "Proposals Relating to the Education of Youth in Pensilvania" (Philadelphia, 1747), 22, accessed on Web site of National Humanities Resource Toolbox, Becoming American, The British Atlantic Colonies, 1690–1763, National Humanities Center, March 2010, http://nationalhumanitiescenter.org/pds/becomingamer/ideas/text4/franklinproposals.pdf.

55. Benjamin Franklin, "Speech to the Constitutional Convention," June 28, 1787, Library of Congress Online, http://www.loc.gov/exhibits/religion/rel06.html.

56. *Everson v. Board of Education of the Township of Ewing et al.,* Supreme Court of the United States, 330 US 1, http://www.law.umkc.edu/faculty/projects/ftrials/conlaw/everson.html.

57. Benjamin Rush to John Armstrong, March 19, 1783, and his *On the Mode of Education Proper in a Republic,* 1806, in Melton, *Quotable Founding Fathers,* 300, 313.

58. Albert Ellery Bergy, ed., *The Writings of Thomas Jefferson* (Washington, D.C.: Thomas Jefferson Memorial Association of the United States, 1907), 14:320–32; http://etext.virginia.edu/jefferson/quotations/jeff1650.htm.

59. Thomas Jefferson, *Summary View of the Rights of British America,* quoted in Melton, *Quotable Founding Fathers,* 301.

60. John Witherspoon, 1776, and John Adams to Thomas Jefferson, June 20, 1815, ibid., 301, 315.

QUESTION #2: WHAT IS THE FUNCTION OF EDUCATION AND HOW MUCH CONTROL SHOULD THE FEDERAL GOVERNMENT HAVE OVER IT?

1. John Adams, *Dissertation on the Canon and Feudal Law,* in Buckner F. Melton Jr., *The Quotable Founding Fathers* (New York: Fall River Press, 2004), 83.

2. "School of Education Faculty Find National Poll Reveals Public Desire for Quality, Need for Info," http://newsinfo.iu.edu/news/page/normal/11710.html.

3. "Americans Discouraged by Public School Performance," http://newsinfo.iu.edu/news/page/normal/11710.html; "Special Analysis 2009," U.S. Department of Education Institute of Education Sciences, http://nces.ed.gov/programs/coe/2009/analysis/, which showed "U.S. 15-year-old students' average science literacy score . . . was lower than the OECD average . . . and placed U.S. 15-year-olds in the bottom third of participating OECD nations."

4. George Washington to William Augustine Washington, February 27, 1798, in John C. Fitzpatrick, ed., *The Writings of George Washington from the Original Manuscript Sources, 1745–1799* (Washington, D.C.: United States Government Printing Office, 1940), 36:172.

5. Fitzpatrick, *Writings of George Washington,* 36:172.

6. George Washington to George Chapman, December 15, 1784, ibid., 28:13.

7. George Washington to Steptoe Washington, December 5, 1790, http://www.marksquotes.com/Founding-Fathers/Washington/index6.htm.

8. James Madison to Edward Everett, March 19, 1823, in James Madison, *Letters and Other Writings of James Madison* (Philadelphia: J. B. Lippincott, 1865), 3:309.

9. Melton, *Quotable Founding Fathers,* 30.

10. Ibid., 31.

11. Fitzpatrick, *Writings of George Washington,* 27:268–69.

12. Benjamin Rush to the citizens of Philadelphia, March 28, 1787, in L. H. Butterfield, ed., *Letters of Benjamin Rush* (Princeton, NJ: American Philosophical Society, 1951), 1:413.

13. Benjamin Rush to John Armstrong, March 19, 1783, ibid., 1:294.

14. James W. Fraser, *Between Church and State: Religion and Public Education in Multicultural America* (New York: St. Martin's/Griffin, 1999), 10.

15. James Monroe to John Kirkland, July 12, 1817, in Daniel Preston, ed., *The Papers of James Monroe: A Documentary History of the Presidential Tours of James Monroe, 1817, 1818, 1819* (Westport, CT: Greenwood Press, 2003), 1:235.

16. Benjamin Franklin, "Proposals Relating to the Education of Youth in Pennsylvania," in Leonard Larabee, ed., *The Papers of Benjamin Franklin* (New Haven, CT: Yale University Press, 1961), 3:413.

17. Fisher Ames, *The Works of Fisher Ames* (Boston: T. B. Wait and Company, 1809), 134; Benjamin Rush, *Essays, Literary, Moral, and Philosophical* (Schenectady, NY: Union College Press, 1988), 55–66; David Barton, *Education and the Founding Fathers* (Aledo, TX: Wallbuilder Press, 1998), 22.

18. John Adams, *Defense of the Constitutions*, 1787, in Melton, *Quotable Founding Fathers*, 87.

19. John Adams, *Dissertation on the Canon and Federal Law*, 1765, ibid., 83.

20. James Madison, "Second Annual Message to Congress," December 5, 1810, ibid., 86.

21. James Monroe, "Address to the Virginia General Assembly," December 6, 1801, quoted in Harry Ammon, *James Monroe, the Quest for National Identity* (Charlottesville, VA: University of Virginia Press, 1990), 177.

22. Thomas Jefferson to William Charles Jarvis, September 28, 1820, in Andrew A. Lipscomb and Albert Ellery Bergh, *The Writings of Thomas Jefferson* (Washington, D.C.: Thomas Jefferson Memorial Association, 1903–1904), 15:276.

23. James Madison to George Washington, 1825, in Melton, *Quotable Founding Fathers*, 87.

24. Nathaniel Greene to Samuel Ward Jr., 1771, Richard K. Showman, ed., *The Papers of General Nathaniel Greene* (Chapel Hill, NC: University of North Carolina Press, 1976), 1:24.

25. James Madison to William Eustis, July 8, 1819, and to Reynolds Chapman, January 25, 1821, both in Melton, *Quotable Founding Fathers*, 161.

26. Thomas Jefferson to John Norvell, June 14, 1807, in Lipscomb and Bergh, *Writings of Thomas Jefferson*, 11:223.

27. Thomas Paine, *The American Crisis*, no. 3, April 19, 1777, in Eric Foner, ed., *Collected Writings* (Des Moines, IA: Library of America, 1995), 116.

28. Thomas Jefferson to John Norvell, June 14, 1807, in Lipscomb and Bergh, *Writings of Thomas* Jefferson, 11:222–26.

29. John Adams, 1819, *Travels in Canada and the United States in 1816 and 1817*, and John Quincy Adams, diary, November 9, 1822, both in Melton, *Quotable Founding Fathers*, 161.

30. David Freeman Hawke, *Benjamin Rush: Revolutionary Gadfly* (Indianapolis: Bobbs-Merrill, 1971), 297; Benjamin Rush, *The Autobiography of Benjamin Rush: His "Trav-*

els Through Life" Together with His Commonplace Book for 1789–1813, George W. Corner, ed. (Princeton, NJ: American Philosophical Society and Princeton University Press, 1948).

31. Hawke, *Benjamin Rush*, 297.

32. Ibid.

33. Larabee, *Papers of Benjamin Franklin*, 3:420–21.

34. Benjamin Franklin to Samuel Johnson, August 23, 1750, ibid., 4:41.

35. Ibid.

36. John Adams to Thomas Jefferson, October 28, 1813, in Lester J. Cappon, ed., *The Adams-Jefferson Letters: The Complete Correspondence Between Thomas Jefferson and Abigail and John Adams* (New York: Simon and Schuster, 1971), 443.

37. Samuel Phillips Payson, in Charles S. Hyneman and Donald S. Lutz, eds., *American Political Writing During the Founding Era* (Indianapolis: Free Press, 1983), 526–27.

38. Carl L. Bankston III, and Stephen J. Caldas, *Public Education—America's Civil Religion: A Social History* (New York: Teachers College Press, 2009), 22.

39. John Adams to Thomas Jefferson, June 22, 1815, in Cappon, *Adams-Jefferson Letters*, 446.

40. Bankston and Caldas, *Public Education*, 22–23; R. L. Church, *Education in the United States: An Interpretive History* (New York: Free Press, 1976).

41. Thomas Jefferson to George Wyeth, August 13, 1786, in Julian P. Boyd, ed., *The Papers of Thomas Jefferson* (Princeton, NJ: Princeton University Press, 1954), 10:244–45.

42. Robert Coram to George Washington, March 5, 1791, *The Papers of George Washington: Presidential Series*, 7:512–13, http://www.consource.org/index.asp?bid=582&fid=600&documentid=59011.

43. Benjamin Rush to Richard Price, May 25, 1786, in Butterfield, *Letters of Benjamin Rush*, 1:388.

44. Bankston and Caldas, *Public Education*, 23.

45. Samuel Harrison Smith, "Remarks on Education," 1798, in Frederick Rudolph, ed., *Essays on Education in the Early Republic* (Harvard: Belknap, 1965), 173.

46. Ibid., 176.

47. Ibid., 189.

48. Ibid., 194.

49. Ibid., 207.

50. Ibid., 222.

51. Samuel Knox, "An Essay on the Best System of Liberal Education," 1799, in Rudolph, *Essays on Education*, 326.

52. Ibid., 297.

53. Ibid., 352.

54. Bankston and Caldas, *Public Education*, 23.

55. Noah Webster, "On the Education of Youth in America," 1790, in Rudolph, *Essays on Education*, 66.

56. Ibid.

57. James Madison, *The Writings of James Madison, Comprising His Public Papers and His Private Correspondence . . .* , Gaillard Hunt, ed. (New York: G. P. Putnam's Sons, 1900), vol. 3. "Journal of the Constitutional Convention," 1787, http://oll.liberty fund.org/index.php?option=com_staticxt&staticfile=advanced_search.php. Madison's only revision was that Pinckney's draft did not give any protection for authors (vol. 9, "To W. A. DUER"), http://oll.libertyfund.org/title/1940/119395/2406272.

58. John Adams to Thomas Jefferson, June 22, 1815, in Cappon, *Adams-Jefferson Letters,* 446.

59. George Washington, "First Annual Address to Congress," January 8, 1790, in Fitzpatrick, *Writings of George Washington,* 30:494.

60. George Washington to John Adams, November 27, 1794, in James Parton, *Words of Washington* (Boston: Joseph Knight, 1871), 166.

61. George Washington, "Eighth Annual Address to Congress," December 7, 1796, ibid., 35:317.

62. George Washington to St. George Tucker, May 30, 1797, ibid., 35:458.

63. Fraser, *Between Church and State,* 23.

64. Ibid.

65. Ibid.

66. Ibid., 34.

67. Ibid., 36.

68. Ibid., 38.

69. Ibid.

70. Ibid., 137.

71. Ibid.

72. Bankston and Caldas, *Public Education,* 105.

73. Ibid., 109.

74. Charles Murray, *Losing Ground, American Social Policy, 1950–1980,* Tenth-Anniversary Edition (New York: Basic Books, 1994).

75. William C. Ringenberg, *The Christian College: A History of Protestant Higher Education in America,* 2nd ed. (Grand Rapids, MI: Baker Academic, 2006), 38.

76. Ibid., 39.

77. Ibid., 47.

78. Thus, authors such as Mark Whitten (*The Myth of Christian America* [Macon, GA: Smyth & Helwys, 1999], 2–4), insist that "the Founders did not intend to establish the United States of America as a Christian nation [and] the assertion that the United States . . . was founded as a 'Christian nation' is itself a myth." I have rebutted this in *48 Liberal Lies About American History (That You Probably Learned in School)* (New York: Sentinel, 2009), 72–77.

79. Joseph Story, *Commentaries on the Constitution of the United States,* quoted in William J. Federer, *The Original 13* (St. Louis, MO: Ameriresearch, 2007), 15.

80. Henry Mayer, *A Son of Thunder: Patrick Henry and the American Republic* (New York: Grove, 1991), 49.

81. George Washington to Joseph Willard, March 22, 1781, in Fizpatrick, *Writings of George Washington,* 21:352.

82.. George Washington to the trustees of Washington Academy, June 17, 1798, ibid., 36:293.

83. Thomas Jefferson to James Madison, September 20, 1785, in Boyd, *Papers of Thomas Jefferson,* 8:535.

84. Thomas Jefferson, "Traveling Notes for Mr. Rutledge and Mr. Shippen," June 3, 1788, in Lipscomb and Bergh, *Writings of Thomas Jefferson,* 17:290.

85. Melton, *Quotable Founding Fathers,* 26.

86. Ibid.

87. Ibid.

88. John Adams to Abigail Adams, February 28, 1789, in *The Letters of John Adams* (New York: Penguin, 2004), 378.

QUESTION #3: IS THE GOVERNMENT RESPONSIBLE FOR PROTECTING THE LAND AND THE ENVIRONMENT?

1. Thomas Jefferson to Samuel Kercheval, 1816, Andrew A. Lipscombe and Albert Ellery Bergh, eds., *The Writings of Thomas Jefferson* (Washington, D.C.: Thomas Jefferson Memorial Association, 1903–1904), 15:36.

2. Thomas Jefferson to Pierre Samuel Dupont de Nemours, 1816, ibid., 14:490.

3. Reverend Elisha Williams, *A Seasonable Plea,* 1744, in Buckner F. Melton Jr., *The Quotable Founding Fathers* (New York: Fall River Press, 2004), 284.

4. Ibid.

5. Thomas Jefferson to James Madison, October 28, 1785, in Julian P. Boyd, ed., *The Papers of Thomas Jefferson* (Princeton, NJ: Princeton University Press, 1950–), 8:682; John Lauritz Larson, "Jefferson's Union and the Problem of Internal Improvements," in Peter S. Onuf, ed., *Jeffersonian Legacies* (Charlottesville, VA: University of Virginia Press, 1993), 345.

6. Boyd, *Papers,* 1:329–44; Larson, "Jefferson's Union," 343.

7. Robert F. Berkofer Jr., "Jefferson, the Ordinance of 1784, and the Origins of the American Territorial System," *William and Mary Quarterly* 29, April 1972, 231–62.

8. Thomas Jefferson to James Madison, February 20, 1784, in Boyd, *Papers,* 6:547.

9. Thomas Jefferson to George Washington, March 15, 1784, in Boyd, *Papers,* 7:25. There is this amazing phrase in the Confederation Congress's language: all new states (created thereafter) "shall for ever remain a part of the United States of America. That in their persons, property and territory they [the governments] shall be subject to the government of the United states [*sic*] in Congress assembled, and to the Articles of confederation [*sic*] in all those cases to which the original states shall

be so subject." This clause explicitly prohibits secession as early as 1784 and explicitly subjects all "new" states (certainly at least including Florida, Texas, Arkansas, Mississippi, Louisiana, Alabama, and Tennessee, or more than half of the Confederacy) to the Constitution and to Congress. Whatever "pact" neo-Confederates think the original constitutional compact comprised, it absolutely couldn't possibly have permitted the secession of the remaining states. Thus, because by that time Jefferson was shaping the Confederation Congress's wording, it was essentially Thomas Jefferson *himself* who discarded the prospect of secession!

10. Thomas Jefferson to Elbridge Gerry, November 11, 1784, ibid., 7:502; to Adams, May 16, 1777, ibid., 2:18–19; and his annotations to a copy of the Articles of Confederation, ibid., 1:177–82, cited in Larson, "Jefferson's Union," 347.

11. Worthington C. Ford et al., eds., *Journals of the Continental Congress, 1774–1789* (Washington, D.C.: Government Printing Office, 1904–1937), 2:196.

12. Hernando de Soto, *The Mystery of Capital* (New York: Basic Books, 2003).

13. Thomas Jefferson, "Fourth Annual Message to Congress," November 8, 1804, in Richard Holland Johnson, *The Writings of Thomas Jefferson* (Washington, D.C.: Thomas Jefferson Memorial Association, 1907), 365–69.

14. Larson, "Jefferson's Union," 357.

15. Thomas Jefferson, "Fifth Annual Message to Congress," December 3, 1805, in Johnson, *Writings of Thomas Jefferson*, 375–79.

16. Ibid.

17. Melton, *Quotable Founding Fathers*, 284.

18. Merrill Jensen, *The Articles of Confederation: An Interpretation of the Social-Constitutional History of the American Revolution, 1774–1781* (Madison, WI: University of Wisconsin Press, 1948); R. B. Bernstein, "Parliamentary Principles, American Realities: The Continental and Confederation Congresses, 1774–1789," in Kenneth R. Bowling and Donald R. Kennon, eds., *Inventing Congress: Origins & Establishment of First Federal Congress* (Athens, OH: United States Capitol Historical Society, 1999), 76–108.

19. Jonathan Hughes and Louis P. Cain, *American Economic History*, 4th ed. (New York: HarperCollins, 1994), 87.

20. Thomas Jefferson to James Madison, September 6, 1789, in Boyd, *Papers,* 15:392–97.

21. Ibid.

22. Bernard H. Siegan, *Property and Freedom: The Constitution, the Courts, and Land-Use Regulation* (New Brunswick, NJ: Transaction Publishers, 1997), 15; Stanley N. Katz, "Thomas Jefferson and the Right to Property in Revolutionary America," *Journal of Law and Economy* 19, October 1976, 467–88.

23. James Madison, remarks in the *National Gazette,* March 29, 1792, in Saul K. Padover, ed., *The Complete Madison* (New York: Harper, 1953), 267–68.

24. Ibid., 268–69.

25. William M. Treanor, "The Origins and Original Significance of the Just Compensation Clause of the Fifth Amendment," *Yale Law Journal* 94 (1983): 694, 710.

26. Madison quoted in Siegan, *Property and Freedom,* 14.

27. John Adams, "Thoughts on Government," 1776, in Melton, *Quotable Founding Fathers,* 284.

28. John Adams, "A Defense of the American Constitutions, 1787, ibid., 285.

29. Noah Webster, "An Examination of the Leading Principles of the Federal Constitution," October 17, 1787, ibid., 285.

30. Max Farrand, ed., *The Records of the Federal Convention of 1787* (New Haven, CT: Yale University Press, 1913), 450.

31. John Locke, *Two Treatises of Government,* Peter Laslett, ed. (Cambridge, MA: Cambridge University Press, 1960), section 124, quoted in Siegan, *Property and Freedom,* 16.

32. Ibid., 17.

33. Ibid.

34. Ibid., 25.

35. Ibid.

36. Herman Schwartz, *Property Rights and the Constitution: Will the Ugly Duckling Become a Swan?* (Washington, D.C.: Washington Institute Press, 1987), 11.

37. Richard A. Epstein, *Takings: Private Property and the Power of Eminent Domain* (Cambridge, MA: Harvard University Press, 1985), 168.

38. Ibid., 169.

39. Siegan, *Property and Freedom,* 30

40. Karen R. Merrill, *Public Lands and Political Meaning: Ranchers, the Government, and the Property Between Them* (Berkeley, CA: University of California Press, 2002). For variations on these debates, see James Willard Hurst, *Law and the Conditions of Freedom in the Nineteenth-Century United States* (Madison, WI: University of Wisconsin Press, 1964). One of the most recent violations of private property rights came in the *Kelo v. New London* decision, discussed at length in Carla T. Main, *Bulldozed: "Kelo," Eminent Domain, and the American Lust for Land* (New York: Encounter Books, 2007).

41. See Merrill, *Public Lands and Political Meaning,* passim.

42. Robert L. Glicksman and George Cameron Coggins, *Modern Public Land Law in a Nutshell,* 3rd ed. (St. Paul, MN: Thomson/West Publishing, 1995), 1–2.

43. Joseph P. Overton, "Does Giving Government Unlimited Power Really Protect the Environment?" Mackinac Center, January 9, 2001, http://www.mackinac.org/3202.

44. Larry Schweikart, *The Entrepreneurial Adventure: A History of Business in the United States* (Fort Worth, TX: Harcourt, 2000), 469.

45. Thomas D. Hopkins, "A Guide to the Regulatory Landscape," *Jobs & Capital* 4 (Fall 1995): 28–31. "Does Giving Government Unlimited Power Really Protect the Environment?" Mackinac Center, January 9, 2001, http://www.mackinac.org/3202.

46. Jack B. Seinstein, "Why Protect the Environment for Others?" *St. John's Law Review,* April 1, 2003, http://www.allbusiness.com/legal/laws-government-regulations-environmental/994165-1.html; Edith Brown Weiss, *In Fairness to Future Generations:*

International Law, Common Patrimony, and Intergenerational Equity (Boston: Brill/ Hotei, 1989).

47.   J. R. Dunn, "Rachel Carson and the Deaths of Millions," *American Thinker,* May 25, 2007,   http://www.americanthinker.com/2007/05/rachel_carson_and_the_deaths _o.html.

48.   Speech by Maurice Strong at 1992 UN Rio Earth Summit, *Deweere Report,* August 2009, vol. 15, issue 8, 3; V. H. Heywood, ed., *Global Biodiversity Assessment* (Cambridge, MA: Cambridge University Press, 1995), 350–51, 728–30, 767, and 782.

49.   Heywood, *Global Biodiversity Assessment,* 779.

QUESTION #4: IS THE HEALTH OF THE PEOPLE CONSIDERED PART OF THE "GENERAL WELFARE"?

1.   "Full Texts of Health Care Summit Opening Remarks: Obama, Alexander, Pelosi, Reid" (updated), February 25, 2010, http://latimesblogs.latimes.com/washing ton/2010/02/obama-lamar-alexander-healthcare-texts.html.

2.   "Health Care Summit," February 25, 2010, http://www.huffingtonpost.com/2010 /02/25/health-care-summit-openin_n_476650.html.

3.   "Kennedy on Health Care, 1978," http://www.youtube.com/watch?v=LhYtMmw9OVk.

4.   "Massachusetts Faces a Test on Health Care," *New York Times,* November 25, 2007.

5.   Marc Lalonde, *A New Perspective on the Health of Canadians* (Ottawa, Canada: Government of Canada, 1975).

6.   John Knowles, "The Responsibility of the Individual," *Daedalus* (Winter 1979): 80.

7.   Joseph Califano, "Introduction," *Healthy People: The Surgeon General's Report on Health Promotion and Disease Prevention* (Washington, D.C.: U.S. Government Printing Office, 1979), ix.

8.   Cited in Dan E. Beauchamp, "The State, the Individual, and the Common Good: The Constitutional Roots of Public Health," in *Health Promotion: Ethical and Social Dilemmas of Government Policy,* National Center for Health Services Research, no. SO4522.

9.   Norman H. Clark, *Deliver Us from Evil* (Boston: W. W. Norton, 1976), notes that, in fact, some "public health" did improve, particularly liver-related diseases and, obviously, alcoholism.

10.   "Seat Belts Save Lives," http://www.car-accidents.com/pages/seat_belts.html; R. Rutledge et al., "The Cost of Not Wearing Seat Belts: A Comparison of Outcome in 3396 Patients," *Annals of Surgery* 217 (February 199): 122–27.

11.   "Palin Paints Picture of 'Obama Death Panel' Giving Thumbs Down to Trig," http://blogs.abcnews.com/politicalpunch/2009/08/palin-paints-picture-of-obama -death-panel-giving-thumbs-down-to-trig.html.

12.   Thomas Paine quoted in Buckner F. Melton, Jr., ed., *The Quotable Founding Fathers* (New York: Fall River Press, 2004), 137.

13. Ibid., 277.

14. Waverly Root and Richard de Rochemont, *Eating in America: A History* (Hopewell, NJ: Ecco Press, 1995), 90.

15. John C. Miller, *Origins of the American Revolution* (Boston: Little Brown and Company, 1943); Robert Middlekauf, *The Glorious Cause: The American Revolution, 1763–1789* (New York: Oxford University Press, 2007).

16. Robert J. Chaffin, "The Townshend Acts Crisis, 1767–1770," in Jack P. Greene and J. R. Pole, eds., *The Blackwell Encyclopedia of the American Revolution* (Malden, MA: Blackwell, 1999); Peter D. G.. Thomas, *The Townshend Duties Crisis: The Second Phase of the American Revolution, 1767–1733* (Oxford: Oxford University Press, 1987); Oliver M. Dickerson, *The Navigation Acts and the American Revolution* (Philadelphia: University of Pennsylvania Press, 1951); Merrill Jensen, *The Founding of a Nation: A History of the American Revolution, 1763–1776* (New York: Oxford University Press, 1979).

17. "Debate in Virginia Ratifying Convention," June 15, 1788, in "The Founders Constitution," http://press-pubs.uchicago.edu/founders/documents/a1_9_1s14.html.

18. William H. Fowler, *Samuel Adams: Radical Puritan* (New York: Longman, 1997), 51–52.

19. Jefferson to Thomas Appleton, January 14, 1816, in "The Thomas Jefferson Papers Series 1, General Correspondence, 1651–1827," http://memory.loc.gov/cgi-bin/amp age?collId=mtj1&fileName=mtj1page048.db&recNum=760. Note the phrase often misquoted in other compilations of Jefferson's writings as "necessity of life."

20. Thomas Jewett, "The Healthful Habits of Thomas Jefferson," *Early America Review,* Winter 2006, http://www.earlyamerica.com/review/winter2006/health.html.

21. Ibid.

22. "The Order and the Economy of the House," Monticello official Web site, http://www.monticello.org/jefferson/dayinlife/dining/dig.html.

23. "Seated on My Throne in the Kitchen," Monticello official Web site, http://www.monticello.org/jefferson/dayinlife/dining/dig.html.

24. Root and Rochemont, *Eating in America,* 94.

25. Thomas Jewett, "The Healthful Habits of Thomas Jefferson."

26. Root and Rochemont, *Eating in America,* 95.

27. "Dined at the President's," Monticello official Web site, http://www.monticello.org/jefferson/dayinlife/dining/home.html.

28. Root and Rochemont, *Eating in America,* 115.

29. Ibid., 424.

30. "Faunal Remains," George Washington's Mount Vernon, http://www.mountvernon.org/visit/plan/index.cfm/pid/753/.

31. Ibid.

32. See, for example, "Wainerights Acct of Non-naturals—1 vol." (Jeremiah Waine-

wright, *A Mechanical Account of the Non-naturals: Being a Brief Explication of the Changes Made in Humane Bodies, by Air, Diet, &c.* London: np, 1707.)

33. George Washington to John Robinson, November 9, 1756, and to Robert Dinwiddie, April 29, 1757, in "The Papers of George Washington," digital edition, http://rotunda.upress.virginia.edu:8080/pgwde/dflt.xqy?keys=search-Col04d3&hi=diet.

34. Edmond Atkin to George Washington, July 20, 1757, ibid.

35. George Washington to Robert Dinwiddie, in John C. Fitzpatrick, ed., *The Writings of George Washington from the Original Manuscript Sources, 1745–1799* (Washington, D.C.: Government Printing Office, 1940), 1:50.

36. "General Orders," July 26, 1775, ibid., 5:340.

37. Ibid.

38. "General Orders: Headquarters, Cambridge," November 22, 1775, ibid., 4:109.

39. George Washington to Horatio Gates, September 1, 1777, ibid., 9:154.

40. George Washington to Alexander McDougall, May 23, 1777, in "The Papers of George Washington," digital edition.

41. George Washington to the Continental Congress Committee to inquire into the state of the army, July 19, 1777, ibid.

42. George Washington to Joseph Reed, May 28, 1780, in William Allen, ed., *George Washington: A Collection* (Indianapolis, IN: Liberty Fund, 1988), 149.

43. George Washington, "Circular to the States," August 27, 1780, ibid., 154–55.

44. Ibid, 155.

45. George Washington to Horatio Gates, September 1, 1777, in "The Papers of George Washington," digital edition.

46. "General Orders: Headquarters, Cambridge," May 16, 1782, in Fitzpatrick, *Writings of George Washington,* 24:261.

47. John R. Bumgarner, *The Health of the Presidents: The 41 United States Presidents Through 1993 from a Physician's Point of View* (Jefferson, NC: MacFarland & Company, 1994), 10.

48. Ibid., 12; John Ferling and Lewis E. Braverman, "John Adams's Health Reconsidered," *William and Mary Quarterly* 15 (1998): 83–104.

49. George Morgan, *The True Patrick Henry* (Philadelphia: J. B. Lippincott, 1907), 404.

50. Ben Franklin from *Poor Richard, 1742,* in Leonard W. Labaree. ed., *The Papers of Benjamin Franklin, 1706–1783* (New Haven, CT: Yale University Press, 1960), 2:340–41.

51. Ibid., 341.

52. Benjamin Franklin to Deborah Franklin, December 1, 1772, in Larabee, *Papers of Benjamin Franklin,* 19:395.

53. Melton, *Quotable Founding Fathers,* 207.

54. Root and Rochemont, *Eating in America,* 115.

55. Ibid., 358.

56. Ibid., 363.

57. Ibid., 365.

58. Ibid.

59. Ibid., 366.

60. Ibid., 368.

61. Edmund Contoski, *Makers and Takers: How Wealth and Progress Are Made and How They Are Taken Away or Prevented* (Minneapolis, MN: American Liberty Publishers, 1997), 163.

62. Ibid.

63. U.S. Congress, House Committee on Agriculture, *Hearings on the So-Called "Beveridge Amendment" to the Agriculture Appropriation Bill,* 59th Cong., 1st Sess. (Washington, D.C.: Government Printing Office, 1906), 194.

64. Fran Hawthorne, *Inside the FDA: The Business and Politics Behind the Drugs We Take and the Food We Eat* (New York: John Wiley, 2005), 37.

65. Frederick W. Allen, *Secret Formula* (New York: HarperBusiness, 1994), 28–66; Mark Pendergast, *For God, Country, and Coca-Cola: The Unauthorized History of the Great American Soft Drink and the Company That Makes It* (New York: Collier, 1993); Larry Schweikart and Lynne Pierson Doti, *American Entrepreneur* (New York: Amacom, 2009), 236.

66. Bette Hileman, "Human Testing: 'Poison Squads' Tested Chemical Preservatives," *Chemical & Engineering News,* September 18, 2006, http://pubs.acs.org/cen/coverstory/84/8438coverbox.html.

67. Ibid.

68. Carol Lewis, "The 'Poison Squad' and the Advent of Food and Drug Regulation," *U.S. Food and Drug Administration Consumer Magazine,* November–December 2002, http://www.toxicology.org/gp/21_PoisonSquadFDA.pdf.

69. Norman H. Clark, *Deliver Us from Evil: An Interpretation of American Prohibition* (New York: W. W. Norton, 1976); John C. Burnham, *Bad Habits: Drinking, Smoking, Taking Drugs, Gambling, Sexual Misbehavior and Swearing in American History* (New York: New York University Press, 1994).

70. Larry Schweikart, *Seven Events That Made America America* (New York: Sentinel, 2010).

71. Gary Taubes, *Good Calories, Bad Calories* (New York: Knopf, 2007).

72. Benjamin Rush, *The Autobiography of Benjamin Rush, His "Travels Through Life" Together with his Commonplace Book for 1789–1813,* George W. Corner, ed. (Princeton, NJ: American Philosophical Society and Princeton University Press, 1948), "Commonplace Book" entry for January 1, 1798, 240.

73. "New York Considers Legislation to Ban Salt in Restaurants," March 9, 2010, http://consumerfreedom.com/news_detail.cfm/h/4122-new-york-considers-legislation-to-ban-salt-in-restaurants.

74. Thomas Jefferson, *Autobiography,* 1821, in Andrew A. Lipscombe and Albert Ellery

Bergh, eds., *The Writings of Thomas Jefferson* (Washington, D.C.: Thomas Jefferson Memorial Association, 1903–1904), 1:121.

QUESTION #5: SHOULD THE GOVERNMENT STIMULATE THE ECONOMY AND OTHERWISE ENSURE FULL EMPLOYMENT?

1. Benjamin Franklin to Peter Collinson, May 9, 1753, http://www.marksquotes.com/Founding-Fathers/Franklin/index2.htm.
2. Richard Sylla, Robert E. Wright, and David J. Cowen, "Alexander Hamilton, Central Banker: Crisis Management During the U.S. Financial Panic of 1792," *Business History Review* 83 (Spring 2009): 61–84 (quotation on 63); Charles Kindleberger, *Manias, Panics and Crashes: A History of Financial Crises* (New York: John Wiley, 2005); and Edwin J. Perkins, *American Public Finance and Financial Services, 1700–1815* (Columbus, OH: Ohio State University Press, 1997, 1994).
3. Albert Gallatin to Thomas Jefferson, December 1807, in Henry Adams, *The Writings of Albert Gallatin* (Philadelphia: J. B. Lippincott, 1879), 1:368.
4. Murray N. Rothbard, *The Panic of 1819: Reactions and Policies* (New York: Columbia University Press, 1962), 15.
5. Ibid., 27.
6. Ibid.
7. James Monroe, Second Inaugural Address, March 5, 1821, http://www.vlib.us/amdocs/texts/09monr2.htm.
8. "Cumberland Road," http://www.econlib.org/library/YPDBooks/Lalor/llCy338.html.
9. Rothbard, *The Panic of 1819,* 20.
10. Ibid.
11. Ibid., 21.
12. Ibid., 34.
13. Ibid., 163.
14. Ibid., 165.
15. James L. Huston, *The Panic of 1857 and the Coming of the Civil War* (Baton Rouge, LA: Louisiana State University Press, 1987), 25.
16. *New York Times,* October 23 and 27, 1857.
17. New York *Herald,* November 3, 1857, and New York *Daily Tribune,* November 3, 6, and 7, 1857.
18. Huston, *The Panic of 1857,* chapter 3, passim; Charles Calormiris and Larry Schweikart, "The Panic of 1857: Causes, Transmission, and Containment," *Journal of Economic History* 51 (December 1990): 807–34. Huston gets the causes of the panic wrong, but correctly analyzes the impact.
19. William Wirt, *The Life and Character of Patrick Henry* (Chicago: John C. Winston, ca. 1912).

20. George Willison, *Patrick Henry and His World* (New York: Doubleday, 1969), 24–45.

21. Hamilton quoted in Ron Chernow, *Alexander Hamilton* (New York: Penguin Press, 2004), 30–31.

22. Ibid., 31.

23. Joseph J. Ellis, *His Excellency: George Washington* (New York: Vintage, 2005), 9.

24. George Washington, letter to Benjamin Harrison, October 10, 1784, http://www .marksquotes.com/Founding-Fathers/Washington/.

25. George Washington, "General Orders," April 18, 1783, and an address to Congress on resigning his commission, December 23, 1783, http://www.marksquotes.com/ Founding-Fathers/Washington/.

26. Richard Brookheiser, *George Washington on Leadership* (New York: Basic Books, 2008), 57–58.

27. George Washington, letter to William Gordon, October 15, 1797, in Buckner F. Melton Jr., *The Quotable Founding Fathers* (New York: Fall River Press, 2004), 190.

28. Brookheiser, *George Washington on Leadership*, 55.

29. Harlow Giles Under, *The Last Founding Father: James Monroe and a Nation's Call to Greatness* (New York: Da Capo Press, 2009), 13.

30. Benjamin Rush, *The Autobiography of Benjamin Rush: His "Travels Through Life" Together with His Commonplace Book for 1789–1813,* George W. Corner, ed. (Princeton, NJ: American Philosophical Society and Princeton University Press, 1948), 38.

31. Ibid.

32. Ibid.

33. David Freeman Hawke, *Benjamin Rush: Revolutionary Gadfly* (Indianapolis, IN: Bobbs-Merrill, 1971), 298.

34. Page Smith, *John Adams: Vol. 1:1735–1784* (Garden City, NY: Doubleday, 1962), 30–31. Adams had so little to say about physical labor or work that there are no index entries for either subject in Page Smith's two-volume biography.

35. Gertrude Himmelfarb, *The Idea of Poverty* (New York: Knopf, 1984), 23–41.

36. Adam Smith, *An Inquiry into the Nature and Causes of the Wealth of Nations*, Edwin Cannan, ed. (New York: Modern Library, 1937), 81.

37. Bagehot quoted in Himmelfarb, *The Idea of Poverty*, 43.

38. Smith, *Wealth of Nations*, 78–79.

39. Ibid., 11.

40. Ibid., 121–22.

41. Ibid.

42. See, for example, Robert Heilbroner, *The Worldly Philosophers* (New York: Simon & Schuster, 1986).

43. Smith, *Wealth of Nations*, 248, 740, 823.

44. Himmelfarb, *The Idea of Poverty*, 65.

45. Ibid., 66.

46. Ibid., 67.

47. Ibid., 68.

48. Ibid., 86; Henry Collins, introduction to Thomas Paine, *Rights of Man* (London: Penguin, 1969), 37; Eric Foner, *Tom Paine and Revolutionary America* (New York: Oxford University Press, 2004); Francis Canavan, "The Relevance of the Burke-Paine Controversy to American Thought," *Review of Politics* 49 (1987): 163–76, and his "The Burke-Paine Controversy," *Political Science Reviewer* 6 (1976): 389–420 (quotation on 403); and S. Maccoby, *English Radicalism, 1786–1832* (London: Allen & Unwin, 1955), 53.

49. Thomas Paine, *Rights of Man* (London: J. S. Jordan, 1791).

50. Benjamin Franklin, *Poor Richard's Almanac,* quoted in Melton, *Quotable Founding Fathers,* 202.

51. Jefferson quoted in ibid., 370.

52. Jefferson quoted in ibid., 157.

53. Benjamin Franklin, *Autobiography,* quoted in ibid., 189.

54. Michel Guillaume Jean de Crevecoeur, *Letters from an American Farmer,* quoted in ibid., 189.

55. Webster quoted in ibid., 190.

56. Thomas M. Doerflinger, *A Vigorous Spirit of Enterprise: Merchants and Economic Development in Revolutionary Philadelphia* (New York: W. W. Norton, 1986), 345.

57. John Spencer Basset, ed., *The Writings of Colonel William Byrd* (New York: B. Franklin, 1970); and Pierre Marambaud, *William Byrd of Westover, 1674–1744* (Charlottesville, VA: University Press of Virginia, 1971).

58. Basset, *The Writings of Colonel William Byrd,* 207–8.

59. Larry Schweikart, *The Entrepreneurial Adventure: A History of Business in the United States* (Fort Worth, TX: Harcourt, 2000), 41; John M. Dobson, *A History of American Enterprise* (Englewood Cliffs, NJ: Prentice-Hall, 1988), 24; *Paul Revere, Pioneer Industrialist,* pamphlet by Revere Copper and Brass Incorporated, n.d., ca. 1957.

60. Esther Forbes, *Paul Revere and the World He Lived In* (Boston: Houghton Mifflin, 1969), 377–97; Keith L. Bryant and Henry C. Dethloff, *A History of American Business,* 2nd ed. (Englewood Cliffs, NJ: Prentice-Hall, 1990), 43.

61. Dobson, *A History of American Enterprise,* 24.

62. Richard Walsh, "The Revolutionary Charleston Mechanic," in Stuart Bruchey, ed., *Small Business in American Life* (New York: Columbia University Press, 1980), 49–79.

63. Schweikart, *The Entrepreneurial Adventure,* 40.

QUESTION #6: DOES THE GOVERNMENT HAVE A
RESPONSIBILITY TO KEEP LARGE BUSINESSES SOLVENT
IN ORDER TO PROTECT AMERICAN INDUSTRY?

1. George Washington speech to Congress, January 8, 1790, http://www.not
    able-quotes.com/w/washington_george_vii.html.
2. Ron Chernow, *Alexander Hamilton* (New York: Penguin Press, 2007).
3. George Washington, "Farewell Address," 1796, http://avalon.law.yale.edu/18th_
    century/washing.asp.
4. George Washington to Governor Morris, December 22, 1795, in John C. Fitzpat-
    rick, ed., *The Writings of George Washington from the Original Manuscript Sources,
    1745–1799* (Washington, D.C.: Government Printing Office, 1931–1944), 34: 401.
5. Chernow, *Alexander Hamilton,* 375.
6. Ibid., 378.
7. Larry Schweikart and Lynne Pierson Doti, *American Entrepreneur* (New York: Ama-
    com, 2009), chapter 3, passim.
8. Richard Sylla, Robert E. Wright, and David J. Cowen, "Alexander Hamilton, Cen-
    tral Banker: Crisis Management during the U.S. Financial Panic of 1792," *Business
    History Review* 83 (Spring 2009): 64–86.
9. Richard H. Timberlake Jr., *The Origins of Central Banking in the United States*
    (Cambridge, MA: Harvard University Press, 1978); Fritz Redlich, *The Molding of
    American Banking: Men and Ideas* (New York: Johnson Reprint, 1968).
10. Albert Gallatin, *Reports on Roads and Canals,* 10th Cong., 1st sess., 1808, document
    no. 250, reprinted in *New American State Papers—Transportation,* 1 (Wilmington,
    DE: Scholarly Resources, 1972).
11. Burton W. Folsom Jr., *Myth of the Robber Barons* (Hearndon, VA: Young America's
    Foundation, 1991), 5.
12. Ibid., 6.
13. Ibid.
14. Ibid., 9.
15. Burton Folsom Jr., *The Empire Builders: How Michigan Entrepreneurs Helped Make
    America Great* (Traverse City, MI: Rhodes & Easton, 1998), 10.
16. Ibid., 26–27.
17. Harold Evans with Gail Buckland and David Lefer, *They Made America: From the
    Steam Engine to the Search Engine* (New York: Little, Brown, 2004), 20–36.
18. Burton Folsom Jr., *New Deal or Raw Deal? How FDR's Economic Legacy Has Dam-
    aged America* (New York: Threshold, 2008), 39.
19. Ibid., 175.
20. Ibid., 181.
21. Barry Ritholtz with Aaron Task, *Bailout Nation* (New York: John Wiley & Sons,
    2009), 29; Barrie A. Wigmore, "The Crash and Its Aftermath: A History of Secu-

rities Markets in the United States, 1929–1933," *Contributions in Economics and Economic History,* no. 58 (Westport, CT: Greenwood Publishing Group, 1985), 540.

22. Folsom, *New Deal or Raw Deal?,* 5.

23. Ibid., 35.

24. Ibid.

25. Ritholtz, *Bailout Nation,* 32.

26. Larry Schweikart, *The Entrepreneurial Adventure: A History of Business in the United States* (Fort Worth, TX: Harcourt, 2000), 72–75; Donald Hoke, *Ingenious Yankees: The Rise of the American System of Manufacturing in the Private Sector* (New York: Columbia, 1989). These conclusions are in sharp contrast to the traditional view presented by Merrit Roe Smith, *Harpers Ferry Armory and the New Technology* (Ithaca, NY: Cornell University Press, 1977), which holds that government should receive credit for the innovation in arms manufacturing.

27. William B. Edwards, *The Story of Colt's Revolver: The Biography of Col. Samuel Colt* (Harrisonburg, PA: Stackpole Co., 1953); William Hosely, *Colt: The Making of an American Legend* (Amherst, MA: University of Massachusetts Press, 1996).

28. William E. Birkhimer, *Historical Sketch of the Organization, Administration, Matérial and Tactics of the Artillery* (Washington, D.C.: United States Army, 1884); Albert Mancucy, *Artillery Through the Ages: A Short Illustrated History of Cannon, Emphasizing Types Used in America* (Washington, D.C.: Government Printing Office, 1855).

29. Schweikart, *Entrepreneurial Adventure,* 186.

30. Richard H. Bensel, *Yankee Leviathan: The Origins of Central State Authority in America, 1859–1877* (Cambridge: Cambridge University Press, 1990), 94–95.

31. Folsom, *Myth of the Robber Barons,* 17–39.

32. James K. Hickel, "The Chrysler Bail-out Bust," July 13, 1983, Heritage Foundation, *Backgrounder* #276, http://www.heritage.org/research/regulation/bg276.cfm.

33. Richard Mendel, "The First Chrysler Bail-out; the M-1 Tank," *Washington Monthly,* February 1987, http://findarticles.com/p/articles/mi_m1316/is_v19/ai_4696991/?tag=content;col1.

34. Ritholtz, *Bailout Nation,* 157.

35. Ibid.

36. James Monroe, seventh annual message to Congress, December 2, 1823, http://www.infoplease.com/ipa/A0900137.html.

37. Adam Smith, *An Inquiry into the Nature and Causes of the Wealth of Nations* (London: Joseph Shield Nicholson, T. Nelson and Sons, 1884), 142.

38. Alexander Hamilton, *The Farmer Refuted,* February 1775, in Harold C. Syrett, *The Papers of Alexander Hamilton* (New York: Columbia University Press, 1961–1987), 1:126.

QUESTION #7: DOESN'T THE GOVERNMENT HAVE A SPECIFIC STAKE IN PROTECTING THE MONEY SUPPLY AND THE BANKING SYSTEM?

1. John B. Egger, "Alexander Hamilton, Economist," 2006, http://docs.google.com /viewer?a=v&q=cache:3iwUr0Fw_78J:pages.towson.edu/egger/ah_economist _200605011516a.pdf+Alexander+Hamilton+and+Adam+Smith&hl=en&gl=us& pid=bl&srcid=ADGEESg26_rUYdv0p3GF6gCOff9tlSRUKzIaGeRLfXTul0s 9VQFCtLziiWKIds1s588gsEt3dCcsn3Z-jUwXf1Z0h3bQNNBvoBQLB c05WR3icvKvveoB64i3IRch6_pnYBrtxMggsiT0&sig=AHIEtbT7XdRIzB4lPirsp SOiPNck_8cECA, 13.

2. Ibid.

3. John Jay Knox, *A History of Banking in the United States* (New York: Bradford Rhodes, 1900), 40. Some confusion existed among the officers as to whether the bank operated as a state or a national bank. Thomas Smith, the president of the Bank of North America, applying for a charter as a national bank in 1864, claimed the bank always had a national charter (33).

4. Larry Schweikart, *The Entrepreneurial Adventure: A History of Business in the United States* (Fort Worth, TX: Harcourt, 2000), 61; E. James Ferguson, *The Power of the Purse: A History of American Public Finance, 1776–1790* (Chapel Hill, NC: University of North Carolina Press, 1961).

5. B. R. Burg, "The Bank of North America," in Larry Schweikart, ed., *The Encyclopedia of American Business History and Biography: Banking and Finance to 1913* (New York: Facts on File, 1993), 33–35 (quotation on 34); Lawrence Lewis, *A History of the Bank of North America* (Philadelphia: J. B. Lippincott, 1982).

6. Knox, *A History of Banking in the United States,* 32.

7. Richard Sylla, "Political Economy of US Financial Development," 2005, http://docs .google.com/viewer?a=v&q=cache:Sjvbefb4JrkJ:www.cfr.org/content/thinktank/ Depression/Sylla_2.pdf+Hamilton+immediate+interest+of+the+monied+men&hl =en&gl=us&sig=AHIEtbS0Cw9QG5kQDSidNsxQID_SPJt9HA.

8. Richard Sylla, Robert E. Wright, and David J. Cowen, "Alexander Hamilton, Central Banker: Crisis Management During the U.S. Financial Panic of 1792," *Business History Review* 83 (Spring 2009): 61–84.

9. Ibid., 66.

10. Ibid., 67. See also Richard Sylla and Jack W. Wilson, "Sinking Funds as Credible Commitments: Two Centuries of U.S. National-Debt Experience," *Japan and the World Economy* 11 (April 1999): 199–222.

11. Quoted in Sylla et al., "Alexander Hamilton," 74.

12. Ibid., 81.

13. Jeffrey Rogers Hummel, "First Bank of the United States," in Schweikart, *Encyclopedia of Business History and Biography,* 181–83. See also James O. Wettereau, "New

Light on the First Bank of the United States," *Pennsylvania Magazine of History and Biography* 61 (July 1937): 236–85; and John Thom Holdsworth, *The First Bank of the United States* (Washington, D.C.: National Monetary Commission, 1910).

14. Thomas J. DiLorenzo, "It's Time to End Hamilton's Curse," http://www.lewrock well.com/dilorenzo/dilorenzo136.html. Of course, it was Thomas Jefferson, not John Adams, Alexander Hamilton, or George Washington—whom DiLorenzo despises—who actually engaged in "military adventurism" with great success in the Barbary Wars.

15. See Lawrence H. White, *Free Banking in Britain: Theory, Experience, and Debate, 1800–1845* (Cambridge: Cambridge University Press, 1984); and Murray N. Roth-bard, *The Mystery of Banking*, 2nd ed. (Auburn, AL: Ludwig von Mises Institute, 2008), 269–291.

16. Hummel, "First Bank of the United States," 182.

17. Thomas Jefferson to John Taylor, 1816, in Andrew A. Lipscombe and Albert Ellery Bergh, eds., *The Writings of Thomas Jefferson* (Washington, D.C.: Thomas Jefferson Memorial Association, 1903–1904), 15:23.

18. Edwin Perkins, *American Public Finance and Financial Services, 1700–1815* (Colum-bus, OH: Ohio State University Press, 1994); Benjamin Klubes, "The First Federal Congress and the First National Bank: A Case Study in Constitutional History," *Journal of the Early American Republic*, 10 (1990):19–41; Fritz Redlich, "The Mold-ing of American Banking" (New York: Johnson Reprint, 1968); and Richard Sylla, "U.S. Securities Markets and the Banking System, 1790–1840," *Federal Reserve Bank of St. Louis Review* 80 (1998).

19. Bray Hammond, *Banks and Politics in America from the Revolution to the Civil War* (Princeton, NJ: Princeton University Press, 1957); and Peter Temin, *The Jacksonian Economy* (New York: W. W. Norton, 1969).

20. See Larry Schweikart, *Banking in the American South from the Age of Jackson to Reconstruc-tion* (Baton Rouge, LA: Louisiana State University Press, 1997); Richard H. Timberlake Jr., *The Origins of Central Banking in the United States* (Cambridge, MA: Harvard Uni-versity Press, 1978); Murray N. Rothbard, *The Panic of 1819: Reactions and Policies* (New York: Columbia University Press, 1962); and Hugh Rockoff, "Money, Prices, and Banks in the Jacksonian Era," in Robert Fogel and Stanley Engerman, eds., *The Reinterpretation of American Economic History* (New York: Harper & Row, 1971).

21. Larry Schweikart and Lynne Doti, *American Entrepreneur* (New York: Amacom, 2009), 156–58.

22. Richard H. Timberlake, "Federal Reserve Act," in Schweikart, *Encyclopedia of Amer-ican Business History and Biography,* 174–76 (quotation on 174).

23. Ibid.

24. Milton Friedman and Anna Jacobsen Schwartz, *A Monetary History of the United States, 1867–1960* (Princeton, NJ: Princeton University Press, 1963).

25. Even Friedman's coauthor, Anna Schwartz, argued that "a more important role [than the Bank of United States' failure] was played by the failure of [Caldwell & Company]." But, she noted, "what is not in dispute is that the banking panic late in that year changed the monetary character of the business cycle then under way." (Anna J. Schwartz, "Bank of United States," in Larry Schweikart, *Encyclopedia of American Business History and Biography: Banking and Finance Since 1913* [New York: Facts on File, 1990], 22–25.)

26. Ibid., 25.

27. Eugene Nelson White, *The Regulation and Reform of the American Banking System, 1900–1929* (Princeton, NJ: Princeton University Press, 1983).

28. Allan H. Meltzer, *A History of the Federal Reserve,* vol. 1:1913–1951 (Chicago: University of Chicago Press, 2004), 4–5.

29. Barry Eichengreen, *Golden Fetters: The Gold Standard and the Great Depression, 1919–1939* (New York: Oxford University Press, 1992).

30. Larry Schweikart, "Penn Square/Continental Illinois Bank Failures," in Schweikart, *Encyclopedia of American Business History and Biography,* 349–51; Irvine H. Sprague, *Bailout: An Insider's Account of Bank Failures and Bank Rescues* (New York: Basic Books, 1986).

31. George Washington to Samuel Washington in John C. Fitzpatrick, ed., *The Writings of George Washington from the Original Manuscript Sources* (Washington, D.C.: Government Printing Office, 1931–1944), 35:498.

32. James Madison to Clarkson Crolius, December 1819, in Galiard Hunt, ed., *The Writings of James Madison: 1819–1836* (New York: G. P. Putnam's Sons, 1910), 9:16.

33. Ibid.

34. James Monroe, speech to the Virginia Constitutional Ratifying Convention, June 20, 1788, quoted in Buckner F. Melton Jr., ed., *The Quotable Founding Fathers* (New York: Fall River Press, 2004), 81.

35. Anthony Chan, "The Savings and Loan Crisis," in Schweikart, *Encyclopedia of American Business History and Biography,* 378–82; George Benston and George Kaufman, "Understanding the Savings and Loan Debacle," *The Public Interest* 99 (Spring 1990): 79–95; Lawrence J. White, "A Cautionary Tale of Deregulation Gone Awry: The S&L Debacle," *Southern Economic Journal* 59 (January 1993): 496–514, and his *The S&L Debacle: Public Policy Lessons for Bank and Thrift Regulation* (New York: Oxford University Press, 1991); and Charles Calomiris and Eugene N. White, "The Origins of Federal Deposit Insurance," in Claudia Goldin and Gary D. Liebecap, eds., *The Regulated Economy: A Historical Approach to Political Economy* (Chicago: University of Chicago Press, 1994).

36. Larry Schweikart, *The Entrepreneurial Adventure,* 444.

37. Vernon L. Smith, "The Clinton Housing Bubble," *Wall Street Journal,* December 18, 2007.

38. Carol D. Leonnig, "How HUD Mortgage Policy Fed the Crisis: Subprime Loans Labeled 'Affordable,'" *Washington Post,* June 10, 2008.

39. Ibid.

40. "New Agency Proposed to Oversee Freddie Mac and Fannie Mae," *New York Times,*
     September 11, 2003.

41. Ibid.

42. "Bailout Is a Windfall to Banks, if Not to Borrowers," *New York Times,* January 17,
     2009.

43. "Officials Say Tracking Bailout Money Difficult," *Deseret News,* January 1, 2009.

QUESTION #8: SHOULD THE UNITED STATES TOLERATE HIGH DEFICITS AND A LARGE NATIONAL DEBT?

1.   For a discussion of the economic world of the day, see Christine Rider, *An Introduc-
     tion to Economic History* (Cincinnati, OH: SouthWestern Publishing, 1995); Robert
     B. Ekelund Jr. et al., *Sacred Trust: The Medieval Church as an Economic Firm* (New
     York: Oxford University Press, 1996); Henry W. Spiegel, *The Growth of Economic
     Thought* (New York: Prentice-Hall, 1971); and Jonathan R. T. Hughes, *The Vital
     Few: The Entrepreneurs and American Economic Progress* (New York: Oxford Univer-
     sity Press, 1986).

2.   Larry Schweikart and Lynne Pierson Doti, *American Entrepreneur* (New York: Ama-
     com, 2009), 24.

3.   John J. McCusker and Russel R. Menard, *The Economy of British America, 1607–
     1789* (Chapel Hill, NC: Institute of Early American History and the University of
     North Carolina Press, 1985).

4.   Saul K. Padover, *Jefferson* (New York: Harcourt, Brace, 1942), 232.

5.   Ibid., 235.

6.   Ibid., 233.

7.   Quoted in ibid., 309.

8.   Thomas Jefferson to Alexander Donald, July 28, 1787, in Richard H. Johnston
     and Andrew Lipscomb, eds., *The Writings of Thomas Jefferson* (Washington, D.C.:
     Thomas Jefferson Memorial Association, 1907), 2:192.

9.   Thomas Jefferson to John Taylor, November 26, 1798, in ibid., 12:64–65.

10. Quoted in Padover, *Jefferson,* 310.

11. Thomas Jefferson to James Madison, September 6, 1789, in Julian P. Boyd et al.,
     eds., *The Papers of Thomas Jefferson* (Princeton, NJ: Princeton University Press,
     1950–), 15:392–97.

12. Ibid., 15:395.

13. Herbert Sloan, "The Earth Belongs in Usufruct to the Living," in Peter S. Onuf,
     ed., *Jeffersonian Legacies* (Charlottesville, VA: University Press of Virginia, 1993),
     281–315.

14. Boyd, *Papers,* 15:396.

15. Sloan, "The Earth Belongs in Usufruct to the Living," 289.

16. Thomas Jefferson to Nicholas Lewis, July 29 and September 17, 1787, in Boyd, *Papers,* 11:135, 639–42; Myra L. Rich, "Speculations on the Significance of Debt: Virginia, 1781–1789," *Virginia Magazine of History and Biography,* 76 (1968): 301–17; T. H. Breen, *Tobacco Culture: The Mentality of the Great Tidewater Planters on the Eve of the Revolution* (Princeton, NJ: Princeton University Press, 1985); and Stephen Harold Hochman, "Thomas Jefferson: A Personal Financial History," Ph.D. dissertation, University of Virginia, 1987.

17. Willard Sterne Randall, *Thomas Jefferson: A Life* (New York: HarperCollins, 1994), 179.

18. James Madison to Thomas Jefferson, February 4, 1790, in William Hutchinson, ed., *The Papers of James Madison* (Chicago: University of Chicago Press, 1962), 13:18–21; James Madison, The Federalist, no. 49, February 2, 1788, in "The Founders' Constitution," http://press-pubs.uchicago.edu/founders/documents/a5s8.html.

19. Thomas Jefferson, second inaugural address, March 4, 1805, in Andrew A. Lipscomb and Albert Ellery Bergh, eds., *The Writings of Thomas Jefferson,* Memorial Edition (Washington, D.C.: Thomas Jefferson Memorial Association, 1903–1904), 3:375–83.

20. Larry Schweikart, *48 Liberal Lies About American History (That You Probably Learned in School)* (New York: Sentinel, 2009), 78–81; Larry Schweikart and Lynne Pierson Doti, *American Entrepreneur* (New York: Amacom, 2009), 82–83.

21. John Lauritz Larson, "Jefferson's Union and the Problem of Internal Improvements," in Onuf, *Jeffersonian Legacies,* 340–69.

22. Ibid., 341.

23. Benjamin Franklin, *Poor Richard's Almanac,* quoted in *The Autobiography of Benjamin Franklin* (New York: American Book Company, 1896), 198.

24. James Madison to Henry Lee, April 13, 1790, in Galliard Hunt, ed., *The Writings of James Madison, Comprising His Public Papers and Private Correspondence,* vol. 6 (New York: G. P. Putnam's Sons, 1906), 11.

25. Thomas Paine, *Common Sense* (Charleston, SC: Forgotten Books, 1942), 42.

26. Ron Chernow, *Alexander Hamilton* (New York: Penguin Press, 2007), 26.

27. Quoted in Buckner F. Melton Jr., ed., *The Quotable Founding Fathers* (New York: Fall River Press, 2004), 150.

28. Harold C. Syrett, *The Papers of Alexander Hamilton,* vol. 2 (New York: Columbia University Press, 1961), 244–45.

29. Alexander Hamilton in *Report Relative to a Provision for the Support of Public Credit,* in Syrett, *Papers,* 6:80–81.

30. Melton, *Quotable Founding Fathers,* 150.

31. Alexander Hamilton, "The Continentalist," July 4, 1782, in John Church Hamilton, ed., *The Works of Alexander Hamilton: Comprising His Correspondence,* vol. 2 (New York: C. Francis & Co., 1850), 84.

32. Ibid., 2:198.

33. Hamilton, *Report on Public Credit*, 6:106.

34. Ibid.

35. Clinton Rossiter, ed., *The Federalist Papers* (New York: Signet, 2003), Federalist no. 21.

36. Hamilton to the electors of the State of New York, March 1801, in http://www
     .marksquotes.com/Founding-Fathers/Hamilton.

37. The best discussion of these concepts remains the classic book by George Gilder,
     Wealth & Poverty (New York: Bantam Books, 1982).

38. Alexander Hamilton, "The Farmer Refuted," February 5, 1775, in Hamilton, *Works
     of Alexander Hamilton*, 2:84.

39. Quoted in Melton, *Quotable Founding Fathers*, 276.

40. Alexander Hamilton to Robert Morris, April 30, 1781, in Syrett, *Papers*, 2:618.

41. Alexander Hamilton in *Opinion on the Constitutionality of an Act to Establish a Bank*,
     February 23, 1791, in Syrett, *Papers*, 7:126.

42. Ibid.

43. George Washington, message to the House of Representatives, December 3, 1793,
     http://www.marksquotes.com/Founding-Fathers/Washington/index3.htm.

44. George Washington to James Welch, April 7, 1799, in John C. Fitzpatrick, ed., *The
     Writings of George Washington, 1732–1799*, vol. 37 (Washington, D.C.: Government
     Printing Office, 1939–1944), 177.

45. George Washington, "Farewell Address," 1796, http://avalon.law.yale.edu/18th_
     century/washing.asp.

46. Ibid.

47. Ibid.

48. Ibid.

49. Alexander Hamilton to James Duane, September 3, 1780, in Syrett, *Papers*, 2:414.

50. Ibid.

51. William Penn, in Samuel McPherson Janney, *The Life of William Penn: With Selec-
     tions from His Correspondence and Autobiography* (Philadelphia: Friends' Book As-
     sociation, 1882), 187.

52. "U.S. National Debt, 1790–2008: Debt to Output," http://www.docstoc.com/
     docs/2852093/US-National-Debt-1790-2008.

QUESTION #9: WHAT IS THE PURPOSE OF WAR
AND SHOULD IT BE AVOIDED?

1. Ron Chernow, *Alexander Hamilton* (New York: Penguin Press, 2007), 74–79, and
    passim.

2. Ibid.

3. Arthur S. Lefkowitz, *George Washington's Indispensable Men, The 32 Aides-de-Camp
    Who Helped Win American Independence* (Mechanicsburg, PA: Stackpole Books,
    2003), 110.

4. Chernow, *Alexander Hamilton,* 79.

5. Ibid., 562.

6. Dave R. Palmer, *1794 America, Its Army, and the Birth of the Nation* (San Francisco: Presidio Press, 1994), 92.

7. Chernow, *Alexander Hamilton,* 565.

8. Ibid., 579.

9. Henry (Light Horse Harry) Lee, *The American Revolution in the South* (New York: Arno Press, 1969), passim.

10. James V. Marshall, *The United States Manual of Biography and History* (Philadelphia: James Smith & Co., 1856), 177–78.

11. Theodore Sedgwick Jr., *Memoir of the Life of William Livingston* (New York: Kessinger Publishing Co., 2008), passim.

12. North Callahan, *Henry Knox: General Washington's General* (New York: A. S. Barnes & Co., 1958), 33–60.

13. Thomas J. McGuire, *The Philadelphia Campaign: Germantown and the Roads to Valley Forge,* vol. 2 (Mechanicsburg, PA: Stackpole Books, 2007), 87.

14. Callahan, *Henry Knox,* passim.

15. Lefkowitz, *George Washington's Indispensable Men,* 26.

16. John Reardon, *Edmond Randolph* (New York: Macmillan, 1975), passim.

17. Palmer, *1794 America,* 92–93.

18. James Ripley Jacobs, *The Beginning of the U.S. Army, 1783–1812* (Cranbury, NJ: The Scholar's Bookshelf, 2006), 244–45.

19. Thomas Jefferson to John Clarke, January 27, 1814, in Andrew Lipscomb and Albert Ellery Bergh, *The Writings of Thomas Jefferson,* Memorial Edition, vol. 14 (Washington, D.C.: Thomas Jefferson Memorial Association, 1903–1904), 79–80.

20. Thomas Jefferson to John Adams, September 12, 1821, ibid., 15:334.

21. Thomas Jefferson's reply to Lord North's proposition, July 31, 1775, in Julian P. Boyd et al., eds., *The Papers of Thomas Jefferson,* vol. 1 (Princeton, NJ: Princeton University Press, 1950–), 231; Thomas Jefferson, "First Annual Message," 1801, in Lipscomb and Bergh, *Writings of Thomas Jefferson,* 3:334.

22. Thomas Jefferson, first inaugural address, December 8, 1801, http://bartleby .net/124/pres16.html.

23. Thomas Jefferson, "Sixth Annual Message," December 2, 1806, Lipscomb and Bergh, *Writings of Thomas Jefferson,* 3:425.

24. Thomas Jefferson, "Eighth Annual Message to Congress," November 8, 1808, ibid., 3:482.

25. Thomas Jefferson to James Monroe, June 18, 1813, ibid., 13:261.

26. Thomas Jefferson to Thaddeus Kosciusko, February 26, 1810, ibid., 12:368.

27. Thomas Jefferson to James Madison, October 15, 1814, ibid., 14:202.

28. Thomas Jefferson to James Madison, May 5, 1807, ibid., 11:202.

29. Donald Jackson, "Jefferson, Meriwether Lewis, and the Reduction of the United States Army," *Proceedings of the American Philosophical Society* 124 (1980): 91–96.

30. Jacobs, *The Beginning of the U.S. Army,* 279.

31. Thomas Jefferson, "Notes Concerning the Right of Removal from Office," 1780, in Boyd, *Papers,* 4:282.

32. Thomas Jefferson to Chandler Price, February 28, 1807, ibid., 11:160.

33. Thomas Jefferson to James Monroe, August 11, 1786, ibid., 5:386.

34. Thomas Jefferson to Elbridge Gerry, January 26, 1799, ibid., 10:77.

35. Thomas Jefferson to John Adams, November 1, 1822, ibid., 15:402. This was the second time Jefferson used the phrase "burn the navy," writing to Richard Henry Lee in 1799 that "we should be gainers were we to burn our whole navy, and build what we should be able on plans approved by experience and not warped to the whimsical ideas of individuals, who do not consider that if their projects miscarry their country is in a manner undone" (Boyd, *Papers,* 3:39).

36. Larry Schweikart, *48 Liberal Lies About American History (That You Probably Learned in School)* (New York: Sentinel, 2008), 14.

37. George Washington, "Farewell Address," http://www.yale.edu/lawweb/avalon/washing.htm.

38. Ibid.

39. George Washington, "General Orders," July 2, 1776, in W. B. Allen, compiler and ed., *George Washington: A Collection* (Indianapolis, IN: Liberty Fund, 1988), 70.

40. George Washington, "To the President of Congress," September 24, 1776, ibid., 77–78.

41. Harry M. Ward, *George Washington's Enforcers: Policing the Continental Army* (Carbondale, IL: Southern Illinois University Press, 2006), 162.

42. Frederick William Baron von Steuben, *Baron von Steuben's Revolutionary Drill Manual* (New York: Dover Publications, Inc, 1985).

43. George Washington to Charles Armand-Tuffin, October 7, 1785, in John C. Fitzpatrick, ed., *The Writings of George Washington* (Washington, D.C.: Government Printing Office, 1939–1944), 28:289.

44. George Washington to Reverend John Lathrop, June 22, 1788, ibid., 30:5.

45. George Washington to William Vans Murray, October 26, 1799, ibid., 37:399–400.

46. George Washington to Benjamin Goodhue, October 15, 1797, ibid., 36:48.

47. George Washington to Marquis De Chastellux, September 5, 1785, ibid., 28:254.

48. George Washington to Comte De Rochambeau, Mount Vernon, January 29, 1789, ibid., 30:188–89.

49. George Washington, *Sentiments on a Peace Establishment,* accessed on Web site www.potowmack.ord/washsent.html, March 2010.

50. Washington, "Farewell Address."

51. http://memory.loc.gov/ammem/collections/jefferson_papers/mtjprece.html.

52. William Ray, *Horrors of Slavery, or, The American Tars in Tripoli* (Troy, NY: Oliver Lyon, 1808); and Joseph Wheelan, *Jefferson's War: America's First War on Terror, 1801–1805* (New York: Carroll & Graf, 2003).

53. Jacobs, *Beginning of the U.S. Army,* 362.

54. Chernow, *Alexander Hamilton,* 602.

QUESTION #10: SHOULD FEDERAL, STATE, OR LOCAL GOVERNMENTS COLLECTIVELY OR INDIVIDUALLY HAVE THE AUTHORITY TO REGULATE GUN OWNERSHIP?

1. Robert J. Spitzer, ed., *Gun Control: A Documentary and Reference Guide* (Westport, CT: Greenwood Press, 2009), xv.

2. John R. Lott Jr., *The Bias Against Guns: Why Almost Everything You've Heard About Gun Control Is Wrong* (Washington, D.C.: Regnery, 2003).

3. Norman H. Clark, *Deliver Us from Evil: An Interpretation of Prohibition* (New York: W. W. Norton, 1976); *Bad Habits: Drinking, Smoking, Taking Drugs, Gambling, Sexual Misbehavior* (New York: New York University Press, 1994); among others.

4. Spitzer, *Gun Control,* 247.

5. National Firearms Act of 1934, June 26, 1934, ibid.

6. Ibid., 160.

7. Clayton E. Cramer, *Armed America: The Story of How and Why Guns Became as American as Apple Pie* (Nashville, TN: Nelson-Current, 2006), 9.

8. Ibid.

9. Ibid.

10. I dealt with the massive evidentiary issues of Bellesiles's book in *48 Liberal Lies About American History (That You Probably Learned in School)* (New York: Sentinel, 2008), 113–18. Since it is unreliable at best, a formal reference to Bellesiles is perhaps meaningless, but is provided here nonetheless: Michael Bellesiles, *Arming America: The Origins of a National Gun Culture* (New York: Knopf, 2000).

11. David E. Young, *The Founders' View of the Right to Bear Arms: A Definitive History of the Second Amendment* (Ontonagon, MI: Golden Oak Books, 2007), 4–6.

12. Ibid., 6.

13. Stephen P. Halbrook, *That Every Man Be Armed: The Evolution of a Constitutional Right* (Oakland, CA: The Independent Institute, 1994), 7.

14. Ibid., 8.

15. Niccolo Machiavelli, *The Prince*, Luigi Ricci, trans. (New York: Signet, 1952), 72.

16. Thomas Esper, "The Replacement of the Longbow by Firearms in the English Army," *Technology and Culture* 6 (1965): 382–93.

17. John Locke, *Second Treatise of Civil Government* (Chicago: University of Chicago Press, 1955), 114–15.

18. Algernon Sidney, *Discourses Concerning Government*, 2:21, http://www.constitution
     .org/as/dcg_221.htm.

19. James Burgh, *Political Disquisitions: or, An Enquiry into Public Errors, Defects, and
     Abuses, Illustrated by and Established Upon Facts and Remarks, Extracted from a Vari-
     ety of Authors, Ancient and Modern* (London: E. and C. Dilly, 1774), 399.

20. Ibid., 405.

21. Young, *The Founders' View of the Right to Bear Arms*, 8.

22. Cramer, *Armed America*, 26.

23. Young, *The Founders' View of the Right to Bear Arms*, 12.

24. Ibid., 15.

25. Larry Schweikart and Lynne Pierson Doti, *American Entrepreneur* (New York: Ama-
     com, 2009), 124.

26. Young, *The Founders' View of the Right to Bear Arms*, 40.

27. Cramer, *Armed America*, 16.

28. Young, *The Founders' View of the Right to Bear Arms*, 28.

29. Ibid., 31.

30. Josiah Quincy, *Memoir of the Life of Josiah Quincy* (New York: Da Capo Press, 1971),
     413.

31. Young, *The Founders' View of the Right to Bear Arms*, 43.

32. Robert A. Rutland and Charles F. Hobson, eds., *The Papers of James Madison* (Chi-
     cago: University of Chicago Press, 1962–1977), 1:153; Young, *The Founders' View of
     the Right to Bear Arms*, 58.

33. Victor Davis Hanson, *Carnage and Culture: Landmark Battles in the Rise of Western
     Power* (New York: Anchor, 2002); and Larry Schweikart, *America's Victories: Why the
     U.S. Wins Wars and Will Win the War on Terror* (New York: Sentinel, 2006).

34. Paul H. Smith, ed., *Letters of Delegates to Congress* (Washington, D.C.: Library of
     Congress, 1976), 1:587.

35. Cramer, *Armed America*, 38. This number amounted to seventy-seven total out of a
     population in the thousands, most of whom were *required* to own guns.

36. Ibid., 39.

37. Ibid., 48.

38. Ibid., 12.

39. Ibid., 14.

40. Young, *The Founders' View of the Right to Bear Arms*, 60.

41. Ibid., 62.

42. Ibid., 64.

43. Ibid., 83.

44. Thomas Jefferson to James Madison, July 31, 1788, and December 20, 1787, in Mer-
     rill Jensen, Robert A. Becker, and Gordon Denboer et al., eds., *The Documentary
     History of the First Federal Elections, 1788–1790* (Madison, WI: Wisconsin State
     Historical Society, 1976–2005), 2:327–28.

45. Young, *The Founders' View of the Right to Bear Arms,* 217.

46. James T. Lindgren, "Fall from Grace: Arming America and the Bellesiles Scandal," *Yale Law Journal* 111 (2002), quoted online at http://papers.Ssrn.com/sol.3/papers.cfm/abstract_id=692421.

47. "Gun Sales Surge After Obama's Election," cnn.com/crim, November 11, 2008, http://www.cnn.com/2008/CRIME/11/11/obama.gun.sales/index.html.

48. "Gun Sales Shoot up Amid America's Fear of Rising Crime and Terrorism, UK *Times,* November 16, 2009, http://business.timesonline.co.uk/tol/business/industry_sectors/engineering/article6917828.ece.

49. "Crime Rates Shown to Be Falling," *U.S. News & World Report,* June 11, 2008, http://www.usnews.com/articles/news/national/2008/06/11/crime-rates-shown-to-be-falling.html.

50. To cite just a few of which I detailed in *48 Liberal Lies About American History,* 227 n., see David B. Kopel, *Gun Control in Great Britain: Saving Lives or Constricting Liberties?* (Huntsville, TX: Office of International Criminal Justice, 1992); Gary Kleck and Don B. Kates, *Armed: New Perspectives on Gun Control* (Amherst, NY: Prometheus Books, 2001); and Martin Killias, John van Kesteren, and Martin Rindlisbacher, "Guns, Violent Crime, and Suicide in 21 Countries," *Canadian Journal of Criminology* 43 (October 2001): 1721–25.

51. John R. Lott Jr., *The Bias Against Guns: Why Almost Everything You've Heard About Gun Control Is Wrong* (Washington, D.C.: Regnery, 2003), 57.

52. Ibid.

53. Ibid., 59.

54. Ibid., 61. (Moore is quoted by Lott on this page, from http://michaelmoore.com/2001_0922.html.)

55. Ibid., 65.

56. William M. Landes, "An Economic Study of U.S. Airline Hijacking, 1961–1976," *Journal of Law and Economics* 21 (April 1978): 1–32.

57. This is generally attributed to Paine, writing as "A Lover of Peace," in *Pennsylvania* magazine, July 1775, http://en.wikiquote.org/wiki/Thomas_Paine.

INDEX